We Who Took a Leap

From Where Our Mothers Left Off

Pam Burns-Clair, MFT

Cover Art: Shiloh Sophia McCloud
Cover Design: Chelsea Clair Livingston

Website: www.pamburnsclair.com
Facebook: www.facebook.com/WeLeapBook

ISBN: 978-1-938886-99-7

Dedicated to my mama's memory, Harriet Burns, and to my amazing daughters Chelsea Clair Livingston and Haley Clair, already carrying the torch forward.

Thank You Mama

*Thank you for everything
Seen and unseen that you
Have always done for me.*

*Especially for believing in
me and my dreams.*

*Thank you for being the
kind of woman I could look
up to and learn from.*

*I don't always have the
Words to tell you how I feel,
But in this moment
I want you to know,
I truly, truly, love you!*

By Shiloh Sophia McCloud
(reprinted with permission)

Praised be your father and mother

Who loved you before you were;

And trusted to call you here

With no idea of who you would be.

Blessed be those who have loved you

Into becoming who you were meant to be,

Blessed be those who have crossed your life

With dark gifts of hurt and loss

That have helped to school your mind

In the art of disappointment.

From "For your Birthday" by John O'Donohue,
Benedictus: A Book of Blessings and *To Bless the Space Between Us*

Table of Contents

Introduction by Pam Burns-Clair, MFT

*H*ow have a few "mid-life" women made a giant departure in consciousness... lifestyle...goals and ambitions...and values about what it means to be a woman? How are their journeys as "mid-life women" (40-something to 70) distinguished from their mothers' journeys...and what have they gleaned from their mothers' virtues and the gifts they gave us? In the interviews that follow, you'll read how the seeds their mothers planted have contributed to who they are.

For over 30 years I have had the privilege of listening to the stories and struggles of "mid-life women" in my therapy practice attempting to redefine womanhood in a way that is very different from how it was presented to them. I consider myself a mid-life woman also and sometimes find myself sharing bits and pieces of my own story or that of others in hopes of affirming...encouraging...validating that we're all in this effort together! This departure from our mothers' "platforms" allows us to create a new vision and in turn offer a variety of options for the next generation of women we're raising and witnessing "taking off" after us.

This shift in consciousness was part of the "60s movement" as we entered the workforce instead of being cast as housewives and moms, dependent on men to support us. Like many before us, we wrestled with society's expectations and labels. We have felt alone, and many of us still struggle with the battle within: between the definition of womanhood that was imprinted, such as pleasing others at all costs, versus the concept of self care, of recognizing and expressing our authentic selves. For those of us who raised or are raising daughters, we struggle with how to strike a better balance for the next generation of women. It can be confusing and lonely.

Since I hold a sacred and legal confidentiality with my clients, the women I have interviewed are not among them. The women who agreed to this exploration* are groundbreakers and have leaped far from their foundations. I have as well and will include my story among them. In both circumstances and attitudes, this small group of women has taken a leap and ventured into territory that has contributed to expanding the vision of womanhood.

I take the opportunity here to humbly thank these courageous women who allowed me to interview them. Two of them prefer to keep their identities private so their names and identifying features have been altered. Each woman found this process at times intense and challenging. Yet they all kept their commitment to this dialogue and exploration with me, for which I am grateful. I hope you will be too as you ride along with us.

I include my own journey because I identify with these risk takers. This small sampling of women is by no means representative of the wide variety of mid-lifers, socio-economically, culturally, ethnically, or by other such standard. But it includes a tapestry of perspectives from women with whom I hope most readers can readily identify. In concluding remarks, each woman shares what she is most proud of so far and what she hopes the next generation of women will carry forth.

We took a leap…sometimes over flames and hot coals…and here are our stories:

  * Each interviewee was asked the same questions, which they received prior to being interviewed. Their responses are woven into the interview as they flowed in our conversation. Each has provided a bio "snapshot" in their own style.

Anne Uemura

Biography

Birth date: 6/8/43

Mother: Fumino (Toyama) Uemura, Birth date: 12/29/1909, deceased: '94

I was born in Honolulu, Hawaii, several years after the bombing of Pearl Harbor. Second born in a Japanese-American family that was eventually of four daughters, I was unaware that the lack of a son was such a disappointment, especially to my father's mother. When my twin sisters were born in August 1945, my grandmother expressed a dual lament about two more girls in the family and the distress of Japan losing the war. Nonetheless, we four didn't know any of this and enjoyed growing up in a lush valley next to a mountain with a bountiful stream running by. It was idyllic, a paradise.

An important memory I have from childhood was looking up at the skies wondering where God was. It was a longing that would surface from time to time explaining why I became a Christian as a teenager, moving away from the Shinto-Buddhist ritual chant practices of my parents and grandmother. And why decades later in healing school, I was deeply grateful to learn that we'd spend the coming year focusing on our relationship to the Divine. It touched an important memory and purpose. Today this is my most important priority: finding my home in God.

Although my parents never said anything about the importance of education, it was clearly an important pursuit for me for many years. After a BA and MA in Philosophy, I taught Philosophy to college students for ten years until I decided to return to school to get my doctorate in Clinical Psychology. In these years I had gotten married, had two children, a son and a daughter, and we had moved from Hawaii to Indiana to Maine. My pre-doctoral internship at UC-San Francisco brought me back across the country to California where I've lived since. The immersion in clinical training in that year convinced me that I wanted to be a practitioner rather than an academician so I found a post-doctoral fellowship at UC-Berkeley. This was followed by 13 years as a Counseling Psychologist in Counseling and Psychological Services where I saw students in groups and individually.

In the economic distress years for UCs in the 1990s I elected early retirement. After that I continued my private practice and began exploring little by little at first, then more and more, non-traditional practices. This moving out-of-the-box culminated in choosing to train again to be a hands-on healer and later to be certified as a life coach.

Currently, I feel so pleased by my life and by the wonderful people in it—especially my partner, Doug; my children, Blandon ('68) and Laurice ('71); my two granddaughters, Noelani and Alana, and my precious friends. My hobbies keep me busy: singing, taiko drumming, cooking, quilting, writing, studying, gardening, and some volunteer work. Pervasive in all this activity is to discover something new, to gain a new mastery, to rely more on intuition, to be freer and to allow myself to be who I really am.

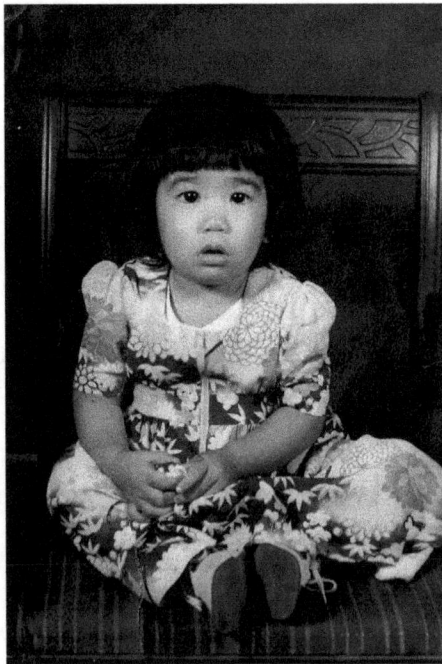

Anne as a little girl

Anne's mother and sister

Anne as a teenager

Anne today

Interview

March 2012

PBC: Anne, I would love to hear how you see yourself contributing to the evolution of the times a woman who is making a leap in your journey compared to the consciousness and cultural backdrop that you were raised in. Do you identify?

Anne: Yes. It's about moving beyond the limits and beliefs I started with…from my family and from my lineage, which is Japanese, Hawaiian, and American. Just to illustrate what I mean by that, let me describe my family a bit.

My parents are both second-generation Japanese, which means that their parents were the first to emigrate from Japan to Hawaii. Although my parents were born American citizens as "Nisei" or second generation Japanese-Americans, their values and beliefs were very Japanese and not American. Perhaps some of this can be explained by their limited education. My father was schooled until grades eight, and my mother, possibly grade five.

I think that in the course of my adult life, I've uncovered certain beliefs that they transmitted to me and have moved beyond them. This leaves me with choices and the possibility of thinking and living outside the "box" of conventionality and acculturation. In contrast, I don't see that my parents were as free to make their own choices.

My parents' story: my father was born in 1904 and my mother in 1909. So my grandparents, my father's parents, must have come from Japan to Hawaii shortly after 1900.

With my mother, I don't have such specificity of dates because we learned a lot more about the history of my father. This is typical in Asian culture. There's an interesting cultural bias that favors the male. For example, my grandmother, my father's mother, lived with us in her senior years because that was the duty of the eldest son. While this position in the family carries such a responsibility, it also carries the privilege of being the eldest male in the family. That's part of the Asian influence.

Because there weren't any male descendants among her siblings, my grandmother had to carry the family name—otherwise it would die out. When she married—instead of getting her husband's name, she kept her family name U-E-M-U-R-A—which would be pronounced "oo-amoo-ra." Here we Americanize it, pronouncing the U as a long vowel sound. There's a lot in the Japanese tradition about carrying on the family name and lineage—going back through the centuries. To illustrate what I mean about moving beyond my mother's experience of life, I want to describe an incident when, as an adult, I encountered a kind of crossroads with my lineage. It occurred while we were engaged in "personal process" in a large group setting while I was a student at the Barbara Brennan Healing School during our third year in 2002. I was not one to volunteer for such exposure. People would often volunteer to do "process" of their own issues or history before the group, depending on their personalities and their needs. There was never a lack of volunteers. Early on this particular day, for some reason I decided I needed to do get involved with this group experience so I volunteered. I don't remember what topic I was going to talk about, but as time was running out for the group process with maybe five minutes left, one of my teachers said, "Anne hasn't had a chance to speak." As I thought about it later, that was just so perfect because the way I grew up, so influenced by my parents' behavior and values, you *never* brought attention to yourself. You, as an individual, were not important. This is part of the Confucian culture that is part of my Asian heritage where the needs of the group far outweigh the needs of any individual. You really are subservient to the group and the group's needs. Your individuality is not celebrated. I don't know what I ended up talking about. But within seconds, the whole impact of my lineage, the suppression of needs and desires of women was there to feel and experience…I felt the mantle of pain, anguish…regret, sadness, all of that—all at once. I was just standing there overcome with tears and a kind of wailing. It was an incredibly emotional and intense experience. I don't even know what was articulated, what I said, what people witnessed or any detail. It wasn't an intellectual thing—it just descended upon me.

PBC: Right—one of those turning points...

Anne: Yes, because that experience defied the rule of not bringing attention to myself. And yes, because in that experience, I had somehow transcended my usual, conventional approach. With full awareness, I felt what I had in common with my female ancestors and somehow that experience freed me. I realized then that one of my purposes in this lifetime was to heal the wounds of my lineage—which I hope isn't viewed as arrogant. I imagined all the women in my lineage applauding my voice—my expression—and I imagined that through my experience of giving expression to these deeply suppressed feelings, all of my female ancestors were acknowledged and freed.

I didn't know until that moment about this particular impact of my heritage and lineage. I can't emphasize enough the gift of this particular experience. I was privileged to feel the mantle of my legacy—the collective cultural unconscious of my female ancestors. And by acknowledging and expressing this heavy emotional burden, I began to see its widespread and deep influence dissolving.

While other Asian women may not have experienced what I describe, I know that the acculturation and collective unconscious binds on our individuality and expression are widespread. To be able to speak our truth...express our creativity and individuality, I believe that these limits must be overcome.

By the time I started at the Brennan Healing School, I had already been on the quest of learning what limitations I had picked up—especially as a female. I am guessing that all of that acculturation led to my experience of feeling "less than," and males were seen as the important ones. It was their word, their control—they dictated verbally or more subtly. As a female, my needs were not important...my self-expression was not important. That's what I experienced as a limitation. And I'll tell you an experience later on about how I learned the consequences of this limitation.

PBC: In terms of your mother's values and the women behind her, let's look back at this question of cultural norms during your formative years—zero to seven. You were no doubt experiencing that message of women are not important, girls are not important, you are to be quiet and subservient, yes?

Anne: Evidently.

PBC: What gifts do you feel your mother may have given you that did take hold...that contributed to your becoming in a positive or meaningful way?

Anne: My mom was conventional and traditional. If I were to pinpoint one value that totally influenced her whole life, it is the idea of duty to family. We, her daughters, benefited from that. Her devotion seemed to be total, providing us with the basics of security, food, home, clothing, and trying to support the opportunities that were available for us. In other words, providing a foundation of safety so that we could have our individual lives.

PBC: Even though in the Japanese-Hawaiian culture, individuality was not emphasized or welcomed?

Anne: Right. I'm not saying that it was nurtured. I'm just saying in terms of our individuality, whatever my three sisters and I did with our lives, the strong roots of security became the foundation for our lives.

Back to duty, I didn't know this story about my mom until later on as an adult. I think it was after my father died—my dad died when he was 85, and my mother was five years younger—that she told us this story:

When my mother was a teenager, I'm guessing about 12 or 13, one of her aunts in Japan who didn't have any children, wanted to adopt my mother. My mother was one of nine children in Hawaii and growing up in that culture, apparently this (being adopted by a relative) was something acceptable. So she was sent to Japan to get more of her education and her training. She and her classmates went to school to learn how to sew tailored shirts, so that was going to be her occupation. But the more important thing is that in her later teens—I don't know at what age, it might have been 18…maybe even 19 or 20—she met the love of her life. We had a photo of the two of them. And they had openly declared themselves to be the loves of each other's lives. (I don't know if my aunt actually did adopt my mother.)

But before they could get married, my mother's father died, leaving my mother to be the logical one to care for all the younger siblings. She was the oldest unmarried daughter because her older sister had already married and left home. There was no one old enough to take care of the younger kids. So my mother had to move back to Hawaii and leave the love of her life behind. She only knew duty—she never spoke about the choice she made to return—or that was made for her. She seemed to have taken comfort in this man's promise to her, that though he would marry someone else because that's what was expected, he would never have children, in honor of their love. I believe she learned through various family connections that he kept this promise so we can speculate this was her consolation—she was left with the memories and she had his promise.

My belief is, however, that I was born to a mother who was really depressed as a consequence of this loss and heartbreak. She could not live a life different than what was dictated by duty to the family. I realize that my sisters may have a different story about our mother. This is my story about her—how I saw and experienced her.

PBC: It's certainly a reflection of the times and the culture.

Anne: Right…it never occurred to her that she could say no, nor did it occur to her that she had any other choices or how compliance would inhibit her life expression. I can see how her actions and this value of duty to family affected me.

I've worked hard to tie my mother's story and my experiences with her in piecing my own life together. So when you ask about who she was in my formative years, she was just a shadow. She was just doing the washing, the cooking…the work. My perception is that she just wasn't available, apart from doing her role and providing that foundation.

PBC: Obviously there was something substantial about the foundation even so. Though a big part of her was missing, that foundation has been your foundation to launch from and express from.

Anne: Here's where it gets murky! I agree that despite my mother's withdrawal from life, she somehow communicated to me her constant support of me, no matter what I chose to do.

This is very speculative, but, sometimes in my spiritual questing about the role of my parents and who they are, I got a sense that…I believe my parents' coming together in this lifetime was "karmic," if you will, as part their purpose—to support me. I don't know about my sisters, but I believe they specifically contracted or were assigned to support me and what I was supposed to do in my lifetime. One might ask, "How does one know such truths?" I only know it by my experience of my mother's presence and our history together.

My father was similar. He had his "joie de vivre" taken from him early on, as well. So they were a good match, in that respect. They kind of retired from life early in their adult lives. They were both quite introverted. In our immediate family, their personalities were so quiet, you hardly ever knew what they thought or felt. They rarely, if ever, expressed any opinion. Who they were as distinct individuals was masked from us. They played their roles and that's all there seemed to be. In some ways, it's as if they weren't there. But their intense devotion to supporting us was always there…it was always there. So, more than the actual work they did to provide that foundation, I'm basically saying there was something more—something like an unspoken belief in us and respect for us. This provided me with a strong basis of what became a solid foundation for me.

PBC: Let's move on to what traits or positive experiences did you and your mom share as you were growing up? Is there anything more you want to say about that?

Anne: One expression of how my mother supported us is that, as a young girl, after my older sister had been taking piano lessons for a few years, I wanted to do that, too. So I asked her when I was in third grade if I could take piano lessons, and she supported that idea. My family's pretty musical. My father played the Japanese guitar called the 'shamisen'…my younger sisters took voice lessons, so we were all very musical. That was wonderful, and I remember that my mother didn't hesitate to give that to me. These positive memories of sharing experiences are so few, though.

We lived in a neighborhood where our cousins lived close by, and we spent a great deal of time over at their house—all of us sisters—so much so that my aunt became like a second mother to all of us. She was more vocal than my mother, she had opinions, and we spent more time interacting with her than with our mother.

One summer I had an incident with my cousin whom I played with a lot. I was about age six or seven and he was two years older than me. What I remember is that I climbed up to hang from the top of the threshold of a doorway and my cousin was running under me. At the wrong moment, I slipped and fell on her and she got hurt. She cried inconsolably! My recollection is that she was resentful and didn't really accept my apology for that. I didn't go over to her house for I don't know how long. I don't know how this ever got amended, if it ever did. I remember talking to my mother about it. I don't remember what she said about it, but I was able to talk to her about it, which is the one time I remember ever talking to an adult about anything of importance to me. I can't remember if she was sympathetic, but at least she was available to hear the story.

It turned out to be a pretty big deal for me because it was a turning point in my relationship with my cousin. I knew, from my mother's presence, that I wasn't alone in dealing with that. I believe that in my family, we have a constant theme of dealing with your life on your own and not feeling that you could depend on anyone in an emotional sense at all. Most of the time the message was, "You're on your own—deal with it." It wasn't ever said or written anywhere.

PBC: But that sounds like an exception that made a big impression for you. Can you recall you and your mom having any arguments?

Anne: Arguments never, never happened! My family was a family that we would now call "conflict avoidant." I think of it as an emotionally unexpressive home. My parents never fought.

PBC: Mom didn't argue with you because you were a compliant part of that system.

Anne: YES, exactly. There were no arguments, the only time we disagreed, my parents and I, was in the eighth grade. I was academically tested, and with about four or five others, I was identified as gifted. They planned to have us skip a year in school.

Although I was really pleased to be identified as gifted, I didn't want to skip a grade because I would be leaving all my great friends behind. I asked my parents, "Please, I don't want to do this." They said, "No." I had to do this. And that was that!

The whole experience of being moved up a grade affected my subsequent academic years because it put me one year behind in algebra, so I had to learn algebra in summer school in six weeks. Then I entered a high school, which was far less rigorous than the one I would have gone to, academically. The teachers, the curriculum, the whole spirit…everything was different. My three sisters went to the high school I would have gone to. So, that really had an impact on me. It set me apart in some ways. In many ways they had the advantage I didn't get.

In reflecting on this, I'm surprised that I actually spoke up! I can't imagine how I had the gumption to stick my neck out, and it didn't pay off so well, but I tried!

PBC: It was sort of a moment of departure. And it was lonely when you didn't get recognized or met.

Anne: Until you said that, I never thought of that as an example of trying to step out of the defined role that I was supposed to be in, and then, having the door slammed in my face.

PBC: So, are there any other pivotal moments that left you feeling alone and despairing and either your parents or someone else helping you through the experience? Or does that feel like the most significant moment, that eighth grade turning point?

Anne: One important turning point for me was when I was getting my Ph.D. There came a point where I had passed everything, all my other requirements, and I had to formulate my research topic. It was a daunting moment. This was when I recognized the impact of being raised the way I was raised—I had no opinion. I had no original viewpoint. So to create a thesis that counted on originality to propose a research question was impossible! It was at some level a real low point to realize that my success up to that point was because I could take "in" very well and spit the learning "out." I could analyze, I could compare and all that. But I could not come up with something new to proceed with my dissertation.

It took me a long time to move from that point, which I would consider a turning point for me, because I had to find ways of overcoming the beliefs and limits of my entire life. I had been indoctrinated to follow, not to lead or speak up! Up to that moment, in my late 30s, I was living according to the doctrine: "You're a good student, you're a good daughter, you're a good citizen…just doing what you're supposed to." Then I came to a point where I realized that those kinds of identities or roles had just about wiped out any kind of creativity or originality and individuality I had. So to go from that point to where I am now was quite the journey.

This "aha" moment happened in about 1978. I got my Ph.D. in '81. My journey began with this recognition that I needed to do something different or my life would not be anything other than it was. The missing piece had to do with anger. Given my family culture where anger was very rare, I didn't know anger. It's taken a long time and quite a process to have anger become something natural and normal. Even to this day, it's unusual to allow myself to feel angry—it's usually quite subtle. Sometimes I watch my thoughts and I've come to know that I'm angry because of the thoughts that I have. But it's not like I often viscerally or emotionally experience the anger. But this work with anger represents an important part of the emotional work it took to recover myself.

Besides all the cognitive work that I did in terms of the beliefs that I carried about self, about limitations and possibility and all of that, the work on emotions that began with this "aha" moment was really important.

PBC: I'm curious as to what your Ph.D. topic eventually emerged to be?

Anne: I had helped with emerging research investigating how the hemispheric lateralization of the brain affected abilities like creativity and different cognitive abilities. At this particular point in time, people were just learning about left and right brain functioning. I had been working with a research psychologist who had just entered into this area. We eventually published a research article on hemispheric functioning in schizophrenics. It was an area that I was already familiar with…the research and the background. The challenge was simply coming up with a question that hadn't been addressed before. It was not a creative thesis project but it was enough to allow me get my degree.

PBC: I'm stringing together what I'm hearing as several turning points: the point at which you were in school and wishing you could choose not to skip the grade… when you tried to speak up and weren't really allowed to be recognized…the dissertation topic struggle…culminating in the moment in your healing school where you described you had it all come to the fore…that your people, the women in your lineage were not allowed to speak up or assert themselves in any way. These events all seem to string together as you emerging…evolving out of this "good-girl" training and lineage.

Anne: Hmmm....this is the first time I sat down to gather up these pieces that you're talking about. I see the experience of holding my lineage's anguish as a kind of culmination—yes.

I'd like to mention two other things that come to mind that are important. When I was in seventh grade I had a best friend. We hung out a lot together. For some reason, some of our mutual friends decided that I wasn't a good friend to her and tried to separate us. They intercepted my phone calls to her to keep us apart. They actually confronted me in school to tell me that I wasn't being the kind of friend my friend deserved. All this led to a group of them—there must have been five or six—who tried me in a mock court trial after school, and they found me guilty!

I was so confused! But the important part is that I had become involved with Christianity at that point in my life and, because of this, the idea of forgiveness stood out in my mind. While my orientation or perspective was a pretty fundamentalist view then, somehow I grasped onto the idea of forgiveness, such that I didn't hold it against any of them. I just kept on living as if it didn't happen. Eventually all of that melted away and it was basically forgotten. It still amazes me that I chose to do that.

Looking back now, from a mature perspective, I wonder what allowed me to have that amount of wisdom! Because it didn't come from my background!

PBC: A spirit of generosity at an early age.

Anne: Another incident was in college. I think it was after our first year as we're entering our second year. I was at a retreat with a fellowship group I belonged to for a number of years. As we were ending our evening enjoying snacks one day, an older woman in our group said something to me like, "You're really afraid of people, aren't you?" It shocked me. I'd never really thought of myself this way. Somehow her question created a crack in my armor, in my sense of who I thought I was.

I spent the next twelve or so hours crying. What I experienced over and over was seeing all these images—seeing the personas that I had adopted—and how futile and false they all were. Witnessing that led to seemingly endless tears. When this intense grief process subsided, I felt reduced to a seed or a little egg. I didn't know who I was. All I knew was that everything that I'd created myself to be had been washed away and I now could—or had to—start over again to define or find myself.

Before that I was so lacking in uniqueness...curiosity...expressiveness. So it was a dissolution of my previous identity. In hindsight, this now seems a total gift in disguise, coming seemingly from out of the blue.

PBC: Was there anyone in that experience that came to your side, who perhaps helped you through that moment? Or was this transformation and emergence all from within?

Anne: The process just unfolded at the time, and what I love about it now, reflecting back, it was quite unexpected. Even at the time it was happening it wasn't like I felt, "Oh my God! This awful thing is happening to me," but being plunged into it and not resisting, just allowing it to be. No one came up to support me. It was a process I went through on my own.

PBC: You became a witness to your own process.

Anne: Now in my life if I could invite such a process, it would be an incredible gift. In retrospect, these two experiences of being betrayed and somehow "knowing" the gift of forgiveness and of having a sudden dissolving of "self" help me believe that there's a depth to me that I haven't consciously known most of my life. It's reassuring and validating.

There is one more turning point: This happened about 1995: I read ***An Autobiography of a Yogi***, Yogananda's book. After reading that book, the spirit of it had a profound effect on me like another "aha" in my life. Up to that point, my consciousness had been dominated by rationality and intellect that hadn't served me. I had no answers. I had no path. I decided then that I needed to go along the path of my heart. This has been my journey since then, a path to discovering my heart.

PBC: In your mom's history, was there anything else that you feel changed her attitude in the course of her life while she was still alive, a shape shifting event?

Anne: The death of my father had an impact on her, because my father ruled the house. He was just over 84, so for about five years—before her passing—she certainly experienced a kind of freedom and choices that she had never had before.

PBC: Apparently, it freed her up in some ways?

Anne: Yes, for that remaining period of time…to taste something else. Just being free to make her own decisions and plans, she could do it without having my father's approval. Her personality also emerged. She engaged more readily in conversation with us and with strangers. She was active in her life, not so much defined by roles. Also, I remember being surprised by her wisdom and "outspokenness" that was out of character for her. For example, once when my husband was visibly angry with me for having locked the keys inside the house, my mother said to him, "You make mistakes, too, you know." That gave him pause for thought and helped him move on.

Before we move on, let me share two more stories about my mother. I realize in how I've described her so far, I can see myself as making a leap beyond her. However, when my mother's mother died, I saw how very comfortable Mom was with death. It was a startling comparison to how confused and scared I felt as a teenager. I remember her words and how she behaved with her mother's body. When it came to her own death, I saw more of this aspect of her. Mom had been ill with dementia and a familial pulmonary fibrosis for several years. In January 1994, she was hospitalized on a Friday. That evening complications occurred and she almost died. The following morning she asked me what had happened. After our conversation in which I told her the truth as I saw it, she lapsed into silence for several hours, seemingly unconscious. In the afternoon, she became alert and spoke, thanking me for all we had done for her, and then became silent again. Her physical body let go early the next morning. What I witnessed with my mother I believe was a passage of an old and wise soul who knew how to move on to what was next for her. When I look at my life with her from this vantage point, I can see how she modeled for me a way of being in life that was grounded in a deep knowing of who she was. In this realization I can see myself as moving toward that *knowing* but certainly not leaping beyond her soul "essence" that I witnessed in this moment. I also witnessed my father's passage and it was very similar. Isn't it wonderful to move into these ways of seeing and appreciating later in life?

PBC: Wow! What a special and sacred sendoff. Could I ask you to backtrack a little and focus on how she approached conflicts and relationships throughout her life and its impact on you? You've given some background on the family being unemotional, that there wasn't any arguing, a rather conflict-avoidant style, in clinical terms. Is there anything more you want to say about how she did or didn't approach conflicts and how you handle these issues now?

Anne: I can say very simply that she didn't change her avoidant behavior, and I recognize it as something that really strongly influenced me, that completely quieted me down. I can think of only a few times when I would bring something up that would be conflictual in my previous marriage, well, in both marriages… there were a few times that I couldn't avoid the conflict for various reasons and what emerged is that I couldn't stay silent any more. However, when I spoke up, I couldn't uphold my stance. I didn't fare well in the ensuing exchanges. I caved in for different reasons each time. I didn't have what it took to prevail when someone disagreed with me.

In the case of my second husband, what he expressed in terms of fear was far greater than the fear that I was talking about. I just stopped pursuing my point of view, but it left me hugely angry and almost feeling self-destructive. I was *so* angry.

As I look back on these incidents, what these episodes emphasize to me is when

I did express what was true for me, I still hadn't developed a way of seeing myself that help me hold my ground. I still wasn't important enough to myself. I wasn't able to experience my anger as a way of saying "enough of this." Consequently, I allowed my anger to turn against me. It took many more years of personal development work for a healthy self-love to emerge so I can now stand with my truth.

PBC: Sort of, "Enough of this submission and compliance! Been there, done that—I gotta move along?"

Anne: Currently with Doug, in my current relationship, we're both somewhat conflict avoidant. However, we both are committed to having room for our feelings and to being conscious and truthful. So it's now more a question of whether one of us decides something is important to express. We each accept responsibility for our feelings. We don't blame each other for how we feel. Even if it may seem to lead to a conflict—and sometimes it does—we honor the need for expression. We make space for our feelings and the opportunity to learn and grow from acknowledging and expressing them.

In short, we allow ourselves to speak our truth even if it's potentially conflictual. That has been very freeing. And we know we cannot change each other. Does that make sense?

PBC: Yes—it sounds like you've come out the other side. I have so many questions because you're describing having taken a huge leap from your background. So how did you get from a background in which conflict was not dealt with to being someone who is now in touch with your feelings and willing to speak up? For example, the conflict that your mom experienced as a teenage girl, that the family couldn't take care of the younger kids, so she was called back and there were no questions asked. It was just duty. Then the family you were raised in, where the parents did not argue, where there was no room for conflict processing. Take me through any pivotal moments that shifted you, awakened you, in your first marriage, or second marriage, and now in this third relationship that have allowed you to embrace a healthier model.

Anne: I haven't really given thought to this, but let me see what I can do.

PBC: Here's how I'm sizing it up: You were serious—you were quite angry and suppressed, both as a child and in your first two marriages. I'm struck by the departure from your upbringing and your journey since then in being able to validate your feelings and tackle conflicts in relationship!

Anne: I would emphasize something more—and this is my bias. In that second marriage—this is when I read *Yogananda*—I began to read other kinds of books about healing, alternative health, and such. My world simply expanded with the spiritual and metaphysical material I studied. So much wise guidance is available to us, isn't there? To help us see more choices and possibilities and help to transform ourselves and evolve into mature adulthood and awakening to our true selves.

PBC: It took you down a spiritual path to "expand your repertoire," so to speak?

Anne: Being curious and picking up books that were available: Wayne Dyer, Deepak Chopra, Don Miguel Ruiz, and currently for me, Eckhart Tolle, Robert Scheinfeld and Gary Renard, all of these contribute to a new perspective, a wisdom of sorts.

For example, I like what Deepak Chopra talked about in his **Seven Spiritual Laws of Success**. There was the story about his children, and how, from the very beginning, you have a life purpose that is only your own. Your only duty in life is to find out what that purpose is. To me this is priority placed on one's uniqueness, one's individuality. It is counter to the Confucian culture and value on the group at the expense of the individual that I had absorbed in my family.

So I would say the turning point was the Ph.D. "moment" when I expanded into this journey of finding who I am as a human being—what I wanted, what I needed and what I desired....all my expressions and possibilities as well as my spiritual self...my life purpose. In that process, you really need your feelings. I've had to make room for them since feelings were not treasured in my home or my cultural background.

PBC: Absolutely. So you were able to rise above your background and expand your ingredients.

I'm interested in what relationship lessons you have learned, and what you were describing as having been influenced by this spiritual quest you were on. Are there any other values that you want to identify in your current relationship, or anything you want to mention here about the impact on your values as you watch your adult daughter go through relationships?

Anne: One of my teachers was my post-doctoral clinical psychology supervisor. What he imparted that I found so wonderful was the attitude that you really need to enter the therapy room with extreme respect for the person in the room. It's a perspective and teaching that I try to remember to this day. It's more than respect—it's getting to a place where you treat the other person as the most important person in the world...you give your full attention...you are really present to their situation, their story. You're not there for yourself. You're there to be a witness, a mirror. That kind of attention will hopefully allow a person to get beyond their typical story and become very truthful...come from more depth...so that their relationship with themselves and their stories can be transformed.

PBC: When we are the therapists, setting our own lives aside, we enter into a rather sacred relationship of healing and transformation.

Anne: We have the beauty of knowing what that's like, but it's tricky to apply that, because when you're involved with somebody whose own story or situation picks up your story or triggers you, it's not easy to get there. My own judgment, idea of what's best…my notion of compassion, etc…these can all get in the way of being truly present.

PBC: It's a tall order, isn't it, to fully enter someone else's reality in the journey. And certainly not one that your background trained you for.

Anne: So this is my current story: I believe that relationships are essential to help us transform, especially our intimate love relationships and friendships. In such relationships, we are most clearly and easily triggered. As uncomfortable as being upset is and being in conflict is, these circumstances are important because they can show us where our early wounds are. They show us our unquestioned beliefs and values. Without experiencing these challenges, we cannot hope to grow up or to evolve. We basically operate as adult versions of a two-year-old who wants her way. We as human beings cannot escape these challenges. So thinking that you can get into a better relationship may be avoidance…there may be some conditions that are better than others, but when we leave in order to escape conflict, to escape being rubbed into our own stuff, wounds, baggage…it's not making use of what could be a really valuable situation. If people could see this, the possibility of evolution and transformation would just increase!

PBC: And yet, do you look back on your two marriages as having furthered your growth rather than looking at it as you quit too soon, or you quit for the wrong reason…or you were left for the wrong reasons? Can you apply that journey to your previous marriages?

Anne: My first marriage was very, very wounding.

When I read *The Drama of the Gifted Child* in the first years as a Counseling Psychologist, I couldn't see how my childhood had wounded me. The book was intended to point me back to my family background, but I could relate to it better in terms of my first marriage. So in some ways, that's the experience that marriage provided. It provided the impetus for taking my personal inward journey. Did I leave for the wrong reasons? I don't know… but from what I know of my children's father, he essentially hasn't changed. I'm grateful to have left. Had I stayed in it, I think I would have been hugely diminished or something.

I was young, I was 21 when I was first married, and for whatever reason, I chose that. I was not ready to make use of it as a "teachable moment" at the time, and maybe it's a matter of maturity and age that allows us to have perspective in hindsight?

PBC: Perhaps the lessons yet unlearned revisit us along the way.

Anne: I realize that both of my husbands' values were and remain very, very different from mine. The level of emotional responsibility that they took is quite different compared with my present relationship. So, if you don't have a partner that is willing to take responsibility for the relationship as necessary to keep it healthy, you are limited. I am so blessed with Doug and his values. You can work in isolation on yourself, but from my view, it's better to have a partnership in which both understand that what transpires offers opportunity for both to mature. This perspective is a departure from my background where you do it all on your own and everything that is wrong is to be used for character-building or learning fortitude. It's not the kind of emotional maturity and transformation that I choose today.

PBC: I'm sure others taking in your story will be nodding in agreement, Anne!

As a mother now looking back on your mothering of your two adult children, what are the similarities and/or differences in style from your mother and the values she raised you by?

Anne: I would say that it's amazing how we recreate wounds, given what was happening in my first marriage when my children were born. I see myself having repeated the wounds of my mother, such that I see my daughter as having had a similar experience as I did. While she was in utero, I went through a very traumatic experience with her father. So by the time she was born, I was absent in my own way because of that. Then, when she was about five, I began my Ph.D. program. So I was absent and distracted in another way as well, re-enacting the absent mother.

As a consequence of that, the theme of making everyone's needs more important than your own is something that I see in my daughter. She's tremendously gifted. She's funny, she's very caring, she's very big-hearted, and she gives when her gas tank is way on empty. And, unlike me, she is physically vulnerable. She has recently gone through a year of numerous surgeries and just recently had bleeding ulcers treated. My mother and I did not have any of that. We too, gave at our own expense, but we were physically robust. My daughter, however, is vulnerable for whatever reason…so I'm seeing how dramatically she is affected. I tell her: "Make sure you get rest. Make sure you take care of yourself." And somehow she fights it; she would say her responsibilities—especially caring for her two daughters and others—are more important than self-care.

PBC: Your dream for her would be self-care?

Anne: Yes, and self-love. For years, I've tried everything I know to help my daughter, trying to "save" her from the struggles and suffering I saw her go through. Recently, I began to accept that idea that no one can save another, that is, I can't save her. Although I wanted to spare her pain, it wasn't my responsibility or within my power to do so. I've relinquished, too, the arrogance that I know what is better for her. I can only stand by her and love her.

PBC: As we close, are there any female role models that you could identify as wider known figures in the culture?

Anne: Two women that I admire are Rachel Naomi Remen and Byron Katie. Rachel, through two books, influenced me profoundly: **Kitchen Table Wisdom**, and later **My Grandfather's Blessings**. There was a period about five years ago that I picked up each of those books again and again. I would read five or six pages or so every night so I could spend time with Rachel. When I got through with one book, I'd pick up the other one and when I got through with the second book, I'd pick up the first one. I spent my time with Rachel that way just before going to bed because I loved her spirit, and as a consequence, I think I have moved closer to her sense of her life purpose and how she is in relationship to her clients. It wasn't a conscious intention to use her as a role model. All I knew was that I enjoyed being in "her company."

PBC: For readers that are not familiar with her work, how would you sum up your perception of her life purpose—her focus?

Anne: Rachel began her career by following a traditional track, like the many physicians in her family. And, as she was moving along in her career and being considered for the position of being the chairman of her department at Stanford, I believe, she decided to move to another track that was influenced by her grandfather who was a rabbi. She finally founded and became a part of an independent holistic alternative cancer treatment program in Marin County, California. She has been a counselor there for many years. In **My Grandfather's Blessings**, as she shares her patients' stories from her counseling sessions with them, it is clear that her witness, her presence is so powerful…that though she may not have spoken a word, she had tremendous influence or ability to bring forth the truth that was needed.

PBC: Do you think that her practice or ability you described, of putting the person before her as the most special person in the world and how they feel that is what makes her so special?

Anne: Yes, but it's also more than that. To me, she had evolved in her ability to be in *stillness* and *present-ness*. She's a definite role model that way. There was a point early on in my own journey where I would be arguing with her in my mind, "No, you've got to do more than that, you've got to say this, you got to do this…" Now, after years of experience, I say, "OH, no. She's right." I believe that because of who she is, Rachel Naomi Remen creates a kind of sacred space with her presence and loving compassionate attention.

The other major influence is Byron Katie who has written a number of books such as **A Thousand Names for Joy** and **Loving What Is**. She is also one whose company I appreciated just before going to bed. I would like to think that she transmitted some of her spirit to me as I read and re-read her words. Byron Katie is a wonderful teacher for people seeking their truth. I believe that she has truly awakened. She knows what is *real*. She loves what is. In contrast, we tend to get caught up in our stories and our beliefs, and we get so confused and upset. But Byron Katie teaches us how to discover our truths rather than hold on to what has upset us. She offers the ability to just "shake it out" so we can emotionally grasp what's really important and what's true. She helps us let go of that which no longer serves us. It's absolutely beautiful.

PBC: How do you see yourself contributing to the evolution of the times? What would be your message to readers of this book?

Anne: Currently, I am practicing forgiveness on the deepest level that I know whenever it is necessary—which is many times a day. For me, the only spiritual practice that makes sense is one that can be done every moment of every day. I can only contribute my evolving awakening to these times. "Be the change you want to see." Because the only person I can change is *me*!

PBC: Ahhh….perfect! You're a living example, Anne!

Cyndi Williams-Carter

Biography

55 years old [at publication]

My mother: Ruth Williams born in Bamberg, SC, in 1930, deceased: 1993

- I've had a successful career working for the Federal Government for the last 26 years.

- Graduated from Northeastern University, Boston, MA, Criminal Justice major, BS awarded 1981

- Married to Rayburn Carter 1982-present, whom I met while he was an engineering major at Northeastern. Husband has worked in the engineering field for the past 32 years.

- We have one son, 31 [at publication], BS in Criminal Justice. Currently working as an independent eCommerce dealer.

- I have one brother who is nine years older.

My mother Ruth was the sixth of 10 children. She was raised Baptist and migrated to the Washington, DC, area with her mother, father and siblings when she was a young girl. Mom never married but spent her life working hard providing for herself and her family. Mom often held more than one job at a time, but she primarily worked in the food service industry. Due to failing health, she had to retire early from her job as a Head Cook for the Washington, DC, Public School System, Department of Food Service, before passing away at the age of 63. I was 35 at that time.

Being one of ten children, my mother only went as far as 10th grade in school before her parents took her out to help at home. She learned very early in her life how to provide for her family. So by the time my brother and I were born, she knew hard work and a caring environment were her responsibility to her family. As a result, we learned the importance of a strong work ethic and the significance of family. My mother's struggles and her determination led me to see the difference an education could make in one's struggles. It also inspired me to choose a more traditional family when starting my own.

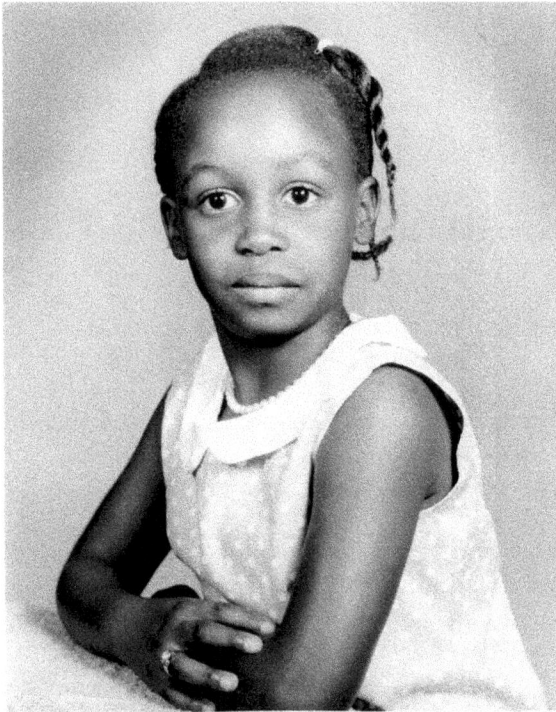

Young Cyndi

Cyndi's mom in her youth

Cyndi's mom

Cyndi today

Interview

November 2012

PBC: As you know, you've been identified as someone who's made a leap in your own evolution of consciousness from where your mother left off. I'm wondering how you view that title [laughs].

Cyndi: It was very thought provoking for me. I'm at that stage of my life during which I'm still discovering who I am—I guess like everybody else. So it's a continual evolution in a lot of ways.

PBC: Lots of soul searching?

Cyndi: Yes. Your proposal to interview me in this light has caused me to think about my family, where I've come from, where I am and my place in my extended family at this point. I come from a family of humble beginnings. My family's worked hard for everything that they've acquired. My mom was the breadwinner of our family. I grew up in a single parent household.

PBC: Where was your dad?

Cyndi: My dad lived in Philadelphia. I didn't grow up with my dad.

PBC: So were they never together and they weren't married?

Cyndi: They were not married, that's correct. I lived in Washington, D. C., but my dad lived in Philadelphia. My mom raised me. I have one older brother. There's a nine-year age difference between him and me. We had a non-traditional family before it was as acceptable as it is today. For many years I was kind of an only child, as my brother was with his father and his family.

PBC: So mom was the breadwinner…were you a latchkey kid or was there a babysitter?

Cyndi: With the exception of going to a babysitter while in kindergarten, I was a latch key kid for the most part. Well, let me back up. My mom worked since the time I can remember, and there was an extended family of other women who helped us along the way. One woman, Miss Quarles, who I fondly referred to as Qua Qua, was the landlord of the rooming house where we lived during my early years, I think from the time I was 10 months through maybe toddler years. She was an honorary godmother who looked after me when my mom was out working over the years. Years after my mom left that house and got her own apartment, I would go back and spend summers with Miss Quarles. It was like a community of elders that was there for me. I became latchkey, as I remember, maybe nine or ten years old.

PBC: So you were left at home after school after that.

Cyndi: Yes.

PBC: And what did mom do for a living?

Cyndi: During my early childhood, Mom worked as a waitress at Key's Restaurant, which was a historical restaurant here next to the historical Howard Theater. She also worked as a waitress at another well-known restaurant. By the time I entered junior high school, she worked as a cook for the DC Public School System until she retired due to failing health. In addition, for approximately three years, she worked as a homecare provider for a family friend's mother who had Alzheimer's—this was not until my adult years.

PBC: And what would you say distinguishes you from your mother, in terms of her personality and yours?

Cyndi: There are a lot of ways that we really are alike. I learned a lot from her. My mom was very good-natured, fun loving, independent, and a hard-working woman. She spent a lot of time working, doing what was necessary to survive.

PBC: And you are a hard worker, as well, I gather?

Cyndi: I am [laughs]—but also I think I'm good-natured. What distinguishes us, I think, was probably education. I was afforded a formal education in a way that she was not. I think about what she might have done or might have been if she had been afforded more education. She came from a large family of sisters and brothers, so she went to school up until tenth grade and then dropped out of school—actually she was taken out of school to help out with the family.

PBC: And you were able to go beyond compulsory education?

Cyndi: Absolutely. I graduated from the DC public school system. I think it was through teachers I met along the way in the DC school system at the time and my own curiosity that made me decide that I wanted to go to college. Education was important to my mom, but she left it up to me to decide how I wanted to chart my own course after high school. And if I had chosen to work after high school, which a lot of my peers chose to do, she would've been okay with that. I was thinking about this recently—I'm the second person in my family, the first in my generation to finish college. From my mom's generation, out of her nine siblings, she had one brother who graduated from college and did quite well.

PBC: You were the first girl to go to college?

Cyndi: Absolutely, I was.

PBC: And how did that happen? Were you sort of mentored by these high school teachers? Was mom able to put any funds toward the college?

Cyndi: Yes, teachers mentored me and I also had a good counselor in high school. It happened a combination of ways—my wherewithal, the choices that I made in high school demonstrated to my teachers that I had what it took to go further than high school.

PBC: To be college material, as they say.

Cyndi: Absolutely. And I credit my mom with kind of giving me that where-withal. She encouraged me to be adventurous. She wanted me to see the world outside of my immediate environs—to go outside of my city. For instance, she would let me go on short trips with my godmother and her boyfriend from time to time. Qua Qua was divorced but had a lifelong boyfriend—Uncle Charlie—until he died. He was a wonderful man and adored her. Mom would let me spend the summers with relatives in Massachusetts, New York and Philadelphia. She had an adventurous nature. She would tell me that when she was a little girl, she loved to "go" on trips to "the country" (her reference to going down south to visit relatives) and when we could, we'd make trips to Philadelphia or New York to visit relatives, too. I think we would've traveled more when I was younger if she didn't have to work as much as she did to maintain our day-to-day existence. After she stopped working, she did do some traveling on her own until she became too sick to do so any more. Throughout school most teachers made me feel as though I was a pretty good student. Mom could only help me so much with school work. So, at times, I had to work harder in some areas than others—school didn't always come easy to me, [laughs]—I had to really work hard at it. I appreciated the teachers pointing out that hard work was part of the journey, and if you could get through that journey, you could move to the next level.

PBC: So, the message both from mom and your teachers was: you can make it… go for it…you've got what it takes to make it.

Cyndi: Yes, it was.

PBC: Well, cool! [laughs] What values do you think either distinguish you or are similar besides those personality traits? Mom passed on a spirit of adventure to you. Were there other values or choices that you feel she influenced?

Cyndi: Her independence and her work ethic: Go out and work hard every day—Be disciplined. She knew she had to provide for us. She did what she needed to do, in order to make sure we had the bare essentials—a roof over our head, food, and clothes. That was engrained in her as she came from such a large family. She had to do what she had to do in order to survive. We saw that. And for me, her hard work made it a little bit easier for me to be able to focus on the next step, which was that education piece.

PBC: So the message was: You do what you have to do to take care of business.

Cyndi: Absolutely, but there was always an emphasis on improving your lot in life, improving who you are.

PBC: It sounds like she actually sort of handed a torch to you, in terms of, "You go far girl! I've paved the way for you!" [laughs]

Cyndi: I'd absolutely say that she did, but not always with words. I also modeled her behavior.

PBC: Yes, her behavior. The way she got up and took seriously her responsibilities became a role model for you.

Cyndi: Absolutely. [laughs] Absolutely.

PBC: As you look at those early years, what are the gifts that you feel she conveyed?

She was a working mom at a time when most mothers didn't work—yes?

Cyndi: Well back then, all the mothers I knew worked, too. She was there for me and she kept me involved in extra-curricular stuff at school if I expressed an interest.

PBC: How?

Cyndi: She supported what I wanted to do. Fortunately, most of my activities centered around school. So transportation wasn't usually a problem. I played instruments, sang in the Glee Club, was a cheerleader, and took dance lessons. There were fees associated with some of these activities. Mom paid for piano lessons and had to purchase my flute and recorder. When I was 14, I was excited to get my first summer job and from that point on, was happy to work during the summers (there's that work ethic) so I could pay for other expenses associated with my activities such as my cheerleading accessories and dance attire. The biggest challenge I remember was when I took piano lessons in elementary school. We felt I needed a piano to be able to practice after school. So we set out to find a used piano but at that time a used piano was more than she could afford. Also, our one bedroom apartment didn't provide enough room to fit a piano. So we nixed that idea.

Mom was there for me when I needed her to be there for me. She just requested advance notice so that she could try to be there for me if she needed to be for school events and that sort of thing.

PBC: What about in your primary years before age seven?

Cyndi: The same—she did what she had to do, and I felt I was always in good care.

PBC: Do you remember times when she was with you, in those early years? Are there any memories that stand out that left an impression on you or that you think may have laid your foundation?

Cyndi: Gosh, something that really stands out was when I was eight years old. We would do things on weekends that she was off, like take in a movie or go downtown. On this particular day she took me to a restaurant downtown called the Blue Mirror for lunch—she dressed me up to take this little portrait. I remember sitting in my cute little light blue and white outfit with the pearl necklace and ring that we bought at the last minute at the local five-and-dime store and feeling more sophisticated than an eight year old. It was a special time. She would do things like that to make the moment special. I don't have many photos of me when I was younger, but that's one of the photos that I'm including.

PBC: Kind of a mom and daughter bonding experience.

Cyndi: Yes. That's one of the earliest memories that I have. Before that, I do remember Momma preparing me for kindergarten—taking me to see the neighborhood school; showing me how to walk to and from school and introducing me to the elderly baby sitter several houses down from our house. Momma would take me to her house before work and I would go there after school and stay until she picked me up after work. I remember the place where I got my first pet, a white cat named Snowball and later a bunny at Easter.

PBC: Would you say that often applied, that instead of being exhausted on her days off, she tried to do things that made your life special and that connected the two of you?

Cyndi: She did, she tried as much as she could to do that. Holidays—Easter, Thanksgiving and Christmas—she would make particularly special. During those early days, I always enjoyed shopping for that special Easter outfit to wear to church and decorating Easter eggs for the Easter basket. And then there was the cooking and decorating the house for Thanksgiving and Christmas that made for special family time together. But most days were spent just getting ready for the next week...the day-to-day things.

PBC: Like doing laundry and chores.

Cyndi: We did go to church sometimes, too. Momma went to church growing up and therefore, thought it was important for me to do the same. We attended church together on a few occasions, but as a young girl I later attended Sunday school on my own. Honestly, I think Sunday was the one day she had to herself when she wasn't working. On the other hand, religion was a big part of my godmother's life and she went to church every Sunday. So when I spent time with her during the summers, we went to church together every Sunday. She would also hold prayer meetings at her house on Wednesday evenings. During those meetings we praised God, sang gospel songs and prayed for everybody and everything!

PBC: In contrast, what did you and your mom argue about when you were growing up that you remember?

Cyndi: Oh gosh. It all seems so trivial.

PBC: Now it does, looking back?

Cyndi: Just the teenage rebellion type stuff...hanging out more...once I started, as I got older, wanting to hang out a little bit later...going to parties, that kind of stuff. Her making sure I was going to parties with the right kids and wasn't in any trouble.

PBC: She was protective.

Cyndi: She was protective, because one of the issues was teen pregnancy. Back then, that was a big, big issue. And she did not, under any circumstances, want me to be a teen mother. She was very clear about what she would and would not accept. So... like any new friends I acquired and—oh, my gosh...if guys got into the mix, "You make sure [laughs] you're not doing anything that's going to cause you to have a baby!" That was the biggest thing.

PBC: Had she been a teen mom with your brother?

Cyndi: She had him when she was, well, 18 or 19.

PBC: Unmarried, right—so it was essentially a teen pregnancy?

Cyndi: Yes.

PBC: And do you think that made her become so protective and determined to make sure you didn't get yourself in those circumstances?

Cyndi: Possibly. And knowing how hard it was to raise children as a single parent, that might have been a factor, but I think it was more about the girls in the neighborhood and my high school. There were some teen mothers there, and I would come home and talk about that. They weren't necessarily friends who were close to me. But you come home and talk about that kind of stuff. So she was aware of that being an issue.

PBC: That was instilled in you. And yet you wanted the freedom to be able to go and do with your friends?

Cyndi: Sure. It wasn't *always* about me going out with guys or anything like that. But I think she thought when you're young, that's got to be a part of it, and perhaps she had also lived through this herself and knew first hand.

PBC: As you look back on it now, they seem trivial, those arguments?

Cyndi: They do. We would sometimes argue over family stuff. It usually had to do with bickering between my mom and one of her sisters. There was drama sometimes. My mom didn't appreciate gossipy, catty women and I think she felt one sister had those tendencies.

PBC: Was there jealousy or rivalry among them as adults?

Cyndi: I can't say there was any jealousy or rivalry, but they certainly had their differences. If my mom didn't particularly care for something her sister said or did they would talk about it and that would sometimes lead to an argument, and they might not speak to each other for weeks or months. I would sometimes be the peacemaker or mediator when this kind of stuff was going on between them. .

PBC: In your teen years or when?

Cyndi: I can remember in my teen years being a peacemaker in some of these issues.

PBC: You were the peacemaker for your aunts and uncles and your mom?

Cyndi: Yes, sometimes.

PBC: Interesting. And was your mom more ambitious than many of her siblings, do you think?

Cyndi: Thinking back, she and her siblings may have had slightly different ambitions depending on where they were in life (for example, whether they were married or not; how many children they had; or the types of jobs they had). But they were all ambitious in their own way. They all just wanted more for their families than they had growing up.

PBC: Sounds like she had that personality of the eldest and an attitude that you do what it takes to get ahead and be successful.

Cyndi: Yes, that was her attitude. But I think because she didn't have a husband and she was responsible for us exclusively, she had to be that way. [laughs] But they all worked. They all knew they had to, and they knew how important that was. Traditional relationships were important. But some of what I've been thinking about recently is that my mom had her children out of wedlock, so she wasn't a traditionalist in that sense. She wanted to be married, but that didn't happen for her. So, she had to view her situation as: "Okay. I have two kids. I need to take care of my kids. I'm gonna do the best I can to provide for my kids instead of trying to bring fathers—or another man—into the mix. I no longer have time to figure that out. I don't have time to make that happen while simultaneously getting out and working, providing for my babies. That's, that!"

She and her brothers and sisters would have disagreements and at times argue over what appeared to be trivial things. They could all be stubborn sometimes. And if they didn't agree on a point, they would fall out. I didn't like to see that going on so I would try to jump in and try to referee or bring them back together whenever they would have these fall-outs.

PBC: And do you think she stopped with you because she became more focused on being a mom than, as you say, having a love life? That, by the time you came along, it took all her energy to be a provider?

Cyndi: Perhaps. She dated and had a love life, but I think she was quick to read men: "If you're not gonna be a family oriented person or be a part of my family, then I don't have a lot of time for that." [laughs]

PBC: Not that you were given a choice.

Cyndi: I always longed for more of a traditional family. And that's one of the ways I feel I've evolved. When I did get married, it was to a fantastic person who came into my life. Well, I ended up getting pregnant before I got married, [laughs] but it matters who you fall for, right [laughs]? He, as we shall say, was the marrying kind, you know? There were a lot of guys who might not have been ready for kids. I mean, I wasn't ready when we got pregnant. I got pregnant at 24, it was shortly after college and I was ready to get out there and forge ahead trying to start a career. But I managed to do that even with a baby in the mix. It just so happened that my son's father wanted this baby and wanted to be with me too, and it was important to me to be married. As a matter of fact, today is my son's 30th birthday! We got married [laughs] in June and he was born in November. So [laughs] my upbringing of not having had that traditional family really impacted my choices.

PBC: So, I'm interested in perhaps a turning point when you may have taken a leap yourself. Any experience that you can think of that shaped you? Was it getting pregnant with your son? Were there experiences of despair, aloneness or crisis that you can pinpoint as having shaped you?

Cyndi: Well, I guess you could say I took a leap when I got married. I could have chosen to have my son and not marry or marry later. I'm sure my family history had some bearing on that choice. That, and the fact that such a good man had come into my life. I also realize, in thinking about that question, that so many years of my life have been marked with loss…of family members and loved ones back to back to back to back. I think in a lot of ways it's probably taught me more about death and dying than I care to really focus on [laughs], and my father died when I was 10.

PBC: Did you know him? Did you have a relationship with him?

Cyndi: I did…I knew where he lived. I knew some of his family members. We communicated from time to time by phone. Mom and I visited from time to time, or sometimes she would send me to Philadelphia. So, yeah, I did know my father but not very well.

When he died, we got a phone call from one of his cousins that he shared a house with, saying he'd gone fishing that day, came home, and died of a heart attack. I remember this was just before my 6th grade graduation. I remembered feeling sad because I heard the words "your father has died", but because he wasn't in my life, the sadness was more from a place of a loss of life of someone who happened to be my father.

Instead of being sad that he wouldn't be attending my graduation, which he wouldn't have done even if he had lived, I later felt relieved that I could put "Father: Deceased" on school forms that required his name, because his name was different than mine. (Now, that seems kinda sad!) As a young child, I was ashamed that he and my mother never married. I felt that whenever I wrote his name and my mother's name on those forms, I was revealing that I was "illegitimate"—the word used for children born out of wedlock during that time.

My mom and I went to Philadelphia, attended his funeral, and came back home all in the same day. We probably attended the funeral more out of obligation to the relatives he lived with because they were always positive towards and more nurturing to my mom and me than my father was.

I think the shift here that I identify with is that my less-than-traditional family made me appreciate and want nothing more than to have a traditional family.

But, the siege of losses started with my father dying and then a few months later, an elderly retired uncle who was my extended family. We lived in the same neighborhood as he did at one point, and he looked after me when my mom was working when I was young. I think I was 12 when he passed away. There were other relatives in the years to come who passed. It forced me to step up and be the spokesperson early on.

PBC: How so?

Cyndi: Like in hospitals, being advocates for these family members. Well, just being there for them…making sure the doctors were doing what they should have been doing.

PBC: That sounds like a grownup responsibility at the young age of 12 or so…

Cyndi: For instance, my Uncle Alfred was the first person that I remember taking on that responsibility for. And like I said, this was the uncle who would take me to playgrounds early on and I kind of palled around with him. He really was a grandfather figure to me. When he went into the hospital, of course, there were adult family members that saw that he was admitted to the hospital. In our family, if somebody got sick, we tried to have round the clock care. Of course, since I was young, I would have to be there with an adult. That's where I first learned to ask questions of the doctor. We visited this particular uncle a lot in the hospital. I remember going back and forth with different family members. If they did not get involved in asking questions about the care, or if they did not like what they were hearing but did not speak up, I guess I kind of learned to ask questions of the doctors. Because seeing this loved one sitting there, lying there, not able to ask for himself, you figure somebody has to be the advocate. I was 12 or 13 when this was going on with this uncle. That was pretty young. I can remember asking questions, making sure that the best was being done for him, under the circumstances. As I grew older, I just kind of became this designated or at times self-appointed person. When my aunt passed away, her kids would call me to keep me abreast of what was going on. I'm usually one of the first people they call whenever there's a family emergency. I seem to have fallen into that role. They also saw how I handled my mom when she was in the hospital before she died and probably called on me because of that experience. So, maybe that's another of the paradigm shifts that's come out of this.

PBC: Somebody's gotta do it, is how you see it? Might as well be me?

Cyndi: Kind of like that…for every decade I can remember—lets' say, starting with the 70s—there's been the need for me to step in that way with a family member…or in some instances, as a friend. My mom passed away in 1993, and I felt had to primarily take on that responsibility for my brother and me both. Before she passed, she was in the hospital for a month. It was every day, constant, going back and forth to the hospital, making sure that she was getting the best possible care under the circumstances. I look back on that now—I wish I could have been there all day. I was 35 when she passed. She was 63. I was just starting the flow of my career with my young son who was 10 when she passed. But she had been sick for at least five years prior to that. Those years leading up to her passing took a lot. But I had to assume that role, because she was my mom. She did need looking after—she was in and out of the hospital.

PBC: Your brother, do you think he leaned on you because you were such a good, advocate and spokesperson?

Cyndi: Well, he helped as well. We were co-advocates in a lot of ways. But I chalk it up to the notion that sometimes females just step into that role differently than males do. I don't know if I would characterize it as him leaning on me, he just let me do or say what I needed to. We talked about whatever the plan of action was when it came to dealing with hospitals and that sort of thing.

PBC: You stepped into this role of advocate and spokesperson…was there anyone there for you that you could lean on with any of these losses?

Cyndi: Yeah, I could lean on my husband. There's usually always somebody that I've been able to lean on. Sometimes you can talk it out with people…you try to put your finger on where the emotions are and determine if you need help with anything like that. I had various outlets—sister-friends, sister-in-laws, and some grief counseling. I probably could have benefited from more counseling. But it's still hard to deal with the sadness and grief sometimes…missing the person or wishing you had more time with people after they're gone or as they're dying. That has never gone away for me in the different losses that I've had.

PBC: Did you ever meet anyone who understood grief in as profound a way as you were learning to? You know, you were sort of thrust into the Grief 101 course. Was there anyone else that you encountered who had a similar experience of multiple or significant losses along the way?

Cyndi: I can't remember meeting anyone having as many personal losses with the amount of frequency that I had over those years. Not on the level that I experienced it. That's been one of my life lessons—grief and loss and recovery. It's probably just that I'm such a humanitarian, not wanting to see bad things happen to people, that I sometimes feel loss so greatly. I wish that maybe life had been better for some of them, or that they had more time. But how you look at it—if your time is up, your time is up—is what matters, in the end. [laughs]

I think what I've learned is that what's important in the end was that those I loved in life and spent time with in their hospital rooms knew that I loved them and that they mattered in my life. The longer I live, I'm realizing that all any of us wants is to know that we matter. And when my time is up, I would hope that I lived my life in a way that others know that they mattered to me and I mattered to them. I really do believe that the spirit lives on. And there are times when I remember those loved ones, or am inspired by them in some way, I realize their spirit never dies.

PBC: Did you sometimes find yourself asking, "Why me and how did this happen …coulda shoulda woulda anything have changed it?" Either how they died or when they did?

Cyndi: I've certainly asked those questions, like what am I supposed to be learning from this? Is this my calling, [laughs] to be an advocate for people…and why do I become so attached? I think what I have learned though, is that even from those hard, hard lessons you can go on with life. You take the best memories you have, and you just go on, keeping their memory alive as best as you can. And certainly, as long as I'm living, all of those people that I've lost are still significant to me.

PBC: Did this bring up issues of faith or spirituality for you?

Cyndi: Yes. I've come to learn that I'm more spiritual than religious—meaning

I connect more with the spirit of a higher being that exists in all of us more than claiming or identifying with any one religion over another. In my life, there are a variety of people of different faiths…friends…the godmother that I lost…the whole question of spirituality is an ongoing quest for me. Mom attended the Baptist church as a young child. She always believed in God, but as an adult, she didn't attend church regularly; she attended sporadically. She, however, chose to be baptized again later in her adult life.

I constantly latch onto anything that can explain us as human beings as well as offer explanations and understanding. I was thinking about who am I and who am I becoming, and one of the things that I really know about myself is that I am a humanitarian at heart….and probably a social worker in my own way [laughs].

PBC: Sounds to me like that Godmother Qua Qua was the closest to someone who took you under wing outside of your mom. Is there anyone else you can think of that took you under wing? So far, it sounds like you've kind of taken it upon yourself to go this alone. Does that ring true for you?

Cyndi: I can't say I had to go it alone entirely. I think I just learned early on when I needed to step in, to add something, or provide support of some kind. Sure, there have definitely been others who took me under their wings. Growing up there were family members, neighbors, teachers, sister-friends, and even some employers, who were interested in and contributed to my development, greatly. One high school teacher, Lynda, who later became my sister-in-law, was also very influential in my late teen and early adult years. Her commitment to social justice and her commitment to her students gave me a broader perspective on social issues, (e.g. politics, education, alternative medicine, family, race) and taught me how having faith and trust in young adults empowers them. I don't mean to sound too cliché, but a village really did raise this child. That being said, I sometimes found it difficult to lean on anyone else. I'm always concerned about being a burden. On the whole, I'd say I'm on a quest of understanding me. I do things, I react and respond to things when necessary, and then I always take a moment to sit back and reflect.

PBC: That sounds like a lot of soul searching.

Cyndi: Certainly I reflect, but I'm always trying to answer the question [laughs] of, "What am I supposed to learn from this?" Or, "Could I have done this better? Could I have done that differently?" Or, "Why that person and not me?"

PBC: Does that seem like one of the ways you've taken a leap beyond your mom? You've been afforded the opportunity to ask more questions than she was, where she had to survive and provide…just put one foot in front of another to make it. It seems your circumstances, being almost an only child, have allowed you to reflect more, and sort of take that torch that she handed to you.

Cyndi: You kind of have to raise your head up above your day-to-day, to be able to say to yourself, "What does this all mean?" I'm not sure my mom really thought to ask herself questions like that. I do feel grateful I was afforded more time to be able to do that. Yes, she was so focused on surviving day-to-day.

PBC: Her focus was, "I gotta provide for these kids". However, you had a little more time and less responsibility as you were growing up to ponder more of the meaning and the choices—relative to her upbringing in which she had to start pitching in for the family instead of finishing high school, yes?

Cyndi: Something else that was a contributing factor for my mom is that she had one sister who had six kids. The two of them were close in age. Yet my mom struggled with her two children! She had to work so hard to make sure that we had what we had. I think the thought of having more kids and to having to struggle was too much. She concluded, "I can't go that route." I think it gave me an appreciation for family planning even though my son arrived sooner than I was quite ready for. It was important to me to make sure that I could sufficiently provide for any children I might have. I look at people who have a lot of kids, not necessarily knowing how they're gonna provide, or if it's gonna be more difficult than they can manage. It was a big consideration for me, whether or not we wanted to expand our family.

PBC: You seeing your mom struggle made you especially conscientious about putting yourself through all that? Rather than allowing the kids to be a hardship or burden, you chose to do it thoughtfully and conscientiously.

Cyndi: Exactly, and I think I got that from mom, too. She did the best she could. She certainly knew that having more kids wouldn't make it more manageable, so I saw her try to be as smart as she could be in raising us right. I think the backdrop that my mom came from a large family where, at times, there wasn't a lot of love and time to go around, influenced how she raised us as conscientiously as she did—she was there even when she wasn't there, if you know what I mean? When she was working and all, she was still there for us. We could depend on her to satisfy our needs. She always let us know, "I'm working hard for you. I'm doing this for us," so we knew we could rely on her.

PBC: So, let's move on to conflict in relationships: how mom handled conflicts as you saw it. It sounds like there were plenty of conflicts with her siblings, and by contrast or comparison, how do you approach conflicts in your relationships?

Cyndi: Well, in a lot of ways I admired her approach, she would always say things like, "There's two sides to every story. You need to get as many sides of the story as possible." And that is my approach when it comes to dealing with conflict. A lot of the conflict that I saw in the family was 'she-said-he said' stuff. So my mom's policy was, try to gather the facts as much as possible and then make your own determination based on that. I think my mom was a pretty good judge of character, and I think that I got some of that.

PBC: For years you were the peacemaker, as you mentioned, with her and her siblings. Do you think that influenced and shaped you into becoming a peacemaker by personality, or in your own adult relationships?

Cyndi: Maybe it did. I guess now I'm trying to improve how to convey my message. A lot of times when the emotions get involved you have to tread lightly on everybody's feelings because you know they're coming from a different place. There was a recent example of this—I visited some cousins and there were some conflicts between them. I told them, "I love all of you and I want to see you all together. When I come to visit, I don't want it to be awkward between any of us. So can you please try to resolve this before I get there?" I usually try and think things through, prepare myself to feel comfortable saying what I need to say when needed, because I saw how that didn't necessarily work out well with my mom. She didn't always make her point in a way that conveyed what she was really feeling in her heart, which was usually coming from a place of love. But it didn't always come across that way.

PBC: In the sense that you didn't really 'sign up' to be the peacemaker, and yet you kind of became designated as such, right? Have you at times asked, "What about me? When is it my turn to receive...to be off duty...to be free?" Or just felt, "I need to take care of me."

Cyndi: Are you asking me who's going to step up and do this if not me?

PBC: Sort of wondering if that role that you've taken on as peacemaker has sometimes backfired or become too limited for you in your adult life.

Cyndi: My caregiver/peacemaker roles have diminished more recently due to a difference in circumstances (e.g. fewer deaths, illnesses, a little more family harmony). But at the time, I was so vested in what was happening and trying to help, that I thought more about finding ways to make the situation better rather than looking for relief. And if/when I became overwhelmed (usually emotionally), there was always someone I could reach out to allow me some time to myself or who might have an idea about trying something different if I was stuck. There've certainly been times that my efforts didn't go over well, [laughs] if that could be a description of these situations backfiring on me. I think I've probably learned more from those instances than anything, and I've tried to improve on them. But if I spotted a no-win situation, yeah I definitely learned to pull myself out of it.

Hopefully I can grow from every experience and have the insight to know when I can be useful. It's definitely a skill I think I'm honing. [laughs] These days I'm less of a family peacemaker. Now I wonder if those skills gained as the peacemaker may have prepared me to become a mediator, perhaps as a job after retirement?

PBC: Is there anything that you want to say about being a mom yourself? You described your mom as being the nurturer and good-natured and hard working—is that the kind of mom you feel you have been to your son? Or are there other aspects of your mothering that distinguish you from her?

Cyndi: I think that I'm more focused. How I approach my son is a little different than how my mom approached me but…well, there are some basic chords. My mom wanted me to do what would make me happy. In that way, I find myself using those same words specifically with my son. He's different than I was in terms of getting to know himself and sharing that with others. He's way less revealing of his thoughts than I was. Therefore, I'm constantly trying to understand what he thinks about and where he wants to go in life. I think that a lot of my wanting to have a traditional lifestyle probably has to do with me wanting to afford him two parents to talk about anything he needed to talk about. Having two parents in his life meant having more than one person for him to rely on. While she didn't always show it, being a single parent and having to decide everything alone was at times a bit overwhelming to mom, I think.

PBC: You feel like you've actually realized the traditional family background that you longed for as a child?

Cyndi: I think it's easier to be a mother to my son because he does have a father in his life. To be able to say, "That's an issue you and your father need to address" after my son and I have addressed it. It kind of takes the weight off of a parent to have a father and a mate to be able to say, "Talk about it with your dad." And I'm gonna come from a different place than my husband would sometimes just because of the gender difference. I'm glad my son has that father willing to provide advice, which I did not have growing up. However, my son will resort to the family before going to outside resources. He's very close to his dad and me, from the standpoint of seeking our advice and wisdom about things. Whereas, I was aware my mom had her limitations for me to go to her for advice or empathy—plus she had so much on her plate. Sometimes another's perspective was helpful to me. The same is probably true of my son on some level, too. After all, as parents we'd like to think we may have all the answers for our children, but I know we don't, for whatever reasons.

PBC: Your son has had more of the contained nuclear family. I'm wondering how your commitment to create a more traditional family has worked for you, given that you do have a career? Have you been able to strike a balance or have you struggled with that? It seems to be one of the paradigm shifts from the post-war years? (50s) that our generation of women has faced. I realize your mom worked and yet you felt she was there for you, but many women who have pursued and achieved *careers*—as opposed to jobs to get by with—struggle with how to attend to work and home in a quality and balanced way.

Cyndi: I think having that traditional, two parent household made it easier to strike a balance between career and family. We both work, so just like a single parent household, we had to depend on childcare. However, if—for instance—my son couldn't go to day care because he was sick, at least one of us could stay home with him. It wouldn't always have to be mom. I had the option of working that out with his dad. That can be a relief from a job and family standpoint. The hard work ethic, coming from that kind of background made me determined to get through college and become a professional.

I have a Bachelors Degree in Criminal Justice, which helped me land my first professional job out of college. I'm grateful for the curiosity that my mom instilled in me. She always wanted us to be exposed to as much as possible, and to do the best we could in our encounters. As I moved from one job to the next in my field, I took on her drive and work ethic to be the best in my profession. My entire career in the Federal Government has involved ensuring the safety of United States and its citizens. I've always taken my work seriously because of the significance of the responsibility. For me, my mom was the epitome of taking her responsibilities seriously.

PBC: You think you get that from your mom's work ethic?

Cyndi: Yeah, I had a lot of respect for her.

PBC: [laughs] So thank you for your high standards in public service!

Cyndi: There are a lot of us hard working, good public servants out there, and there are good and bad in any profession. [laughs] You see it all.

PBC: It's good to hear that your mom's work ethic and that of doing the right thing lives on in you. She was a good role model!

Let's move on to our final topic: the female role models who influenced you. *Now* it's time for you to talk about Oprah! [laughs]

Cyndi: You know, with all that's going on now on a national level…being here in the D.C. area, you certainly get submerged in the politics and all of that. Oprah has long been somebody out there on the national stage that I've admired. I genuinely see her as somebody who is constantly trying to keep us focused on the good in humanity and promoting that we try to do as much as we can so that all of us can live on this planet in the best way possible. I see her as somebody who exemplifies that perspective, and I think that she's the icon she is because a lot of people can identify with her ideas. One little tidbit—I think I identify with her also because she's an Aquarius, [laughs] which is also my astrological sign…we're humanitarians always.

PBC: Oh just so you know, [laughs] my husband is an Aquarius!

Cyndi: I think we are genuinely concerned about the good of everybody. It rings true with me, when I think about all the people in my lifetime that I've met, and what I would do if I had her kind of money. I'd donate to causes that I deem beneficial to society. I'm that person in the family that people come to for advice. I've also helped people financially many, many times when I could. I think they know my heart is genuine, like my mom, coming from a place of love and of good intent.

PBC: And do you also identify with being someone who continued the effort to turn the "lemons" or strife in your mom's background, her very humble roots, into "lemonade"—as in something that involves being able to learn and grow and help people?

Cyndi: Yes, I do identify with turning lemons into lemonade. Seeing how my mom struggled made me see we all have struggles in life, but what counts is how you handle those struggles. (By the way, as a side note, my mom actually made the best homemade, fresh squeezed lemonade, ever!) I'm aware that Oprah came from Mississippi and her grandmother told her she'd have to learn to be a laundry woman. Oprah didn't feel that was true for her. I can remember seeing my mom struggle so hard that I would ask myself how I could do better. Then hearing teachers, my mom, and my friends' parents say education was the key to a better future, I latched onto that message. I think Oprah is a shining example of that fierce determination to transcend her roots, and she is always doing something to try to educate us. She gives us something to think about and puts it out there for us to ponder…challenging us to re-evaluate ourselves…consider…ponder. I like getting those messages of encouragement. I'll be 55 in January, and I'm constantly thinking about my purpose. What is my purpose? Oprah brings that question home a lot. Maybe she's directing it at my age…'Boomer' women. But wherever you are in your life, she urges you to think about having a purpose driven life. I'm still on that path of trying to figure out what my purpose is. So I appreciate her steering our thinking. She definitely is a role model for me; I see some parallels between her life and mine. It's just so wonderful to see an African American women whose life struggles made her determined to be better than her beginnings, so much so that she's an iconic figure known world-wide for striving to make us all think about being better human beings.

PBC: You identify with her journey.

Cyndi: On some level, yes I do—the journey and what we've discovered through the journey. And I'm finding I'm still discovering a lot [laughs] as I go on. I hope I will continue to make discoveries!

PBC: Would your message you'd like to leave the next generation of women be about pursuing an education or going for a purpose driven life?

Cyndi: I think the education message has been emphasized to the point that women know the significance of education. However, I do worry that our society is becoming more insular in its thinking. I think trying to determine the good we can bring to the world and living a purpose driven life is equally as important as education. I'd like to see us think more about being vessels for doing good for others, no matter where we are in our lives. I've been a recipient of kindness from others and because of that, I've given it back. In both instances, the feeling has been awesome. Life's lessons can make for a long journey, but I've found, as you go along the journey in a conscious and reflective way, you're going to discover more about who you are as a person and what your purpose is for that moment. That's how the journey has gone for me. Whoever I was at the time, or whatever the cause was at the time, that's exactly what I was supposed to be doing. And hopefully I'm learning more about that and learning how to take those lessons to the next level, if that makes sense.

PBC: "Hit on your purpose and the journey will guide you forward!" I think that's quite a pearl!

Cyndi: Well I'm curious to read the responses of others in your interviews to know how many of us feel we're alone in what we're going through.

PBC: I think we need to connect to one another's experiences to know that this is the journey of our generation—which is what I hope this book of stories of "we who took a leap" will help contribute to! Cyndi, I also want to restate another pearl you said earlier in our discussion: "When my time is up, it will be good to know that I lived my life in a way that others know that they mattered to me and I mattered to them." How beautiful is that—and you're not done by any means yet!

Biography

Hope Mason Boylston, 6/25/47.

Mother: Emily Mason Boylston, born 1923. Died in 2009.

Graduated from George Washington University in 1969 with a BA in anthropology. Was married first to a Chilean, Felipe Martinez from 1970 to 1981. Married Stephen Beckerman, an anthropology professor I actually meet for the first time in 1967, in 1984 and am still married to him.

I have three children, a boy, and 39 who were born in Chile, a girl 27 and a boy 25 who were born in the US. I have one sister who is 11 years younger than I am.

My career has been pretty random. After college, and the long drive to Chile, I stayed there from early 1970 to mid-1973. I taught English for a while, but eventually began working for the Allende government women's magazine. With another 'gringa' I met there, we worked for nearly a year on an adaptation/translation of Our Bodies Ourselves for publication as a booklet within the magazine. The first installment, about 7 chapters, was ready for publication when the military took over.

In the States from 73–78, I worked transcribing and editing interviews as a research assistant for a journalist and, briefly, because of my mother's mental illness, as part of the DC bureau of In These Times, a social democratic weekly published in Chicago. But mostly, during this time I was an active member of NICH, Non-Intervention in Chile, which had originally been founded to protest CIA involvement in Chile.

From 1978-81, I was back in Chile. I did some translation and editing work and was hired by CARE (a large, international US NGO which sponsors development projects in the third world.) I ran a school garden program, which provided supplies for rural elementary schools. During this time in Chile, I was an active, if somewhat peripheral, member of the Resistance against the Pinochet Dictatorship.

Since coming back to the US in 1981, I've worked mostly as a teacher in a 4th grade classroom and as a Spanish teacher at State College Friends School. I also spent quite a while writing Hay Locos and am currently retired.

It would be hard to find a family any more 'WASP' than mine. Both sides of the family are from New England. My mother's family was Presbyterian and until middle school I went to church every Sunday. Though my paternal grandmother was Quaker, mostly the Boylstons were skeptical of organized religion. My mother was married and separated twice from my father whom she finally divorced and then married a second husband when she was about 55. My father died in 1982 (after they were divorced) and her second husband died when she was in her late 70s.

Finally, thinking of paradigm shifts, I'd say that my mother's life was affected by mental illness, and thus her mindset was dominated by the idea that the US was under constant pressure and aggression from communism (and perhaps later Islam) and must defend itself vigorously against these forces, while mine, in contrast, was that the world was a place where power and wealth were controlled by Western capitalism which resulted in poverty and injustice in much of the world.

Hope as a young girl

Hope with her mother

Hope today

Interview

August 2012

PBC: So, you've been identified as someone who has taken a leap in your own journey of consciousness and I wonder whether you identify with this image of someone who's taken a leap of consciousness in the evolution of the times.

Hope: Yes. I think I do fit that description. I'm now 65 and I can look back on my life and often ask, how did I get here? If I were to be writing another book, it would be to understand that. That's why I thought your project was so interesting.

PBC: Well, thank you. So in terms of the leap of consciousness that you perceive yourself as having made in this journey of yours, what would you say that is in a nutshell?

Hope: I think that I became a person of the planet rather than of the United States. That experience brought me to see my role in the world as a North American in a very different light from the way I grew up.

PBC: How did you perceive it as you were growing up, and now, how do you see the world?

Hope: Well, I was brought up in a very Republican family—the kind of Republicans who are in scarce supply right now whose foreign and economic policies were as drastically to the political right as could be, but whose social views were as progressive as any liberal democratic family. The amount of freedom and responsibility I was allowed to have now astonishes me. My parents fostered an independent young woman in many ways yet without providing any firm footing to that independence, I think. So it led me to wander around the world, and wandering around the world led me to see that there were children dying of hunger all over the place. This altered forever my view of the world.

PBC: I'm aware that you wrote this book about your travels to Chile as you were finishing college, yes? Was that an opening?

Hope: Yes. It was. Even before I left on that trip, I spent my last semester of college abroad in Ecuador in 1969. I think that was when I suddenly realized that the world was a vastly different place than I knew it to be. For example, I would come downstairs in the mornings often and see people sorting through trash to see what they could get out of it.

PBC: Quite a reality check, yes?

Hope: The many towns without plumbing, without electricity, understanding what was going on in this country which was such a contrast to my world…it was a 19th century village I was experiencing. It isn't anymore, but it probably still has more poverty now than it did then in terms of numbers because it's become so much more urban.

PBC: And instead of being alienated by that, you were compelled to adventure further in that territory, yes?

Hope: Yes. That's interesting because I know it doesn't do that to everybody. I would say of the 40 or 50 students who were in the program, run by the University of New Mexico, (and most of them were Chicano and a lot of them had spoken Spanish as children), this exposure made them narrower rather than broader, except for the anthropology students. I think it was what in Spanish would be called 'verguenza ajena,' shame by association. They tended to condemn rather than try to understand the reality of an underdeveloped country: unsafe water, unreliable schedules, and poor facilities. I think some were shocked to see a Spanish speaking world so much poorer than the U.S. All they could see was this kinky little third world country that didn't function very well by our standards. So they rejected it. Whereas I somehow looked out and said, "How could this be?" In my book *Hay Locos* there is one story I share about my walk to school down this road where there was a shop that wasn't a funeral parlor…it was a coffin store…have you ever seen coffins in a storefront?

PBC: I've read a little about that.

Hope: I mean, you don't see coffins on display in the United States. But in addition to these regular looking coffins, there were many more white coffins or some two or three feet long lined in pink and blue satin. It took me a while to put it all together…I realized that these are for children! It was children who died most frequently. If they survived childbirth, the next horrible point in their lives was a transition from mother's milk to unsanitary food and water conditions, so they would die of intestinal diseases. After that exposure, I never could get back to squaring the values I was raised with alongside this new alarming reality. In other words, I couldn't put my world together in a way where what was good for Republicans was good for the world. Even before this trip, I already doubted some of that. I think this is something positive about my family's socially liberal influence on my world view. I knew from the first day I walked into an anthropology class that this was what I wanted to know. I had an absolutely wonderful professor who was chair of the anthropology department whose class got me wondering about the rest of the world. Probably because of that, I decided to go to Ecuador for that semester.

There are a couple of other things that have caused my personal evolution in perspective. One of them was undoubtedly a real influence in my life: that my mother suffered from bipolar disorder.

PBC: So, let's look at what distinguishes you from your mother.

Hope: As a younger teenager, bipolar disorder tends to follow a certain chronological pattern and people who suffer from it tend to have their worst episodes in their mid 30s to 45 or so. As such, my mother was not very well-glued at some of the critical intervals of my childhood.

PBC: And at what point did you become aware of that, and how did you perceive it growing up?

Hope: I became aware of her swings—when she was too up or too down. That, I think, made me different from other children and different from her, and more acutely aware of her.

PBC: Aware that she was different from your friends' mothers, for example?

Hope: Yes, definitely, especially, by the time I was about 12 to 16 which was when the worst of the trouble happened. She went into a few psychotic episodes, manic episodes and was hospitalized a couple of times. My mother's mental illness became a formative experience for me growing up.

PBC: So you found her unpredictable. How did you perceive her mental illness at the time, being so young?

Hope: I think I knew by age 15, certainly and I suspected she had troubles by 11 or 12. Her background played a big role. Her most formative moments were World War II, and she was left with this enduring feeling that the worst that happened in her generation was that the Europeans had thought they could pacify Hitler. After the war, that led her into a very strong McCarthy kind of position, supporting anti-communist conspiracies of people determined to destroy our way of life—kind of a distorted view of the world.

PBC: Would you say she was paranoid?

Hope: She was not that 'well-glued-together.' She easily bought into conspiracy ways of looking at the world.

PBC: Tough on you, yes?

Hope: But by contrast she was not a controlling parent. I often said to friends that in some ways it's better if your mother is occasionally psychotic than if she's constantly neurotic. I think a lot of what made her different was her circumstances, but in some fundamental personality traits, we had many similarities. We were not all that different.

PBC: And what were the circumstances that did distinguish her background from yours, and perhaps left her injured, mentally?

Hope: Her own stage of life and the experience of marrying her boyfriend who went off into the navy in the Second World War.

PBC: Your mother married her boyfriend before or after he went off to war?

Hope: He was already in the Navy when they married, and then, shortly after that, he went off to the Pacific.

Actually my father had…what you would have to say is a fundamentally delightful time in World War II! Which is, utterly bizarre, but he spent a great deal of the war as a Navy pilot in Polynesia, flying from island to island. He was stationed in Samoa. That marriage lasted. She did eventually divorce him much later for odd reasons of her own, which I'll get into later.

PBC: Hmm. And he had a grand time but somehow, his military work experience affected her.

Hope: Yes, that whole idea that we should never compromise…that we had to defend the country against these things, that you couldn't appease communists, and you had to stamp them out somehow.

PBC: Would you say she was more political or plugged in to the mentality that many women and mothers around her had in that time?

Hope: She was definitely more political. She became very involved in the '50s and, and '60s in right wing Republican politics. And they were based on this anti-Communist position. But she didn't have a lot of interest in the economic policy or social policies of the right.

PBC: So did that influence you—her political activism and her anti-communism or conspiracy theories?

Hope: I would say up until I was about 19 or 20 I bought into it then I slowly began to dissent from it. Probably the Vietnam War, being my generation's moment of truth, led me in the other direction. I looked at the war like most of my generation and thought this was a bad war. My attitude was: "This doesn't make any sense. This is none of our business. This is a terrible mistake." I wasn't an anti-war activist at that point. But I was the kind of person who—maybe didn't join SDS (Students for a Democratic Society)—but showed up for all the marches. Where, by contrast, my mother was able to buy into the whole doom-and-gloom theory of 'what ifs': "We have to have this war and we have to drive out these people because if we don't, they're going to come after us."

The other thing that made a difference was that my mother's mother died when she was 10 years old. She was not well for a long time. She had suffered heart damage from having rheumatic fever as a child and eventually my grandmother succumbed. So then my mother was kind of treated as a trophy between her father and her maternal grandparents, who were quite wealthy, and were not above using their financial resources to control my mother's life as much as they could. Though

I don't think we ever talked about it, I think her reaction against that as she became older was perhaps to err in the other direction. This experience instilled in her this idea that you're not supposed to manipulate your children's lives. That was a bad thing to do.

PBC: She reacted to having been over-controlled by her grandparents in raising you, do you think?

Hope: Yes, and my father's family was quite unconventional in many ways. His parents both were brilliant, a chemist and a surgeon, and they seemed to have much less fear of violating traditions than most of their generation. For example, when my father wanted to learn to drive, they said fine, bought him a model T and told him he was welcome to drive it as soon as he learned to take it apart and put it back together—so he did!

PBC: So your mother's background influenced her in such a way that she was deliberately more 'hands off' with you than her parents were with her. Your sister wasn't affected in the same way you were?

Hope: We have the same two parents but were born under very different circumstances by the passage of those the 11 years between us, my being the younger, remember. Her birth contributed to mom's coming further unraveled. We had moved from Grosse Pointe, Michigan, a wealthy 'wasp' suburb of Detroit, to Ft. Lauderdale, Florida…still wealthy but obviously decadent. My father retired at 39 years old and for the rest of his life, managed investments and volunteered in politics. It was an entirely different world.

PBC: Do you think you saw your mom at her worst?

Hope: That's a good question—I don't know. If she had not had another child with some of the hormonal changes in pregnancy, she might have been worse, or if hers was the natural course of being bipolar…I don't know.

PBC: You must have been concerned about your sister as your mom was checking in and out of the reality and checking in out of the hospital? Your sister was so young.

Hope: Yes, I was, at times. Once I can remember clearly I had to rescue her from my mother. I actually had to call my mom's psychiatrist, and they had to come and basically put her in a straightjacket and take her away while I hid my little sister from her. She had escalated to the manic stage where mania turns into paranoia.

PBC: Ooh—kind of scary.

Hope: She had this whole fantasy thing going on, and I had to step in and protect my sister. My father wasn't available at the time, so I had to. Even though I was put in this position of taking responsibility, I also had a lot of freedom. But I was brought up with the notion that with privilege came responsibility, and we had an obligation to act on our beliefs. So even as my parents and I had very different ideas about the political course our country should take, we shared the idea that we were responsible for taking a stand.

PBC: Are there positive memories, gifts that she gave you as well, in contrast to the trouble spots?

Hope: She was a great editor of children's books. She was a phenomenally gifted writer, and instilled in me a love of reading. She read to me as a child. When I was a small child, I think she was a good mother to me in that way and woke up my interest in literature and reading, which we always shared. Much later, I finally decided I ought to let her read the manuscript of my book, **Hay Locos**. She sat and read it almost cover to cover. By this time she was in her late 70s. She said to me when she finished it, "I think we're very much the same, and if I had grown up in your generation and had done what you have done, I might believe exactly what you do." It was a moment I won't forget—I have always been glad that I let her read it. She didn't live too many years after that.

PBC: So, that must have been a gift to you.

Hope: That was a real gift. It was such a gift that she also could see beyond the content of what she believed into who she was, who I was in my own right, and how different generational influences made us what we were.

PBC: She was able to see through your lens.

Hope: See a bit of my lens because, in a great many ways, we were very similar.

PBC: What else was similar about you? The love of literature and that position of taking a stand about what you believe…Those were two similarities—are there others?

Hope: A love of literature and she was a marvelous traveling companion. We traveled together a few times, and we shared a spirit of: Let's go try this! Let's stay away from the big cities and go to the small towns…let's not get caught up in the 10,000 people who are at the Sistine Chapel, let's go to some smaller venues where we are not among the crowds. She did have that spirit of adventure. I don't think she got to act on it as much she probably would have liked to.

PBC: When you were adventuring together, you were able to connect?

Hope: Yes—we had lots of fun together. We made car trips over the years. We went to Greece and Italy together. I cherish those memories. I think she had the same kind of conflict within her that initially drove me away from what my family thought about the world and she wasn't able to get through it.

For instance, she loved coming to stay with me here in Pennsylvania. In fact, if she hadn't died, she was going to move up here. Initially she didn't want to, because she didn't want to go back to northern winters. She was lonely after her second husband died. We had moved to Florida when I was 12, but then she decided she wanted to be nearer to family. My sister had moved to North Carolina, and married this kind of southern 'good ol' boy' after a number of failed marriages, and my mom was living near her there. They shared her politics but were only interested in sports.

PBC: Are you suggesting that your mom had the same conflict in her that you had in you? If so, I'd love to hear more about that.

Hope: It was obvious that she thought it was a lot more fun to live in my house than it was in my sister's. She loved the fact that my husband is a university professor and I have always been a busy social person. People were always dropping in, and when she was at the house, we had frequent dinner parties. People would TALK about things, whereas although my sister agreed more with her politics, she led an extremely unintellectual life compared to me. My mother loved being around university professors and literary conversation. She was an avid reader of British style detective stories, which I got into in my thirties, and we liked exactly the same authors. I could call her up and say, "Have you read this?" and she could say, "Have you read that?" We both were extremely fond of a few good writers of historical fiction as well.

PBC: You were able to transcend the concerns and barriers between you by emphasizing these common interests. In that way, you found ways to connect with her best qualities, yes?

Hope: I think I did. Yes.

PBC: Otherwise, her bipolar condition could be so alienating?

Hope: When it became extreme, yes. For a couple of years she was not in contact with anyone in the family. When she was in what would have been her late 40s and mostly 50s, she had been divorced from my father because she had been pulled into a relationship with a guy who was clearly psychotic and fell in love.

PBC: Your father was aware but took her back??

Hope: Twice actually [laughs]. My father didn't know what to do about it. Poor man, and then she wanted him back the third time. He finally—shortly before he died—said, "I'm sorry Emily. You may always be the love of my life, but I can't do this anymore."

PBC: Were you still living at home when she divorced him?

Hope: I was long out of the house. The worst of this kind of this behavior with my dad started when I was in my thirties. I moved to Florida on and off in 1975 to try to fix it and it cost me a journalism job.

PBC: And there were other men both times?

Hope: Other men twice. I remember thinking that anybody with my mother's intellect would have immediately recognized the individual she was involved with in the first affair was an insanely stupid person to be involved with, but sadly, she couldn't realize it. She fell in with him into a syndrome called 'folie au deux' where two people share a psychiatric delusion or disassociation. In this case, the man was psychotic, a litigating paranoid schizophrenic, and my mom was diagnosed bipolar. She was convinced by his delusions. He managed to convince her that the entire family had stolen millions of dollars that didn't exist.

PBC: It was that shadow side of her that he brought out…it was the worst in her.

Hope: She lived with him for a couple of years I guess. And then somehow she got out of it. I don't know how.

PBC: Not by your influence?

Hope: No indeed. I was the last person in the family that she was talking to. I put all my effort into making her go see her a psychiatrist one last time. I met with him afterwards privately. He said, "She's not in a manic state, but she's bought into this guy." Fortunately, she did eventually get out of that.

PBC: So it was the psychiatrist? Do you suspect he helped her get out of it?

Hope: She was not reachable when I met with the psychiatrist. My meeting with him was a last ditch effort that helped inform me, but she didn't respond at the time. I don't know how she finally got out of it…she never recognized the deviation after it all happened. Well, maybe she did to herself, but she never talked about it. But somehow she got out of it, and then she begged my father to take her back. He took her back, but she started taking ballroom dancing on her own. She was restless…she wanted something more to do in her life. I think this was part of the trouble. She got good at ballroom dance class, and then she had this second affair.

PBC: So dad didn't learn either? He didn't see how he had been taken in by her again?

Hope: He had absolutely no interest in taking ballroom dance classes, so she escaped into that and did it on her own. Then she had this affair and tried to run off with the guy who owned the dance school, and that was insanely stupid too. He was a charlatan, but he wasn't crazy.

PBC: Like the last guy? So, these affairs were hard for you to watch, I gather, but you kept your distance.

Hope: They never actually became a couple, but he was good at milking money out of women like my mother, which he did do. She loaned him lots of money, and he never repaid it. I was not living at home when this was going on, but once she got onto one of these things, you couldn't reach her with how this was a terrible mistake. She had to play it out on her own, and she eventually got through that one too. It was after that one that my father reached his limit and said no, not taking you back again.

PBC: She had to play it out until she reached her 'Enough.'

Hope: Yes, but this was a couple of years before my father died.

PBC: When did he pass away?

Hope: He was young. He was 61—it was 1982.

PBC: So sad!

Hope: Then she was on her own. She moved around a great deal during the rest of her life. She didn't ever seem to establish a good anchor. She did eventually marry.

PBC: Her roller coaster love life certainly reflects a troubled restlessness, doesn't it?

Hope: It was also during a more constricted time for women—had it been our generation, all that energy could have gone into a meaningful career. She clearly had lots of talent.

PBC: So back to you—do you feel you picked up there, that you were able to take that restless adventurous spirit and make a life out of it and a life work out of it, in a nutshell?

Hope: Yes, I think that's it, and I think at some level she wanted me to do that. So, even compared with my own children, I think I was on a pretty loose leash. I mean, the mere fact that somehow, my parents conceded to the idea that my friend 'Toody' and I would buy this Jeep and drive it to Chile…I don't think there's many parents in the world who wouldn't have put up a real fight over that idea.

PBC: As I read little bits of your own published memoir…I got that they didn't take it too seriously but were giving you the benefit of the doubt—or at least your dad was.

Hope: Yeah. They didn't step right in and say, "No." I had a small amount of my money myself then. Both my girlfriend and I had enough means that we could afford this trip. So I didn't need them to fund it directly. But I imagine if they had opposed it strongly enough we would have been dissuaded.

PBC: That she allowed you such freedom might have been a reaction to mom having had too much control in her background?

Hope: Yeah, I think so. We want to give our kids what we didn't have so we counter-balance it. So if we grow up with antique furniture, we like Danish modern instead.

PBC: So true! So it sounds like the seeds that were planted in you of adventure and that restless spirit actually took. They took hold in you and you've been able to use them in a positive way, which I want to hear about more as we get into you, but before I leave your mother completely, I'm interested in hearing about what you and she argued about if there were arguments as you are growing up.

Hope: Other than things like her trying to run off with a dance teacher after I left home…

PBC: But while you were still at home in your growing up years as a teenager, for example.

Hope: I didn't argue with them a lot then. The only point of conflict, and it was significant, was at the end of my sophomore year of high school. I was away for the summer on a student tour of Europe. Somehow in the middle of summer my mother decided—and my father gave up fighting her—that life in Fort Lauderdale was frivolous and not very goal directed, I was under achieving and needed more structure or more intellectual challenge. Or maybe I needed to get away somehow from the overall decadence of growing up in Fort Lauderdale…so she enrolled me in a boarding school.

PBC: Your dad didn't agree but gave in?

Hope: He didn't subscribe to the idea that sending me to a boarding school was a smart idea, but he gave in to her. That was entirely Mother's thing. She sent me away to this boarding school—I remember I wasn't initially opposed to it. I didn't know what it would be like. I hadn't seen the school that was in Philadelphia.

PBC: Was it your view that you were being sent away from her crazy scenes, and was it around that time that you were rescuing your sister from her manic episodes?

Hope: I don't actually remember that being a big piece of it. I think when she wrote me that she had been looking around at these boarding schools, she justified that she had found one where she thought I would do better than I was doing. I think they were afraid I was getting too wild. She had gone to a girl's boarding school, as had her mother, so it didn't seem like a strange thing to do to your children, from her point of view.

PBC: Let's look at the contradiction: they had approved your going to study abroad but then they perceived you as being wild?

Hope: So for example, they found out that a bunch of us fifteen year olds had taken the car on a joyride at night in Fort Lauderdale! That kind of stuff.

PBC: You worried them?

Hope: Typical teenage antics. It was irresponsible teenage behavior, so she sent me to this boarding school that was academically quite rigorous, but it was stifling to me. I went from this trip that they had let me go on with a girlfriend and her older sister with mostly college students, going all around Europe and then I came back to this repressive school. I remember the first day I arrived at the school. My mother had met me in New York, following Europe, and helped me buy clothing for it because, of course, I had no winter clothing, coming from Fort Lauderdale. We did all that and then they put me on a plane to Philadelphia from Ft. Lauderdale, which didn't seem threatening to me at all. I was fine. I got on the plane, I got to the Philadelphia airport and I cabbed it to the school.

The first thing they said to me at the school was, "How did you get here?" I said, "I took a plane from Fort Lauderdale, and I got a cab at the Philadelphia airport." They said, "Well, you can't do that." I was taken aback, "What do you mean?" And they said, "Well, you had to have been met by a chaperone to get here." I said, "I didn't know that, and I'm already here." And that was the tenor of that year. I hated it! It was so restrictive. I responded very negatively to it. It was one of those adolescent things where, in order to show my parents that they had made this terrible mistake by sending me to this horrible place that I couldn't stand, I would fail. I didn't totally fail, but I certainly did badly.

PBC: Did you and your parents or your mom argue about the decision?

Hope: I didn't call up hysterically and say, "You have to bring me home!" I saw the year through, I don't know why. But at the end of the school year I told them I absolutely would not go back to that place, and consequently I went back to the high school that I had gone to in Fort Lauderdale.

Actually my little sister many years later said she wanted to go to this boarding school where they had horses and both boys and girls and she argued for weeks over it; apparently I wasn't home while this discussion was taking place. They gave in to her and sent her to this school, and three weeks later she screamed and yelled and said she had to come home and they let her come home. It didn't occur to me that I could do that. I stuck it out. Ironically, it did actually produce the results my mother wanted. I was so isolated from the kind of world I was used to living in that it was like being sent to a monastery for a year. I did a lot of reading, even though I didn't necessarily read what I was supposed to be reading. I did question what kind of pointlessly frivolous world I had been living in—it made me more philosophical and critical.

But when I came back to Fort Lauderdale, the part of my life that I had enjoyed—the 'joy ride,' per se was over and I basically wrote off high school as a social experience. I kept up social contacts only with my two or three best girlfriends. I took my studies more seriously, having been at the bottom half of the class at boarding school for a year. I ended up graduating I think fourth in my class. So in this very odd way, it worked.

PBC: It sobered you up.

Hope: It did.

PBC: Interesting that you can see that it actually accomplished what they set out to—or at least some of what they set out to accomplish. It felt oppressive and isolated you, but it also sounds like it deepened your consciousness.

Hope: Yes, looking back, I can now see this. I always had that element of individuality. I had participated in being part of the pack with these kids, but some part of me was frequently an outsider before that, and maybe because of my mother's mental problems, I hung out with the in crowd of frivolously silly high school people for distraction, but I was never completely a part of it. After that year away from it, I never had any interest again in being part of it.

PBC: Well, sounds like that was a pivotal moment for you growing up. I'm interested to hear if there were other pivotal moments that I refer to as 'paradigm shifts,' either during your growing up years or later? Those kinds of experiences where your world changed underneath you, or you had to get some help in order to shift from despair…loneliness or crisis to something better?

Hope: So the first week of college, when I walked into Introductory Anthropology 101 and had this spell-binding lecturer, I knew what my major was. I was kind of thinking maybe I would be a philosophy major when I came in. But as soon as I understood that you could see the world in so many different ways, I was hooked. I was fascinated with the flexible scale of human diversity…that things weren't set in stone…they could be very different, and I was fascinated with it. In high school, I had read what actually at some level must have been the first history of human evolution. Robert Ardrey wrote these books about the African origins of all humans. I found that to be fascinating. My father also had wonderful stories about the Samoans whom he loved when he was there. I was curious about non-Western societies.

PBC: Did your dad's stories as well as that college lecture awaken your curiosity about the world?

Hope: Yes, and I became intrigued by how other people looked at the world. I wanted to know more about it. Because I was becoming critical of the way the United States was operating, I wanted to know how the rest of the world operated. Getting into that classroom was pivotal. Reading that book *African Genesis* made me, want to explore it more. I might have read Margaret Mead in high school too.

The political discussions I had in college were also influential. I didn't have political discussions with my family in high school. By college, I was moving away from their politics. I was looking for something else…I probably had some image of wanting to be bohemian, without knowing what that meant. So I chose an urban university.

PBC: In the 70s, bohemian was attractive and 'in.'

Hope: I wanted to find out what cities where like. I wanted to know what was out there. I imagined myself immersed in the world of a novelist or something—it was pretty vague; and I didn't have any experience with any of it. I had this idea of something more expansive. Another big influence was listening to Bob Dylan records. That made a big impact. What I still think of as the best of his work was done as I was graduating from high school. I remember when "Bringing It All Back Home" came out: "Darkness at the break of noon, shadows even the silver spoon—"

I can recite that song, a lot of it, still now. The song was like, "Oh, wow! There are people out there somewhere who see an alternative to what's in front of me." This is what I was moving away from, expanding beyond. The world that I grew up in Fort Lauderdale was remarkably decadent. My father retired at 38 years old. Most of my family's friends retired young and were about martinis and yachts.

PBC: The 'good life' of the privileged.

Hope: Certainly by my senior year of college I was stepping back and questioning my roots, the legitimacy of my culture, its limitations. You're away from everything. I not only looked at the lives of high school kids and the community I grew up in and thought, "If this is the end of the rainbow, it's not what I aspire to." Part of me was restless, but I didn't have any answers to it. I thought, "There has to be something going on in the world that's more important than drinking Bloody Mary's and catching blue marlin." It seemed very superficial.

PBC: Didn't this 'soul searching' coincide with the transition of the 70s free peace and love and checking out from the establishment?

Hope: It was before that—remember, I graduated from high school in 1965, so a lot of these changes happened between 1965 and 1970 for me. I think my first year of college I actually joined the Young Republicans, and that lasted about a year. But by my second year, I hung out with the hippies in the back of the student union. [laughs]

PBC: So, in your first year of college you were trying to embrace the establishment. By the second year, you kicked it.

Hope: I was at a stage where I realized the people who weren't born like me—that is, born to privilege—were much more left wing...student radical types or hippie types...and those were the people I wanted to hang out with. Somewhere in that conflict between what I had been brought up to believe and what kind of people I was attracted to hanging out with, I went with the latter, and eventually, my own questioning of politics caught up with those social decisions.

PBC: So was your mom kind of drawn to the people or the lifestyle that you were carving out for yourself, though she didn't quite realize it or embrace it?

Hope: I think that's right.

PBC: So perhaps you were living out something for her that she wasn't free to live out, which is one reason I'm writing this book! Seems like our generation has been able to pick up a torch that our mothers didn't realize they were carrying, or if they did, many of them weren't free to carry it into its rightful place in the world.

Hope: Yes, I think I was taking advantage of social changes that hadn't happened in her generation. And certainly some of those women did it anyway. Actually, in that vein, on the other side of my family I have to tell you that my father's mother was a surgeon, and she graduated from medical school in 1904. She and my grandfather married very late in life for their generation. They married I think around 1920.

PBC: Wow, that's impressive for those times!

Hope: They were both in their 30s…I think my grandmother was 38 or 39 years old when my father, her only child, was born. She had been a contract surgeon in the First World War, the first group of women who were ever allowed to be army doctors. She served in what would have been the 1st World War equivalent of a MASH unit in France. So there was already some female torch-bearing in my background two generations before! I am not much of a pioneer when I think of what she did. That was quite bold for those times. But she wasn't practicing medicine when I was a child.

PBC: Perhaps subconsciously you knew this was possible. So not only your mother, even though her restless spirit which was unmanaged and unguided, now you're telling me your paternal grandmother was also pivotal or perhaps influential to your spirit of "I can! There's something more out there!" Because she must have had some vision to become a surgeon in the turn of the century.

Hope: Right. Yes, she was an amazing, yet not so easy woman, as you can imagine.

PBC: What was your life like with this grandmother?

Hope: She was nearly 40 when my father was born. She was in her late 60s when I can first remember her. Sometimes she would tell you something about practicing medicine back in the day. Her family was Quaker.

PBC: And what did you think of that growing up?

Hope: Well, she didn't bring up my father as a Quaker. She did continue to go to Quaker meetings sometimes. But she had conflicts with being a Quaker. She wasn't a pacifist—I think that was the problem. [laughs] I don't even think I understood that her family was Quaker until after the fact! Later I realized it was out of her Quaker mentality that she operated from when she thought I was out of control as a child. She would have me sit down and chill out, which is a real Quaker kind of thing to do. Have a moment of silence, be quiet for a bit [laughs]. I've taught in Quaker schools, and that's the thing a Quaker mother or grandmother would ask their children to do. It wasn't so much a punishment like, "Go to your room," kind of thing. It was more like, 'Center yourself.'

PBC: Did you appreciate that about her? You weren't familiar with it?

Hope: I don't think I understood what she was doing until I understood what Quakers were many years later. Then I said, "Oh! [laughs] I get it!"

PBC: When she asked you to take time out in that way, did it actually help you to do so?

Hope: I think she was onto something, but it wasn't until later that I began to grasp it as I was exposed to Quaker meditation. There was this "aha" moment when I said, "That's the part of her being a Quaker that fits into some larger picture."

I didn't see my grandmother that often as I grew up. We never lived in the same town that she did, so she was this occasional presence, except when I was very small. They had a summer house in Massachusetts that is now mine. My family had a little cottage down the road from hers early on, I can't have been more than four. The setting is this little cove that still has an unpaved badly pitted, dirt road, and I would get up and leave the house (which none of my children have ever done)! [laughs] Our dog would always follow me, and I would walk down toward my grandmother's house. Everybody in this little enclave knew who everybody was. I remember I would go to our next door neighbor's because they were more morning people than my parents and they would give me breakfast, then I would wander around!

PBC: So at four you started wandering! [laughs]

Hope: I remember years later when my oldest son, who's now almost 40, and his friend were about six, suddenly nobody knew where they were at this same house at the beach. My husband at the time was a little panicky—"Where are they? We have to do something!" I wasn't too concerned, "We'll find them." I couldn't get behind being terrified by this possibility since I was allowed to wander in this same way in summers as a young child.

PBC: You knew it was OK 'cause you had been there and enjoyed your freedom.

Hope: I've discovered that my daughter has memories of doing things that I had no idea they were doing. [laughs] And I think that's a wonderful thing for children. There's something about the safety of being a child in the 1950s, where I lived in this suburb of Detroit, where we got up and got on our bicycles and were gone all day, or we came back when we were hungry. It's about community, and that's very hard to provide for children now.

PBC: The world is more complicated now—less cohesive communities, yes?

Hope: I remember my grandmother told me once that my father had gone through this phase as a child where the only thing he wanted to eat was, and it was bizarre, like olives and, something else equally silly as the basis for a diet. Almost all families would have reacted to this. My grandmother apparently said, "Well, he'll get tired of that." [laughs] And of course he did get tired of it, and I always remembered as a parent when I watched other friends of mine go through these struggles with their children about what they were going to eat or not eat, how they became power struggles of control. I didn't have the idea that we needed to control everything so much because I had been brought up without it.

PBC: Your grandmother on your dad's side was liberal enough that you were allowed to wander in those very early years at the beach house. It sounds like it paved the way for your adventurous wanderlust as a teenager/young adult, if we look back on the positive messages you received about your wanderings as a young child.

Hope: I think my mother was controlled too much and she didn't value it, so she changed course as a parent, while my father's family wasn't like that to begin with. (laughs) They were pretty much uninterested in conventional opinion. Although they were Republican, they had a sort of anti-authoritarian mindset.

PBC: I'm interested in hearing about other women mentors who may have taken you under wing. Your grandmother didn't exactly take you under wing, but it sounds like she influenced you in such a way that she received you as a young wanderer and created an atmosphere that you managed to duplicate for your children? Were there others along the way?

Hope: For my grandmother, the idea of being dependent on someone was so abhorrent to her that she continued to live in St. Louis for twenty years after my grandfather died. She refused to come and live in Florida—so yes, she appreciated my spirit of independence. I would say that among other women who influenced me, not so much as a personal relationship, was my philosophy professor, Thelma Levine. She was a social philosopher who presented us with a history of philosophical thought. The approach was not the "Let's understand the text," but was, "How do these ideas that these groups of people had fit into this social context," and "How is history a product of these different things and ideas that represent those social constructs." I suppose she held an almost semi-Marxist outlook on the world. But she would provoke us with, "How does this idea fit into that world?" instead of , "What is this idea?" So her influence was intellectually important in my college time of exploration and self discovery.

Later on when I lived in Chile, I met a remarkable woman who was not old enough to be my mother. (I included an essay about her in my book.) Her name was Fabiola Letelier, and she was the sister of the Minister Orlando Letelier who had been the U.S. ambassador from Chile under the Allende government. He was then foreign minister and minister of defense. Fabiola, his sister, became a human rights lawyer. He was exiled, like most of the upper rungs of the Allende government, to this island in Patagonia. Then when he was finally let out, he moved to the United States, where he was an extremely effective lobbyist against the Chilean military government, to the point where they assassinated him in Washington in 1974!

Fabiola was the most incredibly fearless defender of people—trying to get them out of jail and demanding respect for human rights. She was such an amazing woman. I thoroughly admired and still do admire her, and she was a friend and mentor to me.

PBC: She kind of took you under wing or you admired her from afar?

Hope: I was a friend of her son's in the U.S. and when I moved back to Chile in 1977, I looked her up and we became friends. She was an example of strength and determination as she stood up fearlessly and tirelessly against the military dictatorship. By the time I knew her, I was in my 30s. I felt so privileged to know her, and she was the one who actually saved my life when the Chilean military were after me. I don't know if we can cover this in a nutshell…it would probably be another whole interview, but when one's adventure as a 21-22-year-old was so impactful that one writes a book about it, one is compelled to return there!

I was 22, graduated from college and, and my friend, Giselle and I spent six months driving through Chile. I had a boyfriend who was Chilean. So we had always planned that we would spend some time in Chile. Toody and I wanted to meet people who were our peers and live somewhere as opposed to being tourists. So Toody and I settled in Santiago for what we thought would be a few months.

I ended up falling in love with Chile in general. As it was, we arrived there a few months before Salvador Allende was elected in 1970. I lived in Chile during most of that Government, and by that time, my view of the world and the United States' role in the world was such that I jumped in to support the Allende government. I worked for one of the Allende government's women's magazines, and—together with a friend whom I recruited—approached the magazine with ideas. (There's a chapter about this in the book too.) We wrote the first authorized adaptation of *Our Bodies, Ourselves* for publication in Chile. It was a book within the magazine, I think it was going to be published in October or November of 1973, but then the government was overthrown in September. So it actually was never published in Chile—it never materialized. In the process we tried to adapt the content of the book into the context of Chile. We went off in very different directions, which seemed to be fine with the Boston Women's Health Collective who originally wrote the book. In the process we learned a lot about what of this second wave feminist movement was of interest to Chilean women and what wasn't, and it was important to me to bring this feminist movement to help the Chilean women there.

The Allende government published a lot of magazines and had nationalized a big editorial and printing operation, but the magazines had to sell in the market place. They didn't have the money to hand them out for free. The women who were recruited to run this magazine had careers in journalism working on top-ics that were somewhere between Mademoiselle and Good Housekeeping. There wasn't really a feminist component to the movement in support of Chilean social-ism at that time. It hadn't been thought about. People were thinking about large economic themes, not their own lives. When I read the magazine, I felt that they had missed the boat somewhere. From my point of view, the magazine editors had picked up on the fact that if they wanted to reach a broader audience than Chil-ean women's magazines had previously, it should somehow be more democratic than magazines which aimed only at affluent women. So they had fashion pages with inserts of patterns that you could cut out and make...there were simple recipes that did not require fancy ingredients, but all the models of the clothes were these tall, skinny blonde women! Chilean women are not fundamentally tall, skinny and blonde [laughs]. I thought it was dreadful that they were still not able to present an image of what women actually looked like that reflected Chilean reality even though the readers were socialist.

PBC: [laughs]. Wow!

Hope: There's a genre called a 'photo novella.' It's essentially a prolonged soap opera, told with pictures and captions, and the one they had in the first issue was a Peruvian story of this orphan in the Altiplano, the Indian areas of Peru, who was brought up by these nuns. When she was old enough, they sent her to Lima, where she worked as a maid for a rich family, and she ended up marrying the son of the household. Not only that, but he chose her because she was so humble and self-effacing. [laughs] It was ludicrous—I couldn't imagine a worse message. So I wrote a long letter to the editor of the magazine saying this is not right. This doesn't make any sense. How could you be presenting this totally unrealistic story of a woman who escapes her poverty by being humble? [laughs] They published my letter in the next issue. It was a long diatribe written by hand. I didn't even have a typewriter. Since I had not included a return address, the editor wrote a public postscript to me: "Listen, I think this is interesting, and we can't find you, why don't you come by the office." [laughs] So I thought about it for quite a while.

PBC: Wow! That's quite an amusing reflection of a different time, isn't it!

Hope: A lot of people had wandered into Chile in those years, it was the very 'in place to be' for international students interested in changing the world. I had another American girlfriend, Bonnie, who was looking for a way to participate, and I showed her the letter I had written and their response, and we sat down and thought about what could we actually offer these women. I appealed to her to join me, "Before we go over there, lets have a clear idea of what we think this magazine could be doing." And the two main ideas that we had come up with were to do something with "*Our Bodies, Ourselves*," which she had gotten one of the original newsprint copies of. We looked at it and thought about it. We also were interested in bringing in the work of Frances Moore Lappe's ***Diet for a Small Planet***. At this point it's important to realize that there were shortages of meat, and there was this sense, that if you were a good housewife, you should provide meat all the time to your family. [laughs] So we thought, "Here's a way for women to realize that there are other ways to feed your family." We never did that one, because we were more interested in ***Our Bodies, Ourselves***. But that was how we began. Over time we recruited as many Chilean women from as many places as we could in discussion groups to figure out how to approach things. We knew we couldn't do all the chapters from the original in the first installment. We discovered, for example, that for the women from the poor neighborhoods, the shantytown neighborhoods, when they looked at all the different things that this book treated, one of the topics they were interested in was the chapter about self-defense. Chile was a world in which there was a lot of brutal treatment of women and there was concern that maybe they were going to be attacked or raped by someone in their neighborhoods when they were walking home. Or maybe their experience of their husbands was that they got drunk when they got their paychecks, came home and treated them roughly. So for various reasons in their life, the idea that they could learn to physically defend themselves was very appealing—"This is what we want to know," where we had thought of that as being a very minor part of it. So we went in and did that chapter, which we were not actually planning to put in the first installment.

PBC: I feel like we've covered a lot of ground focusing on your 'coming of age' time in your 20s and early 30s. But I want to jump to you as a mother now, and look at any differences that you have manifested in raising your own children or any similarities from the way you were mothered. You gave me a smidgen about letting your kids wander as young children at the summer house. How many kids did you have?

Hope: I've been married twice. My first child by my first husband was Chilean. I married down there and he was born in 1973, and so he's almost 40 now.

Years later I married my present husband Steve whom I'd known forever. He's an anthropology professor, and we have two children who are now 23 and 26.

PBC: What's different, what's similar to your experience of being their mother to your own mother's style of parenting? It seems like you value that your mother allowed you to wander and have an unusual amount of freedom, both as a child and a teenager. Did you raise your children with that same value, especially your daughter, as we look at how the next generation of women who have been raised by 'we who took a leap' is faring so far?

Hope: Yes, let me explain. First, I have two sons—40-year-old Mathias and 23 year old Ben, and one daughter, Jurusha, who will be 27 in November (2012) As to the freedom I grew up with, I think the difference is that my parents almost took that freedom to a kind of benign neglect.

Hope: My first son was raised in a very different social climate than the other two. He has different talents—he's a very visual person and has a different lens from the others. He's in graphic design, and the other two are more intellectual types.

PBC: Do you feel you mothered them differently from one another or mothered them to bring out the characteristics that they have manifested?

Hope: After the coup in Chile, my older son lived in a world in which political activism was a major component of what was going on in those years, and it's been much less so in the lives of my younger children. When we left Chile, my husband, my son Matias and I settled in Washington, D.C., where I'd gone to college and had friends. We each worked at part time jobs and devoted all our free time to exposing the U.S. government role in promoting and financing the brutal dictatorship in Chile, and we became advocates for prisoners and refugees. We also lived in what a friend called "The people's semi-autonomous socialist republics of Adams Morgan and Mt. Pleasant." We lived for about four years in a group household. When Matias was about six, we moved back to Chile. My husband and I eventually separated there. When I moved back to the U.S., we shared custody of Matias and he spent some years here and some years in Chile. He remains in Chile now and has his own family.

But the younger ones...I think that they had the advantage of growing up in a family that always had dinner together and had discussions about what was going on in the world even though there wasn't so much direct political activity. The two younger children went to a little Quaker school that I was quite involved with and taught at for a long time. They were brought up in the world with a social awareness. We didn't use television much when they were growing up, we saw movies on television, but we didn't have cable or anything like that. They read a lot, they're both very curious bright kids, much like I was.

PBC: You read a lot when you were a kid also.

Hope: I did, but they've been around the world a lot more than almost anyone in my generation at their age. When Ben was in 7th grade and Jerusha in 11th grade, we lived in Ecuador for a year. My husband was on sabbatical, so they had that experience of living in a different country, and we took them to different parts of the world also as kids. So, although they grew up in a small town, they grew up knowing there was a bigger world out there from an early age.

PBC: It seems to me that what you cherished and gleaned most from as a child—that spirit of wandering, adventure, and travel that you got despite the mental health challenges your family lived with—you've been able to give that to your children more overtly and consciously than your parents were able to for you.

Hope: Yes my husband, who's an anthropologist, is also a curious traveler about the world, as you would imagine. He has provided more direction without being controlling in our children's lives than my parents provided in mine. As I look at my friends and their children, you're much better off when you bring them up that way with a balance of freedom and direction. Some of my girlfriends still have difficult relationships with their daughters. I think it has to do with control issues. If you let your children go, they come back to you. You hold them back and they have to struggle against you. So my children haven't had to struggle in that way.

PBC: What is your relationship like with your daughter, Hope?

Hope: Wonderful. I have a wonderful relationship with my daughter. We actually went on a 10 day road trip together driving out West and had a wonderful time together. They're all doing what they're doing in their own ways. Jurusha, who was the child with that kind of artsy bohemian impulse that I had, through some odd course of events in her life, became the most political of the three children because she became passionately devoted to children's education. She's about to start teaching in New York City public schools. She was a French major and creative writing major in college, and then she went back to school and has finished a masters degree in education.

PBC: It sounds like the apple doesn't fall far from the tree in her case. Devoted to children's education. That sounds a little like her mama. [laughs] Sweet!

Hope: She's very much like me. But she's serious about what she's doing now. It's wonderful to see that. Like me, she saw things that should be otherwise, education turned out to be her medium and she loves small children. So it was a logical place for her to go. She isn't that interested in overall political work, but as I see it, if you care about children and children's education, in this world, you're an activist. Her grandma was an excellent editor of children's books, remember, so that's in her lineage also.

PBC: That's right—a few seeds came through to her from her grandmother who loved children's literature also.

Hope: Yes. Definitely. We read together. Three generations of women were passionately devoted to Anne of Green Gables for instance. [laughs]

PBC: Well, that brings me to my last question as to any female role models who might have been more cultural figures—people that you think readers might recognize. Is there anyone who influenced you? You already mentioned the philosophy teacher, and your other personal role models...are there others with a broader impact?

Hope: Oh, a big influence as I was looking at life and women in the world was reading Doris Lessing's ***The Golden Notebook***, definitely—which is about the questions women in my generation of feminists and activists asked: how do we interpret the contradictions within progressive movements, combat dogmatism, live as independent women without rejecting men, and have honest relationships. I can't come up with many role models... I loved Janis Joplin's music, but I certainly didn't think of her as a role model.

PBC: Right. But influential?

Hope: Also the music of Judy Collins and Joan Baez. I'm not a musician, but there were appealing and political messages in their songs. Definitely. And there were other musicians who played a big role in my life. [laughs]

Oh, another one who was a cultural influence, this is someone not everyone has heard of, but they should have, is a woman named Violeta Parra. . . She holds a position in the history of folk music in South America that would be somewhere between Pete Seeger and Woody Guthrie. Actually, Joan Baez and Judy Collins have both sung some of her stuff. She has a song that's the name of Joan Baez's album in Spanish called "Here's to Life"—in Spanish, it's "Gracias a la Vida." So she's definitely influential in many ways. I know one of her children.

PBC: Oh, sweet. How do you want the next generation of girls and women to carry the torch of womanhood and what message would you would like to leave them with?

Hope: As someone who's experienced all these different levels of political and social movements who found her way at a time when there was a mass movement, I'm stunned that there aren't women on the streets of all of our campuses protesting against restrictions in women's health care and how we're educating our children.

I think young women need to be a visible presence. I would urge them: Stand up for what you believe! Show up, speak up and vote. History is made by the people who show up.

PBC: There's some hope for ya!

Anita Casalina

Biography

Birthdate: 12/31/53

Mother: Eula Bingham Casalina October 3, 1914

I am the 3rd of 4 children. My brother Steve is 12 years older than I am, my sister Jean is 9 years older than I am. My sister Nancy was 2 years younger—passed away in 2007 from breast cancer. My father was born in Sicily in 1913 and died in 2008.

A friend of mine once told me that she saw my life as being "all about healing and expression." It turns out, she was right. By the age of nine, I had become aware of the great amount of suffering all over the planet. The Christmas before I turned 10, I donated all of the money I'd saved up to buy gifts to the Navaho Reservation, where drought and blizzards were causing a terrible plight for the Navaho people.

In my search for a way to serve, I attended U.C. Davis, in the Pre-Law program. My dad and I both thought I was going to inherit his thriving law practice in Oakland, CA, but I found that the law was far too restrictive, not allowing for actual healing to take place, and often incarcerating people who had experienced trauma and abuse as children. I decided instead to get a degree in Applied Behavioral Science, which emphasized psychotherapy.

I returned to the San Francisco Bay Area, and took two paths simultaneously. I began making social change documentaries, and at the same time I studied various healing modalities. My filmmaking took me to exciting places around the world and I could see that storytelling through that medium could make a difference in people's lives. After I had two children, I realized that I could no longer travel easily, nor work the demanding hours required for documentaries. So my work moved in another direction, and I opened my own practice in the healing arts for many years, until my career path took another turn recently.

In 2011, I met a man who had done great things in Africa and helped thousands of people, showing them how to use their own skills and resources to increase their standard of living. I wrote a book chronicling his remarkable career, and set out once more on the path of global change and ending poverty. I wanted to return to telling stories of peace and prosperity. I co-founded the Billions Rising, Self-Reliance Foundation, a non-profit whose mission is to document and highlight efforts of people and organizations around the world that are empowering others to become self-reliant. Along with my co-founder, I host a weekly radio show, and have written a book ***Billions Rising, Empowering Self-Reliance***, released in November of 2013. In 2014, my team and I begin work on a feature-length documentary about the amazing people and projects we have discovered who are helping to build prosperity around the globe.

I am married to Tony Eldon. We have been married for 26 years [at time of publication], and together for 36 years. We have two children—a girl age 24, and a boy age 22. Tony works as an environmental and building inspector. He is actually a sort of an artist/scientist. He plays many instruments, and invented a hearing test which NASA bought from him, and which is now installed on the International Space Station.

My mother Eula is English and Welsh. Her family can be traced back to William the Conqueror in England. Her ancestors walked across the plains to Utah, and she grew up on the Ute Reservation as a homesteader. Her family is of the Mormon faith, and since my dad's passing in 2008, she has returned to the church and works at the Mormon Temple once a week even at the ripe age of 99 [at time of publication]!

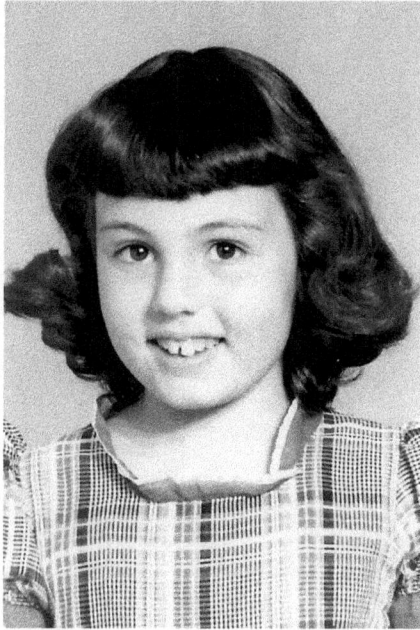

Anita as a little girl

Anita's mom with baby Anita

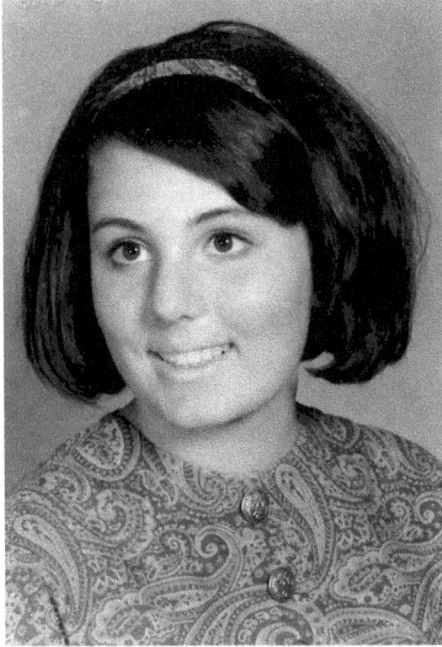

Anita as a teenager

Anita today

Anita and her mom today

Interview

May 2012

PBC: So tell me how you see yourself having been selected and identified as someone who has made a leap from your own background to your current consciousness?

Anita: The way that has shown up in my life is actually through a series of leaps. Even though I was raised to be a traditional woman, I have dedicated myself to social justice and healing. In fact, many years ago, a very wise and insightful woman looked at me and said, "Your life seems to be all about healing and expression." She was right. Everything I have done as an adult has been a combination of healing and expression. When I was probably nine or ten, I realized that not everybody in the world had the same comfort that I had, and materially, that people were suffering the world.

PBC: So at nine or ten, you realized something was different about you?

Anita: Yes, regarding my sense of the greater world around me, I have a brother who is 12 years older than I am and he began reading history to me—a lot of big, weighty textbooks when I was very young, even before I went to school. So I had learned about World War II by the time I was in kindergarten. I had learned about Hitler. I had learned about the suffering of the Jews. I began to understand that there were people in the world who had circumstances that were very dire and very intense...that they were starving or they had no place to live. When I was 10 years old, I took all of my money that I had saved to buy Christmas gifts, and I sent all my cash in an envelope to the Navajo Reservation. I had read an article in Life Magazine about drought, herds of sheep dying, and the Navajo people starving in the cold winter. When my family expected their gift from me, they got a little tag under the Christmas tree saying that I had given away the money I had saved for their present to the Navajo because they needed it more than any of us did.

PBC: [laughs] That's so BIG for a 10 year old! But when you put the notes under the Christmas tree, letting people know you were doing this other thing with the Native Americans Indians and they didn't react so well—what was their reaction?

Anita: The family wasn't necessarily thrilled with that. But by the time I was ten I felt a deep, deep compassion for people that were suffering. I became involved in the Civil Rights Movement by the time I was 11. At 12 years old I began working for the Black Panther Party selling their newspapers to raise money for a children's breakfast program, which served the children who lived in poverty in Oakland. I grew up in Oakland so a very diverse multicultural community surrounded me. My own elementary school was in my neighborhood and everyone was white and middle class, but when I went to junior high, the huge diversity of people in Oakland really hit me. It was right in front of my face every day that there were truly poor children who didn't have more than a couple of outfits to wear to school, and especially the African American community seemed to be suffering. I began listening to late night talk shows that were about racism and my consciousness started to expand. I used to think, "Wow—we have so much money compared with lots of people." My neighborhood around me was middle class. But my own family was wealthier than the people around us. My dad made a lot of money, and we traveled the world on cruise ships ...we were in limousines and villas in Europe. I knew I had a very privileged upbringing, and that I had been given a lot of gifts; a lot of blessings. I also knew that I had been blessed with intelligence, which could be helpful to others as well. In school, I had skipped one and a half grades initially but then slowed myself down a bit so that I would graduate with people more my age.

PBC: What grades did you skip?

Anita: Kindergarten and then they did a split of first and second. They took me out of kindergarten and put me into first grade—and then put me on the second grade side. So I was only five years old doing second grade work. The principal and the teachers told me that I was smart. And later I remembered this as I observed other people's lives. I thought, "You know, I'm smart enough. I can learn what I need to learn to help people."

PBC: You already had a sense of your mission as a young child.

Anita: Yes, but my family had certain expectations of me. It had always been assumed that I would serve in a very traditional way. My dad had a big, successful law practice in downtown Oakland, CA, and he started taking me to his law office when I was very young—about ten years old. I started helping him and he discovered I knew how to write and read legal texts and such, so he just started giving me work to do like I was an assistant or a secretary. He had me do research for cases when I was around eleven. By the time I was 13 or 14, I was doing a lot of work for him. And so, he saw that I had a skill for that, and it became an accepted belief in the family that I was going to inherit his law practice. When I went to the University of California at Davis, it was in the pre-law program. But by early in my senior year, I realized that I would not be able to do something so traditional.

PBC: A lot was expected of you from early on and there was no let-up!

Anita: Yes, and some issues were coming up both in family dynamics and my dad's workplace. I also saw around me from the time I was young that women simply weren't being respected in the way that I thought they should be. I think loneliness sharpens our powers of observation. I would go to my dad's giant office parties. He owned a law office building that he built across from the Hall of Justice in Oakland. So everybody, all the DA's, all the public defenders, as well as the entire police department of Oakland would show up for these parties, and I got to be a fly on the wall.

While observing the behavior of the adults and watching the men get drunk and hit on the women, I felt that something wasn't right. Some of these women were in the District Attorney's Office, or public defender's. These were very intelligent women but they were being treated in a way that felt very demeaning. It was the era of the mini skirt and the women would dress in very provocative ways even though they were professionals who needed to command respect in the courtroom. It really bothered me that this kind of "mixed message" behavior was going on.

At those same office parties, I also overheard a lot of terrible conversations, not just about women, but derogatory remarks about people of color; a lot of racist comments. That got me even more fired me up to somehow advocate for people who were suffering in the world and needed help. I really felt the world was out of balance—it was sexist, it was racist and really needed a lot of help. So, I became very involved as the opportunity and "movement" presented itself.

In high school, I participated in the anti-war movement and continued to be involved when I went to college. But I was disappointed when I discovered that some of the anti-war movement men were just as sexist as my father's business counterparts and expected the women to be making the coffee and getting food for them. We thought we were equals in our protest against violence in the world and yet, we were still being relegated to this role of caregivers for the movement. I was really shocked at some of these young hippie men who acted so badly. I remember saying to a couple of them, "How can you think that this is a revolution against the past when you're behaving just like your dads! You're talking just like your dad would to all of us women." I was really incensed.

PBC: So is this where you started identifying yourself with what later may have been referred to as feminist values?

Anita: When I was a senior at Davis, I realized that the law was 'black and white' and I had this acute ability to see the gray area that sits between black and white. There were circumstances that influenced people to do the things that they did that would not be addressed by the law. So I switched over to get a degree called Applied Behavioral Sciences that was essentially a psychotherapy degree. After I graduated, I began working at the University of California Davis' Women's Center. It was both a feminist counseling center and a clearing-house for women. It was the early days of the feminist movement, so it was very exciting. I worked there as a peer counselor for women who had questions about their lives.

PBC: Back tracking a bit…I want to take you back to your early years with your mother—what personality traits might distinguish you from your mother as you grew up with her?

Anita: She had four children, two of whom were almost teenagers by the time I was born. My sister was nine, and as I said, my brother is 12 years older than I am. So, my mom was distracted a lot when I was growing up. She had a big home and a huge piece of property to take care of as well as all of us children.

My dad wasn't at home a lot because he was building a very successful law practice. He also had a lot of other business interests. As I look back, he really does appear to be a true renaissance man. In addition to being a trial lawyer, he was a building contractor, a realtor, a horticulturalist as well as a vintner. He was away from home most of the time. He was busy in the world, and my mom was distracted by all of her many projects and responsibilities at home. My mother is and was Mormon. She had not been practicing while she was married to my Catholic dad, but she was very religious prior to that and is today, as well, at age 98.

She was used to me being what she always said was 'rebellious.' I was the rebel in the family. I was the one who did whatever I wanted.

PBC: Hmmm...do you think that served you to just be left to do your own thing?

Anita: Oh, I really do. I'm so grateful [laughs] as I think back on that now.

They would always say, "You do whatever you want no matter what we tell you!" And they kind of all rolled their eyes. My older sister was really, in some ways, my second mother. She was my really good, supportive mother all through my childhood because my real mother was so busy and distracted, and my dad was a very difficult person to live with. My mother was depressed while I was growing up. So when I would do things that felt in some ways rebellious or out there or edgy in some way, she just knew that's how I was. She didn't address it a whole lot. She just seemed to accept it with a sigh.

There were times when I was younger I would think, "Gosh it would have been nice to have had a lot more support and a lot more conversation...a lot more loving understanding." But I think it has been my destiny to break the mold and to be the one who looked at the family script and to say, "You know what? This really doesn't fit for me. And I have to do the things that feel right to me." It was like that from the time I was really little. When I look at the old home movies my dad would take of us, I was always just kind of "out there." Everyone would be standing still for the camera and I would start dancing wildly. I felt like they tried to control me a lot and bring me into their tribe, to no avail.

PBC: [laughs] You were determined and guided to do your own thing! You weren't having their control!

Anita: Yeah and when they couldn't control me, they kinda got used to me being so wild. They often said I was wild and rebellious. And I now know that wild and rebellious is what creates the paradigm shift.

PBC: Ah—now that you have looked at it with adult eyes, you see that being wild was a virtue.

Anita: When I was in my 20s, I had the good fortune to spend private time with the brilliant pioneer of developmental psychology, Erik Erikson. My husband Tony and I used to go to his house and swim and have dinner with him and his wife, Joan, when they lived in Tiburon. We read his books ***Young Man Luther***

and **Gandhi's Truth**. Both of those were about people who broke free from societal norms to bring about great change in their cultures. Essentially they were saying, "There are ways in which our world needs to be changed." And really, it is the people who pushed that edge who led the world to change. I think I started pushing the edge of the family at a very young age.

What is interesting about my mother is that there is a deep wisdom and intuition within her that I was not aware of when I was growing up. She was not happy, so she did not communicate much with me. After my dad became ill with Alzheimer's, I began to learn so much more about my mother—who she was and where she came from.

PBC: But do you think she deferred to your dad in terms of raising you Catholic, not Mormon? In other words, did she just kind of let Dad call the shots?

Anita: Oh yes, she kept completely quiet. She let him call the shots for everything and she's discussed that with me a lot now. She admits she felt weak, that she was afraid of him. She did not feel that she could speak up because he had such a violent personality. She said back in those days when a woman got married, the children were always raised in the father's religion. So that's why we were raised Catholic.

PBC: Interesting—I see this paradigm shift, this breaking of the mold on your part, perhaps for you AND your mom! She deferred to dad and you were raised within the box, so to speak. All along, you knew that the box wasn't for you. Your mom even saw you not buying into the box, but she didn't give you too hard a time perhaps because you were living something out that was secretly admirable or beneficial to her somehow.

Anita: Sometimes she really admired me even when I was little and was so free-spirited and other times I believe it frightened her. I can remember when I was 15 years old, we went to Sicily to visit the relatives, and we went up to the top of Mount Etna, which is the active volcano in Sicily. My cousin Massimo and I ran down to the lip of the volcano and down a steep side of the mountain in loose volcanic stone. I remember my younger sister and my mother cowered up at the top and they were both screaming for me to stop—to come back, afraid I'd fall into the crater. They were so frightened, but later on when we were reunited next to the car in the parking lot, my mother said to me, "You were so beautiful as you ran down that hill, your hair was flowing in the wind and it looked like a horse's mane. You looked like a wild free horse running down to the crater..."

And there is a picture that she took of me doing that with my cousin on Mount Etna. When I was five years old I remember standing in the backyard talking with her about something while we were picking flowers or doing something. We had a huge backyard with a beautiful Italian garden. Again, she did all the Italian things. She planted Italian vegetables for my dad. She harvested Italian fruit from the fruit trees.

PBC: He was Italian but she was not, is that right?

Anita: She's 100% English. [laughs] She was like the adopted Italian. But we were back there in the yard, hanging out, and I said to her, "I'm never changing my name, when I get married." And she said, "Oh, honey you will, you'll meet the right guy and you'll change your name." And I said, "No mama, I think it's a really stupid thing to do." And she still laughs about it. She said, "You came out and the first words after you were born were 'I am a feminist!'" [laughs] She teases me about that. I have never changed my name, being married. She also told me, "You never wanted me to call you a girl, after you became 11. You had become a woman by then and you had joined a feminist movement which hadn't really even begun at that point!" That's her memory of it—that I was born a feminist and was a woman by the time I was 11. It's very cute. She has a great sense of humor about all of it now.

PBC: Is a sense of humor something you feel you share with her that she was able to nurture in you, even though she was depressed?

Anita: She didn't laugh when I was growing up at all. She's funny now. She was depressed when we were growing up because my dad was so difficult. One of the things I remember hearing Al Pacino say is that he became such a good actor because his mother and grandmother and aunt wouldn't let him out of the house because they were afraid of New York. They also were so depressed that he began performing like crazy for them, and he, as a result, became a great performer. In some ways I also became very funny—I tried to get my mother to laugh because she was so sad. I have a really strong memory of her sitting at this great big machine that she ironed sheets on called an "Ironright." She seemed like a slave every day. It felt like she worked in the house so hard. This Ironright—if you've never seen one, was about four feet long, tall, like a big box and to a small child it looked huge—you sit at them and feed sheets or other garments into them and a big roller does the ironing. It was one of the monsters of my childhood! Probably because she always looked so depressed when she had to use it. But, I remember drawing this whole cartoon strip for her, while she was sitting there ironing, and bringing it in to show it to her. I was probably seven. I read it out loud to her and tried to humor her. One tiny corner of her mouth moved up into a smile, but that was it.

PBC: You worked hard to get her to crack that smile!

Anita: I remember many times thinking, "Boy, housework is terrible." Because [laughs] I didn't quite understand what was making her sad except that she seemed so burdened all the time. All I can say is I'm happy that we have wrinkle-free sheets because I wouldn't be ironing anything!

PBC: [laughs] Right. You got your fill of ironing back then.

Anita: And it took me a long time to adopt cooking as something I wanted to do because that was another thing that seemed so sad—I felt she was chained to the stove. So I've had to find ways to cook and make it entertaining by putting on music—doing it in a way that feels light and fun instead of burdensome.

PBC: What would you say the positive experiences were that you and your mom shared or the gifts that she gave you at that formative time of your life?

Anita: She was really encouraging of my creativity. I can't say enough about how proud she was of my artistic abilities.

PBC: She saw you as artistic?

Anita: I was always building, always making things. I would wake up every morning early, at sunrise, like little children do. But I would wake up so excited because I always had a project going. It's how I am now. Now, when I wake up and remember my writing or whatever it is I'm doing, whatever my project is now, I still feel very excited about it. My mother really nurtured that and encouraged that. For example, she got my dad to buy a big sheet of 5/8-inch thick plywood and cut it lengthwise so it turned into a huge worktable for me. She laid it down over two bedroom end tables or nightstands, which had little drawers in them. It became this giant worktable for me and for my younger sister, and my mom said, "You can do whatever you want on this. You don't have to worry about hurting the wood—you can carve on it, you can glue on it, you can paint on it, you can do everything you want to do."

PBC: I'm struck by how she was so constrained herself and yet she gave you such a blank slate: "Here you go. It's yours to do what you want with."

Anita: She did, and I feel like that really helped me to grow, not just as an artist but in so many ways because my lens was so big, wide, and open for creative expression. When I look back, I see that was the foundation for everything that I've done creatively. Whether it was to help people as a healer or all of the documentaries that I've produced or the huge amount of stained glass windows I made or the songs I wrote…the books I'm writing… It all seems to have started there.

PBC: It was all written on that worktable.

Anita: Exactly. I vividly remember how every morning I could get up and do whatever I wanted on that table. And I remember my body feeling really relaxed and really open to doing whatever came to me.

And the other thing I can tell you is that my mother was a stellar athlete. She was a pole-vaulter. [laughs] And, you know, to this day, if she sees someone pole vaulting, like in the Olympics—she says, "Oh I just loved pole vaulting!" I think her athleticism comes from how intensely physical her childhood was. Her own mother died when my mom was only eight years old, and that set the tone for hard work on the farm. Her older sister moved away to live with their grandmother and my mom took over all of the housekeeping. That was the turning point of her life. She was put in charge of the family when she was only eight, and it was a really big pioneer family living out on the Ute reservation in Utah. She baked bread every morning for the family. She cleaned. She cooked. Her dad remarried, but my mom still kept doing a huge amount of the housework.

PBC: Oh wow! She grew up in Utah?

Anita: On the Ute reservation. The Mormons moved across the plains to escape persecution. They settled in Utah and many of them began farming on the reservation, with the permission of the tribe, provided they gave portions of their harvest or something else of value back to the tribe. My grandfather was a big support to the Utes and they to him. My mom tells me lovely stories of Ute families coming over to visit. Her family and Ute families shared meals and were friends.

PBC: And then you gave your allowance to the Native Americans when you were 10?

Anita: Yes, the Navajo. Believe it or not, the very first non-English language words I ever learned were Ute. She taught me a few words in Ute when I was a toddler! [laughs] So I knew about the Native Americans from the time I was really tiny. My point is that she became so rugged and so strong, living out there with a dirt floor, no heating, and an outhouse. She had to walk to school. She had the constitution of an Amazon woman. She lived through the 1918 influenza. Her grandmother made sage tea for the family and they all survived even though they contracted it. They were all so sick but they prayed together and drank this brew that her grandmother made. [laughs] And nobody died! She survived, she worked from morning until night, and she is very strong constitutionally. When she went to school, they discovered she could hit a baseball out of the park and of course she could also pole vault! When I was little, she taught me how to really swing a baseball bat. I could hit it out of the park every time when I was in elementary school, too! You know, "Keep your eye on the ball, pull the bat back this far, and then, just hit it as hard as you can." [laughs]

PBC: That sounds symbolic as I hear those words: "Keep your eye on the ball and hit it as hard as you can." [laughs].

Anita: She taught me standing broad jumps. She could jump! My mom gave birth to me when she was 39, so she was an older mother for the time, but she was still athletic. She loved showing me how to jump. She would take me out and show me how to throw your weight forward and not up [laughs] ...and how to jump as far as you possibly can.

PBC: I'm seeing how she planted some seeds perhaps inadvertently that you've taken and "run with!"

Anita: One of my favorite memories with my mom is that I would walk home from school to have lunch with her some days. She'd make sandwiches for us and we would listen to the news together. We'd listen to Paul Harvey's newscast on KGO Radio. We would just laugh because he would tell little jokes about the news.

PBC: And she laughed when she heard that radio show?

Anita: Yes—eating lunch with me—it wasn't work; she wasn't attached to the ball-and-chain of her life. It was a relaxed moment. So these are really sweet memories—having lunch with her. I had her all to myself because normally I had to share her with teenagers and a younger sister. So, to have her all to myself was really fun.

PBC: Can you talk about a turning point where something or someone else besides your mom might have brought you through despair or aloneness or crisis to new hope?

Anita: Yes. The earliest person of influence I remember was a woman who worked at the elementary school as a yard monitor, they used to call them. They were parents or neighbors who would come to the school to just hang out during recess and make sure that the kids behaved—just to help the school as a volunteer. Mrs. Lightner just loved me and I loved her. She became another adult person in my life who taught me fun things. I would go to her house to spend time with her. She just lived half a block away. As I mentioned, my mom was distracted or depressed...my older sister and brother were gone a lot because they were teenagers...my younger sister was "the baby." My dad was gone. So Mrs. Lightner...

PBC: ...took you under wing?

Anita: She taught me how to play the autoharp. That was a really big deal. We used to sing to her little dog. She had a little cocker spaniel and we'd play the autoharp. She taught me how to make beautiful braided rugs. She gave me loving attention and always told me how smart I was—how pretty I was. And that was the first time I remember really feeling like I was getting a different perspective on myself. I wasn't hearing, "Why can't you be like the rest of us?" [laughs].

PBC: She really saw you and liked you.

Anita: She would just hug me and hug me and tell me what a great little girl I was.

PBC: What a great gift she gave you.

Anita: I'm just remembering now another important moment...in the sixth grade, the school secretary picked me to be her assistant to help in the office. She said, "You're so bright, I see how smart you are, I need somebody who can organize these papers for me and run the mimeograph machine and answer the phone. Can you do that for a few hours a week?" It was just a student volunteer job. I remember I was young—in sixth grade. But it was great having so much responsibility. I even had my own little desk next to hers. The principal would come in and smile at me when I was there and tell me what a great job I was doing. So that was a real boost for me, also.

PBC: You have already addressed the turning point of your mom's life—her mother dying—your mom becoming in charge—and the rugged woman that she became. Is there anything else that you feel was significant as a shape-shifting event for her?

Anita: Being raised Mormon shaped her as well as losing her mother. She is 98—she was born in 1914. That was a time long time ago when women were the ones who served the men. And she really learned to serve her family after her mother passed away. But, she has another part of her, too, that emerged when her stepmother told her that she would not be able to go on to high school. She would have to stay home and take care of the family. She was devastated because school was her life. She was a straight A student all through elementary school, when she wasn't baking bread and caring for the family. Her English teacher said, "Eula, you are too smart to stop going to school. I want you to come live with me." So my mom moved out and went to live with her English teacher and was able to attend and finish high school. So, she has a rebellious streak in her that I feel influenced me as well.

PBC: Interesting. That was bold back then. Of teacher AND daughter!

Anita: It's sweet because she still mentions the teacher, Mrs. Aiken, remembering some wise words of advice she would give.

PBC: Role model.

Anita: Mrs. Aiken was a very significant role model—she was like the real mother that my mom needed. My mom's always said the day her mother died, she felt that she lost her only friend in the world. She and her mother were very, very close and her mother died of heart failure at a very young age. So really, that shaped her. She had someone who believed in her in Mrs. Aiken.

PBC: It's so interesting!

Anita: So even as she was telling me not to rebel so much, there was this other story that she had lived.

PBC: That became validating for you even though she didn't broadcast it?

Anita: Exactly. The message was: "This is what you're going to have to do yourself. Really, really push yourself forward." When I met Mrs. Aiken—many times when we'd go to Utah we'd see her—I held her in high esteem. I loved her because I knew that she had helped my mom. She had really saved my mom from a life of drudgery.

PBC: "Do as I do, not as I say." [laughs]

So, as we look at how you approach conflict and how your mom approached conflict, it sounds like your mom approached conflicts in a mixed fashion.

Anita: When I was growing up and conflicts arose at school, she would always tell me, "Oh just ignore them." She wanted me to be more passive. I saw her doing that herself. She just ignored a lot of things that were going on around her.

PBC: But she saw you not so willing to ignore but rather to confront...taking a different approach than she taught you.

Anita: I wanted some strategies, I wanted some ammunition, and I wanted some strength. I felt like I needed protection. I felt like I needed mechanisms something that would serve me—some words, or some behaviors. Because I was so young for my grade, I would be picked on sometimes because I was smaller and I wasn't going through the same social changes and developmental things that the kids around me were. So if somebody was teasing me or such, I could have used some strength. She said, "Just ignore them." She did go to school a couple a times to talk to the teachers on my behalf.

PBC: She would rise to the occasion?

Anita: She would rise to the occasion, but we really didn't make headway because somehow she would back down very quickly. So what I think happened was... I haven't mentioned this part…she had a stepmother after her mother died who was extremely cruel and violent. She grew up in an environment with violence, so she learned to lay low at a very young age. She learned to become a pleaser. She always said that her stepmother, 'Aunt Lila' she called her, loved her because she, my mom, was willing to work hard and help with all the chores. Lila inherited five or six children when she married my grandfather and then had four or five of her own. So my mom grew up in this huge family, and was the one who had the strength, fortitude and the desire to help.

PBC: Oh, lord. She paid dearly for the stepmother's approval. It was conditional love.

Anita: That set the tone for my mother's behavior—how she had learned to be passive.

PBC: It was about survival, yes?

Anita: A few years after she married my dad, he began to act out in anger and became violent. Her immediate response was to keep a low profile to survive. So that's the past history… the backdrop that I have become unwilling to repeat.

She now uses the term "weak" when she speaks of how she was in the years with my dad—weak and passive. She really sees it all now in hindsight.

PBC: Your approach is in direct contrast to your mom's passivity. You saw something wrong with that approach. Tell me how you feel now when you approach conflict and how you further developed those skills.

Anita: It did both shape and scar me, I would say. I had to learn from a very passive place. In spite of that, for some reason, as I said about always being the rebel of the family, I think I've always had a level of strength—of individuality. But when I got older, it was hard for me to resolve conflicts. I had to learn to speak up. In college, for the first time I realized that I had a choice in life that I could say what I wanted to and that the sky wouldn't fall…that I could speak my desires, my truths, my knowledge, and it would be heard. Even if it was pushed back against, I discovered that if we could debate or argue long enough we could sometimes come up with words or ideas of compromise. I didn't know about compromise when I was growing up. Discovering compromise was this great freedom. I felt that I had grown wings when I discovered that it was possible to meet someone halfway…to do nothing more than to lay my cards on the table and have the other person do the same. Then we could say, "Well look at that! Our cards don't match and yet we are still good people." I didn't know that was possible.

PBC: Has this been useful in your current family?

Anita: I have a very good marriage of 25 years. I know that I've learned a lot more about conflict resolution just by remaining married all this time. My husband and I have both learned how to resolve conflicts and compromise. Both of us know how to say, "You're like this and I'm like that, and aren't we interesting…we're so different and we still love each other."

PBC: I'd say this is hard-earned compromise. [laughs] I'm struck that you manifested this out of the childhood that you're describing, because you could have so easily been shushed…quieted, suppressed into submission by the forces that you're describing—both mom's passivity and dad's dominance. It sounds like all along there was this observer in you that you trusted. Somehow you were able to muster up the courage to trust your observations and the spiritual guidance that you received. Do you want to speak about that?

Anita: Frankly it astonishes me sometimes, too…[laughs] that I could raise myself and essentially birth myself into the world as a very unique kind of person. And I continue to have a life that goes against tradition. I think I learned to build bridges as a young child. I think that what you are saying is—yes, it was courage. I also had this really strong sense within me about God. I felt that there was a *goodness* in the Universe. And it was in such strong opposition to what was being shown to me every day—not just in my family but in the traditional society around me. The kids who were popular in school were often mean to other children and I thought that was horrible! I would befriend the fat kids and the unpopular kids. I would give them food. I would be nice to them because I would be so upset by the way they were being treated.

PBC: You were already trying to set straight the values around you.

Anita: I also saw that, with all of this behavior going on, a lot of these traditional people didn't seem particularly happy. I knew somehow there was something better. I just knew there was something powerful and incredible to be had in the world. I don't know how I knew it; I just knew it instinctively.

PBC: That's impressive—that somehow you could trust your inner knowing, your inner seeing and not let it be snuffed by the external, traditional methods and exposure that you had.

Anita: The concept of building bridges became important to me from the time that I was really young. I don't know exactly how I saw it as bridges, but I began to. That I could be myself and still speak or behave in a way that other people could hear and respond to. So I would. It became a strategy in a lot of ways for survival in the family. How could I survive in the society you know, in a very traditional community when I was observing injustice?

PBC: So you were compelled to bridge a gap as you took in both realities?

Anita: Yes—one of the things that I learned to do is talk in a really quiet voice. It's a way to be heard where you speak in a quiet voice that allows you to reach people as you speak the truth that's in your heart. In my family, I learned that the only way to be heard was not to yell. If I spoke from a quiet place of kindness, there was a chance I would really be heard.

PBC: At what point do you think you became aware of that quiet voice being effective?

Anita: [laughs] At a very, very young age and then I began working with it a little more when I was in school. I was tracked with these really high IQ kids—we all took these IQ tests and we were in this gifted program. It was an accelerated program and I was put in a special sixth grade class.

PBC: The gifted and talented program?

Anita: A class where kids were bussed in from all over the city to do this experimental kind of work. There was a group of very racist and loud boys. It was a huge deal to challenge them, given my small stature. I would speak really quietly on purpose to get them to hear me because they had to stop yelling in order to hear anything. I remember them leaning forward in their little school desks in the sixth grade trying to hear me. I was talking about how all of us were God's children and we were created equal. The teachers wouldn't want to talk about God in class because it was a public school. But I would persist: "Well, then let's just say what the Constitution says—all men and women [laughs] are created equal." I remember the kids just staring at me [laughs]—like "Where'd she come from?"

PBC: You saw the gap, and you found a way to cross it. So between you and your mother, how would you summarize the similarities and differences?

Anita: I think the gap has really narrowed since my dad became ill with Alzheimer's and then passed away in 2008. One of the things that I've learned from my mother is how to evolve with the world, and this has narrowed the gap, because she's really moved forward. After my dad died, my mother became a modern woman in her 90s! And what she taught me that I appreciate is that at any age we can continue to move forward in the world. So for my part, I have learned to work with technology a lot rather than being afraid of it. I listen to contemporary music, because I want to be a part of the current thought form of creativity on Earth. I know my mother's own evolution has influenced me to remain current with life. She taught me: don't just get old. Keep moving forward, and, yes, she has been instrumental in shaping my children's lives. She sends them the most insightful letters and has phone conversations with them. She's really helping them. She's like a counselor for them right now.

PBC: This is new since your dad passed away?

Anita: Yes. She's evolved into a more engaged person since then.

PBC: How does your mothering of your own kids compare to the way you were mothered?

Anita: I have had very different circumstances than my mother did, which have given me a foundation for a joyous journey with my two children. The society around me has evolved. I have my own career. And I have a wonderful and supportive husband. He has co-parented with me, which has eased the burden tremendously. And he's been a wonderful dad. There has been no alcohol abuse or out of control violence in our household, as there was in my home growing up. So the environment has been so much more nurturing to begin with.

There've been a couple of other events in my life before I had kids that have shaped me as a woman and a mother. One was going to the University of California at Davis, and finally feeling like I found an amazing group of intellectual peers who were also rebellious yet were leaders in their families, too. We would talk about being leaders and rebels, both. It was interesting because I began to feel like I had a place in the world. Then, of course, it was a natural consequence that the feminist movement in 1971 swept me up. It was that movement becoming so powerful around me which showed me that I had not been alone thinking and feeling as I had about women's roles in society. I had been feeling like I perceived all of these things on my own in a vacuum, but, in fact, it really was time for the world to shift in terms of women. I was part of something enormous, very exciting—a mass consciousness.

As a young woman out of college I began producing social change documentaries. I had the wonderful fortune to work with Helen Caldicott from Physicians for Social Responsibility and David Brower, founder of Friends of the Earth. There were lots of other great organizations and people I met during that time and I always felt that I was able to make a small contribution to the world through documenting the work of these amazing people.

Then I had children and it became clear to me that I would be unable to travel and work the long, crazy hours required in documentary producing. At the same time I was working in filmmaking, I had also begun studying with people who were exploring alternative ways of healing—homeopathy, sound healing, and intuitive healing. I trained with a brilliant intuitive healer and found that I was able to use my own intuition to help people as well. I began working in private practice and led healing retreats.

But to further answering your question, as a mom myself, I have tried to really understand my kids on a deep level. I listened to them, and I gave them the room to make decisions for themselves, even when they were younger. I believe that we learn the most from "Earth Consequences," or the natural outcomes of our decisions, even the bad ones. So, within reason, Tony and I let them both make choices and learn from those. As I said, within reason. That helped them to test the world around them for themselves and taught them so much that in some ways, they are more capable young adults now than they would have been if we were too controlling of their behavior.

I also did my best to add excitement and humor to their lives. I made up a lot of stories and games that amused them. I spent a lot of time at their charter school, too, because I felt that having me there helped create more continuity in their lives between home and school. Both of our kids tell me I (mostly) achieved my goal of helping them to have great childhoods!

PBC: Tell me about any famous role models that may have influenced you in your personal evolution.

Anita: Gloria Steinem, as a feminist, spoke to me more beautifully than any other feminist woman did, because of her brilliance. And Marianne Williamson, author of ***Return to Love*** and other books, as a spiritual woman speaks to me. I listen to all her words and love her.

PBC: Interesting… as they're your contemporaries, but even so, had a profound influence, it sounds like.

Anita: They are both such exemplary women—activists and healers in their own way. My work as a healer for individuals led me back to the planetary healing work I do now.

PBC: Tell me a little about your newest paradigm shift if you'd like—in a nutshell?

Anita: It has evolved out of my individual healing. In 2011, through one of my private clients, I met a man who had worked in Sub-Saharan Africa for 20 years. Over the course of his career, he transformed the lives of many thousands of people by helping them add value to the products and practices they already had in place. Rather than simply giving aid to these various populations, his team showed people how to use their own skills and resources to increase their standard of living. I was so inspired that in the summer of 2012, I wrote a manuscript for a book chronicling his work.

Writing that book inspired me to look for more people or groups who realized that building self-reliance and showing people how to create wealth for themselves is so much more effective, long term, than giving aid. While I found that such programs were enormously successful, I also saw that much of their work did not receive enough attention from the media. So I contacted my friend, best-selling author and social media guru Warren Whitlock and together we founded "Billions Rising, Self-Reliance Foundation." We are dedicated to solving the problems of poverty worldwide through education and action.

I oversee projects and represent the foundation in the media. Our mission has been to learn as much as possible about the programs, organizations and projects that promote "self-reliance" as a means to alleviate poverty, and then to share that information as widely as possible. We have a book *Billions Rising, Empowering Self-Reliance* that releases in November 2013 [now released by date of publication], and we begin production on our feature-length documentary in 2014. When we did the Google Analytics recently, we found that our promotions had literally reached millions of people worldwide. Our weekly radio show is drawing in thousands of listeners each episode. We post about six blogs per week about great things that are happening around the world and get a huge number of comments—so our plan seems to be working! These programs and other non-profits are receiving more attention, support and funding.

PBC: That's fantastic! You've really taken your work to the next level—and I'm sure readers will enjoy tracing your roots back to the various pieces that have all pointed you in this direction now.

Anita: A friend recently remarked that in undertaking running an international non-profit, I have blended all that I have learned this past decade as a filmmaker and healer. I agree with him! And in all honesty, I have never loved any work I have done as much as I do this. I see that my team and I are making a real difference. This is what gets me up in the morning. I leap out of bed early each day, filled with excitement!

PBC: Is there anything that you would like to leave the next generation of women in your closing thoughts?

Anita: What I love most about running the "Billions Rising Foundation" is that I'm finding women who are able to take control of their lives after generations of poverty. The Women's World Bank is a great example of this—their micro loans empower women to build businesses and become independent. There are women in Kenya and Uganda who are building small businesses for themselves with the help of some of the foundations we represent. These women become completely self-sustaining and then reach out to help other families. Women helping women is taking place everywhere around the globe.

As women elevate themselves professionally and politically, we are also given the opportunity to elevate ourselves spiritually in society. I believe we are, in fact, going to become more and more the spiritual leaders of the world. Our female sensibility includes the nurturer, or 'she who brings life,' and it is so critical for our planet now and for humanity. We are the ones who are going to heal the planet—the environment. It's not that men won't play a part in it but, but the Yin—the female part of us—really embraces our planet, embraces humanity and sees the unity and the oneness. So, instinctively, I feel that humanity stands such a great chance of survival the more women take the social, political and spiritual power on earth.

PBC: I'm gonna quote that verbatim: "…Humanity stands such a great chance of survival the more women take the social, political and spiritual power on earth!" [laughs]

"Myrna Yi"

Biography

Born: 1966, 46 (at the time of interview)

Mother: Chinese. Born in China 1926; died 2008 at 82 years

Married, husband (agricultural real estate investor)

Full-time mom

University of California, Bachelor's Degree in Business Economics

2 Daughters, 14 years and 10 years

Youngest of 6 children—siblings:

  Brother – 1950
  Sister – 1954
  Sister – 1957
  Sister – 1960
  Sister – 1962

I was 42 at the time my mother died.

Father: Chinese, born in China 1924, died 2002 at 78 years. I was 36 at the time.

Interview

June 2012

(This is a fictitious name as this interviewee prefers to keep her actual identity private.)

PBC: You've been identified as someone who's made a leap in consciousness from where your mother left off. I'm interested in hearing your take on how you think you fit that category…primarily in terms of the values that her life represented, and the values that your life represents…if we look at human consciousness being a continuum and each generation takes it a little bit further or a different direction.

Myrna: Right. I think for my mother and myself, she raised five daughters and one son. The son—my brother—was the eldest, and five girls to follow.

PBC: She was Chinese, correct?

Myrna: Yes, and my father was also Chinese. She was kind of a traditional Chinese mother in some sense in that she really valued family and she was the matriarch in our family, but she still gave way to my father as the head of the household and gave him that glory and respect. However, she was really the one who ruled the roost, like in many cultures. She instilled in us to be strong, independent women, which I think strayed a little from traditional Chinese culture. The tradition is when you marry—and they have two different words for marry that differentiate the roles of men vs. women. A woman "marries and surrenders" into the man's family. A man "takes" a wife into his family. So, it's similar to here the reference for the groom: you take a wife. In China, the wife becomes part of the husband, and when you marry, the wife becomes part of her husband's family. There is a saying in Chinese that when you (a woman) marry a chicken, you live as a chicken. When you marry a dog, you live as a dog. The meaning is that a woman completely loses her own identity and takes on the identity of her husband and his family.

PBC: So the husband was the dominant aspect. But your mom kind of challenged or expanded tradition?

Myrna: That was always underlying. I think my mother always stressed that you have to be independent, you don't depend on a man to support you and you have to be educated. Education is the means to self-sustenance.

PBC: This attitude, "Don't depend on a man to support you….education as sustenance," that's a big of departure from her Chinese upbringing or tradition, isn't it?

Myrna: It's a departure from the tradition that she was raised. Just to clarify, she was raised in a very traditional family; her mother was married in an arranged marriage where she didn't meet her husband until the wedding day. She was only 16, and my mother's oldest sister was also married in that fashion, and that was, unfortunately, a very tragic marriage. She wasn't treated well by her husband. So, by the time it got to my mother's turn, her parents decided to let her choose her own mate. And so, she met my father on her own. They courted and eventually got married, but my mother was also the first female in her family to be educated. She got a college education and a teaching credential as well. So, she was the go-getter in her family.

PBC: So there was a bit of a paradigm shift, if we want to call it that, within her family of siblings.

Myrna: Right, within her generation. So, she instilled that into us, her children, and this became part of her mission to migrate to the United States. My mother always knew that, being a daughter in China or in Hong Kong, you don't have the equal opportunities as being a son. In her mind, this was a huge paradigm shift for the sake of the children and a better opportunity, especially us daughters. She was always in her mind, temporary in location. When she was in China, she knew she was going to eventually go to Hong Kong. From Hong Kong, she knew she was going to come to the United States for our benefit.

PBC: So, she saw herself on the move.

Myrna: On the move, yes, until she landed in America. That was when she was in her 40s.

PBC: And do you think she was on the move in China wanting to come to America because there was some dream here?

Myrna: Yes, the dream would be to educate her girls.

PBC: Even though she managed to get educated in China, she wanted an American education for her girls.

Myrna: She knew the tough struggle it would be to get five girls educated the way she was.

PBC: She knew she was kinda the exception in China. Correct?

Myrna: Yes, exactly. So, for me growing up, I had all the lessons of being independent, along with being educated. My parents were both educated. My father was a scholar. As I was growing up, he was a Chinese scholar, a calligrapher and artist who basically knew everything about China. [laughs] The Chinese language has about 40,000 characters and the average high functioning educated person knows about 10,000.

PBC: That's interesting, in that we can hardly relate to that in this language and culture.

Myrna: Yeah, I know because everything is down to…initials or acronyms here so it was like…wow! [laughs]

PBC: Yeah, and everybody knows complete English by fourth grade! Where the native language is not so complex such that you'd study the fineries into college that way. Literature or journalism would be the closest counterpart, I suppose.

Myrna: Yeah, right. So my father was a life-long student.

PBC: Interesting. So tell me what age they were when they immigrated here and what age you were.

Myrna: I was 10 months old and my parents were both in their early 40s.

My mother must have been 41, my dad 43, I think, both not speaking the language. My father spoke some English but my mother never spoke any English. They had six children and no money.

PBC: Wow. Both of them were very determined.

Myrna: Very difficult, but very determined. So, back then I think you needed to have a sponsor to immigrate, to be allowed a visa. My mother always knew she was gonna end up in America. Her father was Canadian. I'm sure this gave her the security of knowing she would eventually migrate to be closer to family. Her parents and siblings eventually settled in the Bay Area, which is the reason we settled in San Francisco. It is very interesting, because he married my grandmother when she was 16 and she stayed in China. He came back and forth from Canada to China once every eight years. Therefore, my mother has a sister, and then she has a younger brother. They are all eight years apart.

PBC: Your mother's father was a Canadian? And her parents didn't live together. I see, wow! And this was an arranged marriage, yes?

Myrna: Yes.

PBC: All the more remarkable! Do you know how this was arranged, given his Canadian status?

Myrna: I don't know how it was arranged. Her mother lived in China with the children, her father was in Canada and had a restaurant, and that's how he supported the family, but physically they were only together every eight years and my mother only met him twice in her life, I think.

PBC: He supported the family by sending his checks to China? Wow. How unusual was that then? [laughs]

Myrna: I think it was seen as practical—that's how they fed themselves. It had to be done as a big sacrifice.

PBC: Did her parents who arranged this see this coming, do you have any info??

Myrna: I don't know but this was not uncommon back then. The overseas Chinese were seen as the prosperous ones because conditions in China were bleak and unstable at the time.

PBC: He couldn't or didn't consider bringing them to Canada with him to live together with him?

Myrna: I don't really know the logic behind that, but he and his brothers owned their own business in Saskatchewan, Canada, and they all did the same thing. They all had their wives in the same big house in China. Actually I visited that house in 2010 with my husband and daughters.

Myrna: So my mother lived with her mother, her siblings, her aunt and one cousin. The house was built such that you each wife and children had their own quarters and then the common quarter would be the living room and dining area.

PBC: Very fascinating. We could probably do a whole story on just your mom's history! It's interesting background to look at your roots. I'd like to look at the personality traits that distinguish you from your mom.

Myrna: Her background is certainly very different than how I grew up. But in thinking about our personalities, I really feel like I'm my mother's daughter. I'm very similar to her but fortunate enough to live in a place where I feel I get better opportunities.

PBC: Can we look both at your circumstances that have afforded you more comfort and opportunity as well as any differences in values that have evolved?

Myrna: I am aware I am much more fortunate because of my parents' endurance and drive.

PBC: So in a sense you're able to capitalize on her values and live them out without the obstacles that she had.

Myrna: Yes. Right.

PBC: And what of those personality traits, would you say are similar between you? Would it be valuing education? Determination? What else would you describe yourself as being like her?

Myrna: I think I value family. I value my husband and our relationship and I also value my relationship with my daughters where I feel like my role is…number one, I'm the mother and their protector. I feel compelled to instill in them the same values: you need to be able to sustain yourself…be educated …be a strong woman and be kind. I'm not sure, but I see those as pretty universal. [laughs] But maybe I think it's universal because it's what I grew up with!

PBC: Well, being a strong woman is getting redefined I think—what it means to be a strong woman and what it means to be independent. It seems that independence was a pretty big piece of your background in that it was a departure from Chinese tradition, you think?

Myrna: Yes, I completely agree—it was such a departure from the Chinese tradition. However, it's a complicated question because I think there are now a lot of women in America who define independence as having a job and being a working mother—being able to manage the workplace and the home and to balance that. For me, I'm defining it my own way, which happens to be my mother's way. [laughs] She stayed at home too. That was the priority for her—to make sure that she was home when the kids came home, we were fed, and that she was there to supervise. Similarly to my mother, I feel that this is the same choice I am making - to stay home and be a full time mother and wife. In today's world, with standards of living higher and affordability being a factor, I feel fortunate that staying home is an option for me.

PBC: You're finding it your own way. So you are an at-home mom. Would you say that you are doing that consciously and mindfully?

Myrna: I'm doing that consciously and mindfully for our situation, not because my mother did it. I'm doing it because it works for our family. I recognize that not everyone is able to do that. And I appreciate that I have that opportunity. It is a privilege and a luxury.

PBC: As you look at your values and your mom's values, are there any ways that you feel that you've departed—or further departed, as the case may be—from the traditions that she was in the process of departing from?

For example, what about being raised to please, prioritizing others and putting oneself last, which is typical of the traditions that many of us have come out of in various cultures. So where do you see yourself on that continuum or progression?

Myrna: We were definitely raised to please. However, like I said, my mother was a strong person. We were raised to please my mother and father. We raise our children with a cross between tradition and modern ways. We try to instill in them confidence and a their sense of worth and esteem, which is more modern. However, we hold on to traditional values such as NOT putting yourself first always, pleasing your parents and delayed gratification. It's not easy and we're not always parenting that conscientiously, but we try to do our best in finding a balance between modern and traditional.

PBC: Were there any times when you remember finding that difficult, or you wanted to please them in a way that they weren't so comfortable with, such that they couldn't really offer their approval?

Myrna: Yeah, there were times, many times because, ultimately, I am a mix of the Chinese culture, my parents' teachings, and the American culture. You have the influence of your friends, the influence of your family and then you have the historical influence of your ancestry. So there were always conflicts.

PBC: If there were choices that you made that mom didn't approve of or that you wished she would approve of, are there choices that you're making now that perhaps she didn't approve of or wouldn't approve of, or do you feel like you are pretty much making her proud and always did?

Myrna: [laughs] Definitely not always! So for example, I was 21 when I graduated from college. Then, I moved to Hong Kong because I had a boyfriend there. It progressed until we got married which my parents did not approve of not because they didn't like him—they thought I was too young and they wanted me to continue my education in post-graduate school. So, I should have listened to them, number one. [laughs] I was too young—you go through many changes between 20 and 40. So I do regret that choice, and, in hindsight, I think that going to grad school in my early 20s would have been a great environment for me both academically and socially. I would have learned more technicalities of a field as well as being surrounded by smart people. Mostly, I wish the same for my daughters—to go further with their educations. My mother was right.

PBC: And how did that relationship turn out? 'Cause that's not the man you're with now…

Myrna: No, it ended in divorce shortly after. It lasted two and a half years.

PBC: And you came back to this country, obviously. Did he remain there?

For reference here, we were looking at the departure from your mom's values and what torches you are carrying vs. where you didn't get her approval. Maybe this relationship took it a step further than she could approve? It seems you're talking about what we might look at as a rebellious time in your young adulthood?

Myrna: Right…but his being a Chinese man—I thought that they would be more pleased.

PBC: It was almost like a test of their values, wasn't it? "What do you appreciate more, the Chinese aspect, or that I'm supposed to be independent and educated?"

Myrna: That's right. But I was young, extremely naive and stupid. I would say that I was experimenting. Having said that, my parents loved my current American born and raised current husband. I met him shortly after moving back to San Francisco from Hong Kong. We worked at the same company in San Francisco and we became friends. I enjoyed his curiosity for life, his intelligence and his 'groundedness'. He grew up on a farm with very traditional values, where the boys did the outdoor chores and the girls did the indoor chores. I think he was raised probably more similarly to my mother than to me. Here was this handsome man with many attributes that I admired and he was American! I realized then that I was more American than I had been willing to admit to myself. He and my mother were very much alike. My husband is a very smart man and my mother was a very smart woman. She is still by far the smartest person I have known. [laughs] They both had very analytical minds. They also have—using the present tense—the capacity to read situations really well and also to read people pretty well…they're very intuitive. So, even though they didn't speak the same language, they were still able to see things with the same eyes. For example, my mom would be on my left and my husband would be on my right in a situation, and they would both at the same time speak the same commentary in their respective languages. [laughs]

PBC: Wow. They saw things similarly. So your mom migrated here, but didn't learn English?

Myrna: We lived in San Francisco where you didn't really need to learn English. They never drove; my parents took a bus everywhere. They managed a business. My father was the vice principal of a Chinese Catholic School. He also was an artist and calligrapher. My mother was a homemaker. They worked hard to save their money and eventually owned property in San Francisco. Initially when we moved to San Francisco, we lived in Chinatown, and then eventually we moved into I guess what has become known as the second Chinatown. It was the 'rich man's China Town' at that time we lived there. The second Chinatown is usually where the more established immigrants moved to once they get settled enough to afford a house.

PBC: So it was insulated enough in that time that they could manage with just speaking Chinese. Did Dad learn more English or did he remain uni-lingual in Chinese also?

Myrna: My father actually knew English and he was able to converse and understood a lot, but if anything was complicated, he would ask the kids!

My father was deeply immersed in the Chinese community. He belonged to a lot of associations and benevolent clubs in the community and they didn't need to use much English in their surroundings.

PBC: And so you were bilingual from the beginning since you came here as an infant and you started in school here in the US—is that where you learned English, in school?

Myrna: I spoke Chinese to my parents and learned English through my siblings. So everyday I would go to American school and come home, and between the ages of 1st and 5th grades, get dressed and go to my Chinese Catholic school.

PBC: And were your parents Catholic?

Myrna: No, Buddhist, but they weren't really serious Buddhists. They were kind of fair weather Buddhists.

PBC: Ah. So can you explain why they chose Catholic school for you—your siblings also?

Myrna: The Catholic school was the best option at the time because that's where my dad was the Vice Principal and a teacher. My father, as I told you, was a scholar and also a poet…keep in mind, my mother would kind of spout off these Confucius sayings and other teachings or poems…so my father or my mother would start and the other would finish the verse or quote. So we grew up at the dinner table listening to these kinds of teachings and idioms and such which were life lessons. For me growing up—I didn't find this to be unusual until I was an adult.

PBC: Did you value that? Do you, did you appreciate that?

Myrna: I did and still do. I value the uniqueness and the "culturedness" of the environment that I grew up with.

PBC: It was inspirational?

Myrna: It was dorky and foreign at the time, but now as an adult I appreciate it very much.

PBC: As you got to be teenagers, did you roll your eyes, like [laughs], "There they go again. [laughs] Spouting off their Confucian-isms." [laughs]

Myrna: [laughs] My parents had a good sense of humor, they were both really funny, actually. [laughs]

PBC: And you have that too, yes? [laughs] So at your dinner table now, how old are your girls?

Myrna: My girls are 14 and 10.

PBC: What kind of an atmosphere do you create? Is there any ritual at the dinner table?

Myrna: Being that my girls are young, our family traditions are still evolving. My role as a mother continues to unfold and is constantly changing as our daughters mature and their lives and schedules progress. I very much hope my kids think we have a good sense of humor! [laughs] They are growing up very differently from how I grew up. For example, I grew up in San Francisco so we didn't have a garden. Even if we had, probably nothing would grow because it's so cold and foggy. But my husband grew up in a country setting on a farm, so he does all the gardening including produce that we eat. He also grew up in an extremely religious household.

PBC: What religion?

Myrna: Presbyterian.

PBC: Does he still practice that religion?

Myrna: [laughs] I would say maybe he's a fair weather Protestant now—after being married to me. [laughs] But his family was strict Presbyterian. He wasn't, but he went to church every Sunday until he was 18. His parents still do at 92. [laughs]

PBC: Wow. So he didn't buy in so completely but went through the motions growing up because it was expected.

Myrna: My husband can still recite bible verses and stories like no other. He brings in the lessons and stories at appropriate teaching times for our girls. The teachings are ingrained in him and he is able to pull them out of his hat whenever he is inspired to do so, but he is not a regular church-goer.

Myrna: So at our dinner table, he says grace, which I never grew up with.

PBC: You grew up with Confucianism!

Myrna: [laughs] Yes. I mean, it wouldn't be everyday, but it would be a few days a week that we would say grace at our dinner table now. And he grew up with saying grace, so he'll say, "Thank the Lord for our food" and so on and so forth—that's our ritual, and then—it seems kind of mundane—but we talk about our day… everybody gets a chance to chat and we love it! But I prepare the food like my mother did—my husband doesn't do a lot of cooking. He does the outdoor work, just like his upbringing as a boy.

PBC: But you said he prepares the garden? [laughs]

Myrna: Yes. He has a large garden in town and grows many of our fruits and vegetables. Gardening, farming really, is his connection to his roots and it relaxes him.

PBC: And the girls? Do they participate in the gardening, the setting the table, the preparation, any of that?

Myrna: They do all of that—they help quite a bit. They garden with my husband mostly during the summer when they have time and the garden needs a lot of attention. They also help with cooking and cleaning before and after meals.

PBC: Willingly or with some nagging from you? [laughs]

Myrna: There's a little bit of both. They are willing to do it because we've taught them that being a part of our family means contributing to the family unit—which translates into helping out with chores and tasks. However, sometimes it takes encouragement, which can be interpreted as nagging! [laughs]

PBC: Are there any other traits that your mom had or passed on to you, positive experiences in your formative years, that have stuck with you, and that you are passing along to your children?

Myrna: [laughs] There is one ritual that I wish I could pass along to my children, but this is something that I think is pretty incredible. As an adult now I realize you have to have money to do this, so I'm not holding my breath just yet! But when it was my birthday, I took my mother out to lunch.

PBC: Oh, at what age did this begin?

Myrna: In my 20s, once I started working and making money. Because it was my mother who brought us here into this world and she suffered the many hours of labor, whatever it was....

PBC: You wanted to thank her? Kinda like Mothers Day on your birthday?

Myrna: Yes. Yes. I thought that was a sweet tradition and I hope to hear that my kids would want to pick it up someday. [laughs]

PBC: [laughs] Are they home now, overhearing this?

Myrna: [laughs] I felt it was an honor to be able to do that.

PBC: And what was the Chinese tradition for celebrating birthdays?

Myrna: Not much. When I was young, my family would have dinner followed with a birthday cake. I'd never had a birthday party until I was 30.

PBC: But there was a cake as you were growing up?

Myrna: Yes.

PBC: Were there candles or singing or presents?

Myrna: We'd sing Happy Birthday…maybe a few presents but it would mostly the cake that signified the celebration. There would be a red envelope gift that would have some money in it.

PBC: That's for good luck, good fortune?

Myrna: Yes, the red envelope that you get for New Year's. That's a traditional gift in China—a little bit of money in a red envelope, the ritual Chinese red envelope.

PBC: Ah.

Myrna: Another way to honor and thank your ancestors and your predecessors…

now that my mom has passed away, I like to go to visit her grave on or around my birthday. This is the extension of my taking her to lunch on my birthday.

PBC: You appreciate that?

Myrna: Very much, that's very Confucian. I do appreciate that.

PBC: Respect for the elders.

Myrna: For the elders and ancestors because, well, without them, we wouldn't be here!

PBC: You're addressing a consciousness about ancestors that perhaps isn't much here in this country at this time.

Myrna: No, the focus is on the self.

PBC: Do you ever find a conflict in that? Given the current trends and culture that your girls are exposed to and what you want to raise them with?

Myrna: Yeah, I think as the years have progressed within this culture, our society has become very much a 'me society'!

PBC: How so?

Myrna: Well my daughter's 8th grade graduation was like four days of festivities. I don't remember this when we were graduating from 8th grade. We just kind walked across the stage and that was it. Just my parents were there and my siblings weren't there. It wasn't a big deal.

PBC: What did you think of your daughter's event/s?

Myrna: The focus, the spotlight was really on the children.

PBC: …to their detriment, to some degree?

Myrna: Yes, but that's a whole other story. Yes. I felt that graduating from middle school should be expected of our children. It is a minor milestone that should be recognized and acknowledged simply.

PBC: I'm interested in the difference in what values of your upbringing you're trying to live and hold onto and what values you're feeling in conflict with or trying to adopt anew, in contrast to your upbringing.

Myrna: I think that my husband and I are both relatively conventional compared to a lot of other parents nowadays. For example, my oldest daughter (age 14) just got a cellphone this Christmas and she is the last in her class to have one. Many of the kids have had cell phones for years. We feel you value something more when you've had to be patient and to anticipate it. My husband and I were raised with lots of siblings and not much money. Our parents didn't buy us lots of things and we didn't take fancy vacations. We had to make do with what we had and what our families could afford. My parents worked hard and did not have time to come to school functions nor were they able to communicate with my teachers. I navigated my school and choices on my own. Sometimes not making the best decisions.

PBC: Childhood is becoming so influenced by the material electronic world and kids are growing up earlier in this culture than when we were kids?

Myrna: I think once you introduce technology, the interactive face-to-face seems to these young people secondary or maybe not necessary at all. So those social skills in the traditional meaning become underdeveloped because of the new norm. That's happening to our youngsters—meaning kids as a "society" in general. My older daughter was late in the game and during the times that she did not have a phone yet, she spent observing her friends' behaviors and their actions with their phones. She noted to herself that she will not text or use her phone while she is conversing with someone face to face; other things she found annoying that her friends with phones did, she swore to herself no to repeat.

PBC: I find it interesting, coming out of your multicultural background that you have married an American man who comes out of a traditional background in terms of the agricultural based and the religious mores that he was raised in. Yours and his values seem to match up, yes?

Myrna: They match up very well. They're very similar.

PBC: But interesting how you both came to this meeting place. [laughs] When you look at your backgrounds, you grew up in Chinatown in San Francisco, and he grew up on the farm in 'Presbyterianville.' [laughs]

Myrna: Right—exactly. But my parents grew up on farms too, so I would hear stories of what they experienced and what they appreciated—we didn't have any fast food or junk food at our house when I was growing up. They ate a lot of fresh vegetables and fresh meat growing up on the farm, which is what my husband grew up with too. It's the simplicity of life that we both grew up with and appreciate.

PBC: …and that you're trying to maintain.

Myrna: In many ways, yes.

PBC: In your upbringing, Myrna, what did you and your mom argue or perhaps not see eye-to-eye about? I get that you had to be very respectful to your elders and authority so I'm wondering if there were arguments, or if you kept any feelings of discontent inside?

Myrna: Yes, there were arguments, but at some point I think, my English became excelled beyond my Chinese. Once that happened, I lost a lot of my Chinese at a rapid pace. It became more difficult to argue with my parents in Chinese!

PBC: What age was that?

Myrna: Around nine or 10—it became difficult. The other thing about growing up in a bilingual household—it's great because you have the exposure to the two different languages and you can speak both languages well. But if one or the other doesn't speak a common language well, you miss out on the nuances of the weaker language. I do think it was a barrier to communicating with my parents. It was easier for me to not tell them things because I wasn't able to express the nuances of it and didn't want them to misunderstand my meaning.

PBC: Are you exposing your girls to Chinese with that in mind?

Myrna: Neither of my daughters speaks Chinese. However, my older daughter will be learning Mandarin when she goes to high school.

PBC: Interesting.

Myrna: I feel like I wasn't as above board on the on the language-arts side as I should have been when I was going to school. Looking back, there was a disconnect in my English language ability. While I learned English at school and did well, and spoke English fluently, there was the day-to-day home life that wasn't in English. That bridge that connected my day use of English and my evening use of Chinese was missing growing up.

PBC: How did that affect your relationship with your mom?

Myrna: If I wanted to communicate with my parents, I had to speak Chinese but I didn't communicate with them as much or with as many details as I would have liked…purely due to my language limitation.

PBC: To choose to drop one language or to speak mono-lingual was not allowed. So communication became strained.

Myrna: Limited. And at that time, I was also shifting developmentally.

PBC: So you became limited in being able to communicate the nuances, the subtleties of your experience with mom, you had to switch it to Chinese for her to get it, and you were more adept at English.

Myrna: It was a little more of a struggle. At that age, during my teens, I gravitated towards my school friends more.

PBC: What were the topics that you would have discussed in more depth if you had more of a grasp on the language?

Myrna: Typical arguments [laughs]: "How late I can stay out?" "Why aren't you doing this? Why aren't you cleaning the house? If you want to go to the gym, you might as well clean the house 'cause you get exercise that way too!" Very typical arguments—nothing major.

PBC: [laughs] No scars from those arguments?

Myrna: No. I didn't realize then, but I do now, what wonderful parents I had.

PBC: Hindsight, huh? [laughs] Well in contrast to the wonderful parents you had, I'm wondering if the example that you gave of marrying the Chinese man and moving to China was one of those turning points for you, or if there are others you can see that taught you something, impacted you in a major way.

Myrna: I think that was the big turning point. When I met this Chinese man, I thought how easy it was that he was modern and yet traditional in his Chinese ways, likes and dislikes. He was familiar to me and that was comforting. I felt "all the boxes checked".

PBC: Was there a language issue or did he speak fluent English?

Myrna: No, no. He was completely fluent. He was educated in the US but grew up in a very traditional Chinese household where the women ate after the men. There was a family table but when there were guests, not everyone could sit at the table at the same time. Quarters were very cramped so during parties, meals were staggered and the men would eat first followed by the women. That really stuck with me and felt really crazy and unfair...especially since the women prepared the meal!

PBC: Did he have expectations of you that in some way your values would be in keeping with the patriarchy?

Myrna: Absolutely. At one point, I said, "I would like to get my masters degree." One comment he made which was incomprehensible to me until it sunk in, was "Oh, you can't be smarter than me."

PBC: It was revealing.

Myrna: [laughs] Yes. And like I said, I was young; I was stupid. I should have listened to my gut and also to my parents.

PBC: And what do you think kept you from listening to your gut and your parents at that time?

Myrna: There's definitely a benefit to being taught to please, on the one hand. But on the other hand, it is important to know when to go against the tide and do what's right for you. He and his family really liked me and wanted us to get married. I wanted to please others so much that I lost my sense of what I really wanted.

PBC: Because you were taught to please, you didn't listen to your own gut? Do you think you had become a pleaser to your own detriment at that point?

Myrna: Yes. You don't realize what a sacrifice you're making at the time...you think it's going to all end up just fine.

PBC: But that experience taught you otherwise?

Myrna: [laughs] I should have pleased my parents instead—they had it right!

PBC: In a sense, I feel like we put our parents' values to the test in our teen or young adult years: "So does this win your approval? How about this?" And we learn from those attempts...sometimes in the process of intending to make a statement to our parents—"Okay, I'll be a pleaser. Watch this!" kind of thing, we end up suffering the consequences. It sounds like that relationship was one of those experiments.

Myrna: Right. It taught me to actually look and listen. You have to listen to yourself—to what you really stand for and who you are.

PBC: Were there other points like that that you can think of?

Myrna: I think there was a big turning point when my father died suddenly. That was in June 10 years ago that my father died. It was due to a massive heart attack. Death seems really far away until your parent dies or someone really close to you passes away. I was shocked and saddened—I was 36 years old with a newborn—our second daughter.

PBC: It jolted your world?

Myrna: It brought home that mortality is real. But also it shattered my mom's world completely! My mom loved all of her children, but first and foremost, she adored my father. And my father adored her. So it left a big void in her life.

PBC: Your grandmother had an arranged marriage, where your parents chose each other and were very much a pair. There was deep love between them?

Myrna: They were always there for us kids, but once we grew up and moved out of the house, they were always there for each other. They were very social. They did everything together, so we almost never got to see them unless we scheduled the time. After my father's death, my mother didn't continue in her social world because she lost the love of her life. Mom was deeply saddened. So she kind of reverted back to being in the mom mode and spent a lot of time in the home or visiting her children. Because I was the youngest and was, I'm happy to say, the closest to my mother [laughs], and since I had a baby, it gave her a purpose to come stay with us and help with the baby, as opposed to staying with my other siblings who had no kids at home. My siblings and their spouses all worked so she would spend the days by herself when Mom visited them. My house was the natural place for her to be because I was home and could use Mom's help. She spent a lot of time with us, which allowed me to get to know my mother as an adult…to reconnect with her.

PBC: So those experiences of your first marriage and then losing your dad as an adult both left you hurting, yet in both instances, something turned you from despair or aloneness. Looking back prior to that early marriage, would you describe your childhood as pretty secure and happy?

Myrna: Yes, I had a very secure and happy childhood. My parents guided us well and I knew that they would always be there for us. It wasn't until I was older that I learned of my parents' past struggles and how they were able to overcome the effects of them. To me, knowing how strong a marriage my parents had gave me lots of security as their child and lots of hope that I can too have a strong marriage, which I feel laid the foundation for my current marriage.

I think a big pivotal moment for my mother was when my father was arrested for being a traitor. This was during the communist revolution and my father was working for the Chiang Kai-shek Regime. He was the chief of police. Chiang Kai-shek was the anti-communist and also was a father of Taiwan as we know it today, so my father was working under him. My father subsequently met my mother and then moved back to Mainland China. But then the revolution happened and he was labeled as a traitor to China, and so the Chinese took him to 're-education camp' as a form of jail…decompression from brainwashing. He was in the re-education camp for two years, during which time my mother had my older sister who was conceived before my father was arrested. What I learned later about this time was that the baby died a year later and my father had never met this daughter. My mother experienced this birth and death all by herself, while also supporting the family (herself and my brother) and her mother-in-law. I came about 12 years later than this.

PBC: Wow. There was a baby that died. Do you know how?

Myrna: I don't really know what she died of. I don't think my mother knew what she died of either.

PBC: That must have really tested her inner strength. Do you know how she got through that? Did she have family support?

Myrna: My maternal grandmother helped monetarily, sending money to my mother.

PBC: Did she talk about that time afterward?

Myrna: I was about ten when I learned that I had another sister. But, no, they didn't talked about it at all, they only talked about happy things! [laughs]

PBC: And how was that for you, looking back, that she didn't talk about suffering or pain from such a critical time in her life?

Myrna: Those were really big events that caused deep, deep wounds, and I think those were hard for her to bring up. It was my dad who shared it with us. For my dad I think that was a big turning point too. He didn't talk much about his time in the re-education camp either. He suffered there, separate from my mother's suffering. Separately, they both prevailed, reunited and moved on. Another big turning point was when my family immigrated to America.

PBC: Do you know how that decision was made and what influenced the timing? You were a baby under a year?

Myrna: My parents always knew they wanted to end up in the US because my mother's parents and her siblings were both here. The US, being the land of opportunity, was the place they saw their children growing up and getting an education—and it was within reach because of our family connections.

Another pivotal factor on my father's side was that he was only child of an opium-addicted father. His mother raised him because his father was mostly missing in action, visiting opium dens. My grandfather grew up in the family jade business and his known talent was being able to find jade at its natural source.

PBC: Any speculation as to what drove grandfather to get hooked on opium?

Myrna: My grandfather was an irresponsible husband and father being so distraught and then under the influence, and he died at 46. Opium was rampant in those days and I don't know what drove him to use it. I believe it was the driving factor in my father's motivation to be a proper provider for his family, loving husband and community leader.

PBC: Sometimes a negative role model can be a powerful teacher. Pretty tough on his mom, I can only imagine!

Myrna: For my grandmother, my father was her world. She worked hard to support him and his education. When my parents got married, they lived together with my father's mother.

PBC: So he lived with his mother in her home where he brought his new wife, yes?

Myrna: Right. That was traditional then. You take a wife…the wife comes with you into your family home. And through the six children that my parents had, my grandmother was a part of that. But when my family immigrated, it was through a sponsorship on my mother's side. It was my mother's sister was our sponsor. Because my paternal grandmother was not her blood relative, she had to stay behind. She was so heartbroken to be left alone, she couldn't even go to the airport to say goodbye to her son, daughter-in-law and her six grandchildren. She was so, so sad and she died less than a year after we moved to the US.

PBC: And do you know if your mother felt guilty for essentially abandoning her—for prioritizing her girls over the grandmother?

Myrna: I think so. I'm sure she was sad and I'm sure she felt sorrow but not necessarily guilt because she thought she was doing the right thing looking to the future. The plan was that once my parents obtained citizenship, they would be able to apply for my grandmother to come and join us, but she passed away much too early.

PBC: So, my sense is that your mom was the kind who pulled her bootstraps up during hard times and made the best of it. She valued strength and determination and the attitude, "Be all you can be, be the best you can be" got conveyed to you. But there's an emotional piece that seems to be kind of buried—perhaps by perceived necessity? She wasn't comfortable going into vulnerability or expressing grief because that would weaken her…is that accurate as you look back on it, now?

Myrna: Yes. She was also very much a compassionate and empathic person. She didn't actually speak the words but you could see it in her face or feel it. I believe these were pivotal times in my parents' lives that shaped them into who they were as people and as parents. I was fortunate enough to have my parents be two individuals as separate role models and together as my parents and my support system.

PBC: And would you say that you've been able to carry forth those qualities also? Compassion, empathy and yet strong and determined? Do you see any weaknesses or anything missing in her—perhaps because circumstances or necessity limited her—that you would like to expand or improve on in your life?

Myrna: Being close with my daughters throughout the years—that's what I would like to achieve….so far, so good. We continue to grow. For me with my mom, it was closeness to a certain point and then there was a distance…then we came back together. I would like to be able to continue the closeness with my girls, without a break.

PBC: Distance both because of the language barrier as a teen and then when you and your siblings left home, she and your dad established their own very social life, you almost had to make an appointment to see her? But then you reconnected after your dad passed away and she became part of your family again?

Myrna: Yes. I think this may not be an exception, but a natural developmental evolution of maturity and the cycle of life.

PBC: What do you and your daughters argue about, Myrna?

Myrna: Sleepovers. [laughs]

PBC: [laughs]

Myrna: We don't argue much, actually. [laughs] It's just their social lives that make for any conflicts at this point. There are too many activities and too little time. [laughs] My oldest daughter is just graduating from the 8th grade. Some of her friends are being allowed to go out on their own, without supervision and I'm not comfortable with that.

PBC: And do you have fears as she goes into high school?

Myrna: Absolutely. That she desires more independence.

PBC: That's gonna become more of an issue, isn't it.

Myrna: And because her high school is in another city/county, I won't know many of her friends as well as I know her friends now.

PBC: And yet you still chose to send her to the high school where you did because of the kind of education it will give her?

Myrna: Yeah. It's a tough call to stay local or to go to a school out of town that's a better fit. If we can't seem to make it work, we could choose something different in the future if we need to. We don't see it as a permanent decision.

PBC: The values that you feel that you have instilled in your daughters in their formative years...are you hoping that they will carry them into these years, especially as your older daughter becomes a high school student—that value of family intimacy and connection?

Myrna: I hope I've instilled the value to please without compromising who they are. [laughs] I love who they are!

PBC: Well, they're still becoming who they are! But so far you don't see any reason for them to have to choose between being true to themselves and pleasing others, right? Would that be the improvement you would hope to accomplish from your upbringing—for them to not have to choose between pleasing or being true to oneself and pleasing others at the same time?

Myrna: Yes, absolutely. I now know these are not mutually exclusive attributes. As a matter of fact, under the right circumstances, they can be complimentary attributes.

PBC: In your mom's time as she was raising you to please others, especially in the context of the patriarchy even though she was able to challenge that in some ways herself, but with your first husband, it backfired. You found that pleasing yourself and pleasing him weren't compatible. But I see that as a kind of crossroads in your upbringing. So you are hoping that the way you raised your daughters doesn't put them in such a crossroad or split?

Myrna: And that it's important to know that pleasing others carries longevity only when you are content and not compromising your own dreams. I hope that we've paved the way for our daughters to know this intrinsically. Also, for them to know themselves to make small decisions well because then bigger decisions may not feel as monumental.

PBC: You, being on the younger side of this generation of "Boomers" that has been raised...on one hand with the message of please others, and please yourself last, yet, on the other hand, our generation is trying to re-calibrate that, redefine that... our challenge now is to take care of ourselves, listen to ourselves, trust our instincts, trust the little voice inside kind of thing. Is that what you're hoping to offer your girls?

Myrna: I often ask, "Do I please myself or do I please others?" I sometimes struggle with doubts still. I think the key is to assess each situation as to which way to go. It's hard, because you think, "Pleasing others should please me." And that's a whole circular conundrum. So, you dig deeper and try to figure out, "Okay, does it really please me? And if it doesn't please me, will I be able to live with it?" And yeah, it's hard to know what the next generation will feel about what we've modeled for them.

PBC: With the cellphone "delay" you described with your older daughter and the social pressures to get one sooner, she would not have objected, would she, had you given her one sooner? But it seems you make a sort of value statement in your postponing it, "Not until we're ready," and then, "Now you're established enough" or whatever justified that choice in her maturity. By delaying that electronic form of interaction, you've emphasized a priority of human interaction, yes? So I'm wondering if you are concerned that, now that she's "wired" and equipped with the phone, she'll lose that in some measure?

Myrna: The whole time she didn't have a phone and all of her friends had phones, she saw what they did with them that she found annoying—like texting while having a conversation with their friend, or constantly checking their phone. So I'm hoping that reaction is stored, and those little mannerisms that she found rude will transfer to how she models her behavior.

PBC: ...and distinguish between true friendship as supposed to multi-tasking fractured attention! It's a new parenting challenge and social challenge for many adults as well!

Myrna: Seeing her reaction just made me pleased that I did the right thing. [laughs]

PBC: Let's talk about conflict resolution, how your mom approached such situations and how you approach conflict now.

Myrna: [laughs] Mom's approach was clever and strategic [laughs] when there was conflict with us. Now I would call it "Mom's democracy" which went something like, "Okay, this is what you think and this is what I think ...I've taken a survey of all your siblings and this is what they think which is actually what I think [laughs] so that's the verdict."

PBC: Amazing. [laughs] So it was, "Everyone agrees that my way is the way?" [laughs] That's pretty funny.

Myrna: [laughs] Exactly. [laughs] Yeah, it was funny.

PBC: Dad too? Did she talk him into seeing things her way?

Myrna: Of course!

PBC: And so, how do you approach conflict resolution either similarly or by contrast?

Myrna: I don't like conflicts. [laughs] I guess none of us really do. But I'm definitely not as appeasing as I was because as I get older, I feel I don't need to please for approval. I know now that being a pleaser isn't always the right way. I try to see both sides of a conflict and take a reasonable position.

PBC: More self-assured?

Myrna: A lot more self-assured, but I think I'm probably also more flexible than I was. I know that it's not always worth the battle. I really don't argue that much. With my friends and my daughters, we talk it through and I hope to explain to them what my side is…and they are able to explain to me what their side is and somehow we just make it happen, we work it out.

PBC: That sounds very effective and evolved…is that a departure from your mom's approach?

Myrna: Yes—it was her way or the highway!

PBC: Where you work to find our way through conflict with your others. And what do you think is allowing you to do it this way? That confidence you referred to? You're able to take a kinder, gentler approach to conflict than the way you were raised?

Myrna: I believe it's the benefits of the features in both cultures from my up bringing. I'm able to see some value in both approaches—traditional and a more modern American way of "processing conflict resolution," as they say.

PBC: You're able to apply the virtues of the traditional attitude, the sort of collective "book of common sense" perhaps…as well as the importance of listening to oneself and being true to oneself.

Myrna: Right.

PBC: So, now I wonder if you can name one or two role models beyond your mom—either personal mentors or perhaps cultural figures that have impacted you, inspired or influenced you? Leaders, movie stars, celebrities that others might recognize in name?

Myrna: There was a woman who was a mentor to me who came into my life when I was 14.

PBC: And how did you meet her?

Myrna: I worked for her. She had a children's store in San Francisco. She is hip! She is African-American. [laughs] She is very artistic and appreciated individualism. She was 36 when I was 14. Above all, she was my friend.

PBC: She saw you, she liked you, she came to know you?

Myrna: I felt comfortable telling her things that I was not comfortable telling my mom at that time of my life. [laughs]

PBC: [laughs] Kind of a hip mother figure whom you could relate to? But no other cultural icons that you can think of?

Myrna: Yes, she was a hip mother figure, exactly. But I can't think of another role model.

PBC: Okay. It's interesting isn't it? Again, although you're at the young side of this generation that I'm interviewing, but it seems most women's impressions are similar…that the predominant historical figures presented were males. So I'm curious when I interview you groundbreaking women to learn whether there are any females that you found yourself looking up to, wanting to emulate because you like what they wrote or whatever medium they might have used to reach an audience…and quite often there is a void. You're not the first person to say, "I can't think of anyone."

Myrna: It does seem sort of that way…I think you're right. [laughs]

PBC: You know, I suppose Mother Theresa was a predominant female icon that we were familiar with…in my day Jackie Kennedy was an icon…but it seems like there's a void, and for myself, I want my girls to have some female role models to look up to, not just me. (And when they're young adults, we're not their icons—they need their own!)

So my last question has to do with what you are most proud of, and what do you want the next generation of girls to value? What are the dreams you want them to carry, and what message do you want to send to them collectively?

Myrna: I am proud that I am able to be a woman who is consciously raising a family. I hope to be a role model of pleasing others while at the same time pleasing myself—to find a way for all that to work together.

PBC: To fulfill the dream or vision of being a woman who is able to be a full time mom who is doing it consciously, deliberately, mindfully.

Myrna: For women or for my daughters to choose to work and if that pleases them is totally fine, and I'm not talking about economic necessity where you must work.

PBC: You want to make an impact on your home and family by being present.

Myrna: Right…so I wish for this next generation—to know that (if it is economically possible) it's ok to stay home and care for your family as long as it's a positive contribution.

PBC: Many women among our generation, speaking broadly of these times, 'struggle with the juggle' [laughs] such that they feel guilty not being home enough if they work and they feel drawn to being more of an at-home mom like you. Yet women who create the space to be full time moms often feel in a minority and sometimes feel pressured by society (beyond economic pressures) to work outside the home, as if there is more value there. So in a sense, in this generation of "Boomers", we've created a bind where you're damned if you do and damned if you don't! You have chosen to be a creative at-home mom deliberately but perhaps are among the few who have escaped that bind and are proud of it!

Myrna: Yeah. [laughs] I don't know how creative, but yes. It's extremely difficult to work full time and to care for a family with all that comes with that. To do both work and home well at the same time would be impossible for me because there's only so much brain power, attention, time and energy I can give in one day. The juggle isn't worth it to me or my family.

PBC: Perhaps you're the role model of finding contentment in your choice, Myrna, I would venture to say.

Myrna: I think so.

PBC: The at-home mom that doesn't juggle…who's present and content in her role, whose center is in the home.

Myrna: The term 'stay at home' sounds kind of sheltered [laughs]—like you don't go out!

PBC: So maybe we should re-label it "full time mom!" Though that sounds like you have no life outside of motherhood…we really need a new term, don't we?

Myrna: Maybe so…this is what I chose and I'm happy with my choice.

PBC: Does being a full time mom free you up to be more a part of the kids' communities?

Myrna: Yes for my kids' as well as my husband's. For example, when he has a work function, I can accompany him in the daytime or in the evening.

I've been able to join him on work trips and 'R & R' trips in the past without the kids.

PBC: ....which you are free to arrange because you don't have to juggle your own work schedule. [laughs] It gives you freedom.

And lastly, what would your message to readers of this book be? What do you want this readership of mid-life women to take home?

Myrna: Assess, pick and choose the values from your roots that you want pass on. Practice those values. Just as I found as I cleaned my mom's house out after she passed away in 2008, pick the good things to take with you and value the process.

PBC: That kind of sizes up the journey, I do believe! I refer to it in my therapy practice as 'choosing the pearls, the jewels that we want to take forward and pulling the weeds.' You did it literally, but it also seems a metaphor for yours and your mother's journeys. Yours together is a joint leap, as I see it, that she began in many ways before her time and that you are committed to continuing.

Charlie Toledo

Biography

I am an out-of-state "assimilated" Indian supporting Northern California issues as this is where I have lived since 1972. Napa County, Ca just about 50 miles north of San Francisco. A lovely to place to have my home and family! I am a masseuse and hypnotherapist (since 1986) with background in home births and organic gardening. Since 1995 I've been involved in International Human Rights and since 1997 water and land issues locally and globally. My life vision was to never allow for boredom! Got that one down!

As a young child (three years old) I realized I was a dream walker able to move between the worlds of waking and dream states. This gift enables me to work beyond the physical world in the etheric and astral planes. Since my heritage as a mixed blood (Spanish-Indian) female was culturally sensitive—my family respected my intuitive gifts, allowed me to explore this within the household, but not outside the home or ever to discuss it with strangers. Just recently have I begun to talk about this side of myself in public arenas, as it has become a more broadly accepted vocabulary. My dreams have guided me, my friends, my clients in many decisions and adventures.

Born as the 4th child and 2nd twin in a sibling group of ten has shaped my identity in a group or "us consciousness". My parents made a voluntary move or rural urban migration before I was born. I grew up in Albuquerque, New Mexico, in an adobe house that my father and uncles constructed. Our family moved again to Orange County in 1958. This fulfilled my parents' dream to live by the ocean in California, as well as being more urbanized and mainstream.

I knew I was different from everyone else by the time I was 11 years old. I saw, and see myself as being on the cutting edge rather than a groundbreaker. I'm glad I didn't wait for society to catch up with me. As a dream walker since a very young age I was able to discern an individuated path towards the common good and towards higher evolution.

In early 1970s I became an organic farmer long before it was popular. I traded my vegetables until I was asked to raise and supply my organic produce for a few popular local restaurants. Farming came naturally to me, as my grandfather was a chili farmer in New Mexico.

Here is an excerpt from a bio article written about Charlie from an interview a few years ago:

> *Built on a foundation of small steps, Charlie Toledo has created a lifestyle self-described as on the edge of the mainstream—yet she is connected to a world-wide network of individuals inspired to create positive change for all through grassroots movements, one step at a time.*
>
> *A 40-year resident of Napa County, Charlie Toledo is known for her volunteer work with the Suscol Intertribal Council, regionally and internationally she is known for her women's human rights work through Women's Intercultural Network (WIN). For three years, 1978 to 1981, Toledo was a midwife who helped to bring over 100 new lives into the world. At the end of those three years, she became a certified massage therapist. Toledo continues this practice today as her primary profession.*
>
> *Toledo gave birth to her daughters at home in rural parts of Napa: Rosa in 1976 and Summer in 1978. Home births were illegal in California at that time. It was considered child endangerment. Despite it being illegal, Toledo worked as a midwife between 1978 and 1981, but the emotional and physical drain of midwifery convinced Toledo to look for a new career.*
>
> *As a midwife you're on call 24 hours a day and when you get that call, you have to be prepared that the birth could take from two hours to five days. In concert with the Bay Area Guild of Midwives, Toledo continued her advocacy to improve and humanize the birthing experience at hospitals. She and others fought a seven-year battle to legalize home births and midwifery, which was successful in 1985.*
>
> *In 1981 Toledo began her present career of massage therapy and bodywork. With a laugh she recalled, "At that time, massage and body-work were on the fringe. It was usually associated with massage parlors that were fronts for prostitution. Today my work is considered to be "alternative health care."*
>
> *Having her own business allowed Toledo the flexibility to live a life that suited*

her. By the early 1980s she was a single mother living in the Yountville area. Her two daughters were her first priority.

Her work as a masseuse/hypnotherapist also provided her with a valuable lesson that has been helpful in her volunteer endeavors. With massage she has had the opportunity to work with people from all walks of life, ages and life phases. Toledo has discovered that what works in helping the individual body can also be transposed to the business and political arenas—the global body. They are the same because they are all made up of human beings...

Toledo was able to put that theory to the test in 1992 when she accepted the request from Native American Elders to reactivate the Suscol Council. Toledo candidly admits, "Little did I know when I agreed to accept responsibility of re-activating a local Native American organization how it would consume my life. It's been a lot of work in the last 21 years. Few realize how much time and money it takes to access the Indian community. But now there is less pressure, tension, and more cooperation within the Indian world. It is very exciting challenging work!"

If her life wasn't busy enough already, in 1995 Toledo added another project to her endeavors, women's human rights. Her advocacy and activism on behalf of women, however, actually extends back to the 1970s.

Having such intimate knowledge of an experience unique to women it was only natural that Toledo became a delegate to the 1995 Beijing, women's human rights conference. The results of the conference were networking team building, a 12-point action plan and the commitment to global ratification of the women's human rights referendum.

The U.S. delegates decided to form state committees, such as CAWA (California Women's Agenda), and then refine their focus even more to each county. Toledo is the co-chair of the local chapter who has hosted informational meetings and workshops to increase local awareness. In 2001 a group of Ugandan women shared their culture, experiences and thoughts with interested locals. "Sharing cultures is very exciting," said. Toledo

Recently Toledo became the Chair-elect of WIN, Women's Intercultural Network. In 2002 and 2007 she also fulfilled a longtime dream of traveling to Uganda. During the whirlwind tour, Toledo and the others were treated as dignitaries and visited many remote communities. "The Ugandan women impressed me," she said. "They have overcome adverse political and social conditions to and develop a constitution that mandates 30 percent of every office must be comprised of women. Sometimes when you've struggled so long, you don't realize what you have really accomplished."

In reference to the political unrest in Africa, Toledo said, "I felt safer there than in Indian country here with the army and police being able to come in after you. You're very vulnerable. So you don't want to be too far out on the edge."

As a result of stretching her network globally, Toledo has realized the importance of building international relations. "The first step for the Suscol Council in that arena is sending a group of Pomo dancers to New Zealand," she said. The Maoris, the native people of New Zealand, hosted the 16-member group, including Toledo as principle organizer.

Not mentioned in the article: In 2003 Charlie traveled as a U.S. delegate to Afghanistan to assist in organization of emerging woman leaders to participate in constitutional rebuilding and assisted in the creation of a video-documentary.

Charlie adds the following more current update since that article was written:

Currently I am still deeply involved with development of "Suskol House," a 20-acre site in Northeastern part of Napa County being used to preserve, disseminate and protect the Native American traditions, songs, dances, basketry and ceremonies of indigenous peoples of the Americas (Abyala). The environment is being developed with experimental and state of the art construction innovations that will be a blend of traditional and very modern adaptations, such as straw bale earth plaster. Also under immediate discussion and hopefully implementation a combination of very recently patented methodologies of wall surface applications; bamboo core walls, waffle foundations that would intensely minimize the use of trees (wood) and cement creating a ZERO footprint! Suscol is implementing perma culture garden techniques minimizing need for water by maximizing the use of organic matter and compost.

I also currently serve on Low Income Advisory Board to California Public Utilities Commission to help focus the State on water crisis conservation as principle key solution.

We are involved in film production to highlight all these concerns. Suscol Intertribal Council produced two local films. Both films were premiered at the Napa Valley Opera House in 2013. "The Sky is the Roof" focuses on environmental crisis under scope of historical indigenous destruction in this region and was featured at the Petaluma Film Festival Oct 2013. The second film, "Awakening the Voices of Our Ancestors," which celebrates life perspective on indigenous survivors and the importance of sobriety in preserving culture and traditions, was featured Nov 2013 in San Francisco at the American Indian Film Festival.

So many exciting projects in this "new dawn!"

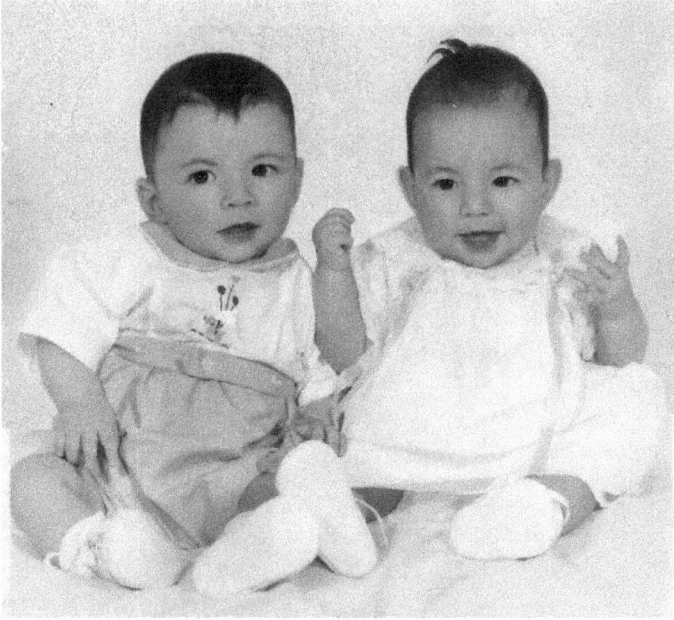

Charlie and her twin brother at 5 months

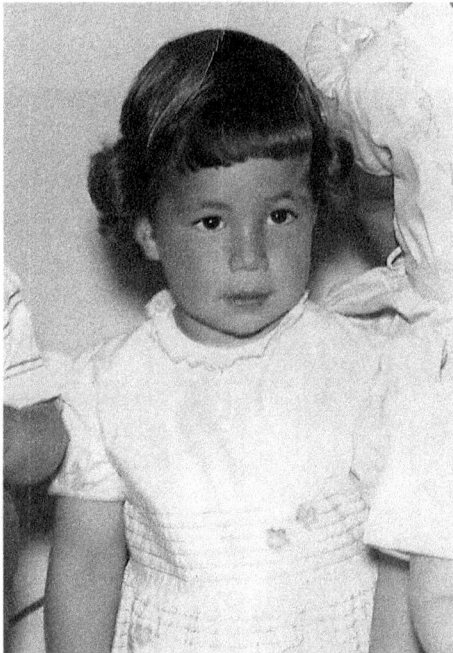

Charlie as a little girl

Charlie's mother

Charlie with her mother and her first baby

Charlie today

Interview

March 2012

PBC: You've been identified as someone who made a leap. Tell me how you see yourself contributing to this evolution, given where you have come in your own journey from the consciousness that your mother was a part of and where you are in your journey. What do you think are the characteristics that you attribute to that leap, the breakthrough in your own journey?

Charlie: At a very young age I had conscious memory of myself as a spiritual being in a physical presence. I was born into this lifetime with a vision of what my personal life was in this dimension. I'm what's referred to as a 'dream walker,' a Native American term. This is in the DNA of my family line. I came with the intention prenatally, a commitment to break a cycle that had been part of my maternal lineage with my own birth which I have been able to do even though it has been a precarious journey. I started having conscious memory of what my life's work was probably in my early forties, but I remember being aware of my own intense spirituality probably between the ages of two and three.

PBC: Did you say your own intense spirituality?

Charlie: Intense because it was very lucid, like what we would call a lucid dream. I was very aware of myself as a presence beyond the physical world in my conscious mind between two and three. It wasn't until about my early 40s that all this came into focused clarity when I started writing, and doing psychotherapy, and working with medicine people and shamans. I became able to recall memory of other lifetimes, to recall memory of my prenatal period, to draw from what we would call the 'star journey'…and the journey of my spirit into this lifetime and this body.

So, I think because I was able to bring that awareness of intention into consciousness at such a young age, I have memory from the time I started to walk. I can remember dreams from when I was a toddler. It was like an awakening or remembering. I think most of us when we're born, through our passage into this lifetime, forget. I think the typical experience as part of our birth is that we forget who we are and where we came from. The fact that I was able to recover that memory at such a young age and then start working with it—I believe that gave me the capacity to make 'the leap.' But my family life was supportive of that also. I was raised in a very traditional Hispanic Catholic environment that believes in angels and saints and a creator God that is overlooking us, helping us. I think having a whole lot of saints and angels that are watching over you and helping you, when you're raised in that environment, makes it easy to recover and maintain a metaphysical awareness.

PBC: Tell me a little here about your ethnic lineage. There was Hispanic, and also some Native American?

Charlie: I'm referred to as a "mixed blood person." Both of my parents were mixed blood. In New Mexico when I was growing up in the 1940s and 1950s, there were just three ethnic groups: Spanish, Native American, and 'mixed blood.' They were usually a mix of Native American and Spanish. On my paternal side, however, there were Basque who were actually 'earth-based' or indigenous people of what is now referred to as Spain and France. Many fled Western Europe during the Inquisition in the late 1400s, early 1500s with no intention of returning. A lot of them settled in New Mexico. They brought the food and the name that my last name, Toledo, comes from. They intermarried with local earth-based people, the Native American people that were living in those geographic areas. Then there were Castilian Spanish who came later in the late 1500s early 1600s into New Mexico. They had the idea of conquering the Indians. They were looking for gold, wells, land and such. They did not intermarry with the Indian people. They saw the Indian people as potential slaves. They came to exploit the Native Americans, taking what they had. There was a group of Hassidic Jews that also fled into New

Mexico. On my maternal side, my full-blooded Native American great-grand-mother married a Hassidic European. Those traditional Jews were distinct with their bowler hats and long curly hair. They were also fleeing persecution from Western Europe, so they were coming with no intention to return. They intermarried with the native people.

So consequently, both of my parents were in that third group of mixed-blood people, because the three groups were so separate, they were kind of defined separately—they didn't mix together.

PBC: Interesting…

Charlie: You see, the native people who did not intermarry did not mix with the mixed-blood people. The Castilian Spanish people held themselves aloof and above the native people. Then the mixed Indian/white people were kind of outcasts on a certain level from both groups. At least this is my current understanding of this time period that preceded my birth.

PBC: Complicated!

Charlie: By the time I was born in the 1950s, these ethnic distinctions weren't quite as strong. By then, Anglo people were starting to immigrate to New Mexico. During my early childhood, I remember starting to meet for the first time around age five to six, what we would call white people—'Anglo-Americans.' They were mostly Hispanic Catholic and Native American. Then, as I was around six, there started to be Anglo people. My family did a voluntary migration from Albuquerque, New Mexico to Southern California where I grew up in an urban setting. So, I would say that I'm an 'assimilated native person.' My grandparents were forced to become 'assimilated,' and then my parents made voluntary movement to Southern California away from a rural lifestyle of the area south of the Tome Land Grant. This is the land of my mother's heritage. The Tome Land Grant was deeded to landless tribes by the United States government.

PBC: And what age were you when your parents moved to Southern California?

Charlie: I was about eight in 1958. It was between my second and third grade in elementary school. We moved into a very different culture of Orange County in 1958 where it was predominantly an Anglo community. We were still involved with the Catholic Church. We were put in a Catholic school, and that's where we got our grounding. I lived there 'til 1969. I went through Catholic high school, and then went to a local community college. Around that time, around '69,'70, I left Orange County and moved to Northern California,. The 'flower child' thing was going on and was quite a big party in Northern California. So I joined it!

PBC: Let's discuss the personality traits that distinguish you from your mother.

Charlie: I think that I'm bolder and more outspoken than my mother was. My mother was very forceful within the home. We had a 'matrilineal heritage' when we were growing up. The Tome land grant and my grandmother's land were to go to the "oldest" girl—my aunt, my mother's oldest sister Josie. So, within the household, my mother was the boss. My father brought his check home to my mother, and she made all the decisions regarding our upbringing and the details of our lives. Within the house she was very strong, but outside the house she wasn't. I think that's where the distinction came: I became much bolder than she was, more outspoken in the public realm.

My mother's values or choices—I think they influenced me a lot. I was asked awhile back how did I grow up in such a big family—10 kids total—and have such a strong identity? I believe because my mother was such a force in our life. When we moved to Orange County, she pulled us together. We became very tight, like a tribe. I was never alone in my childhood—EVER! My mother kept us together very tight in a close group. So when we walked to school, I was responsible for my younger brothers and sisters. At the end of the school day, I'd wait for my younger brothers and sisters, and we would all walk home together as a group. We were expected to be home by 3:20. We had to make that mile walk in 20 minutes, and if we weren't home we'd be in trouble. My mother was strong and forceful—she was fiercely protective of us, though I found it very oppressive as a child. But as an adult, reflecting on this, that's what made all of us—ALL of my siblings—very strong personalities, because what we did, where we did it, who we did it with was all very important. If we weren't doing the right things at the right time in the right place...we would be punished. We would be slapped...we'd be spanked. So there was sharp scrutiny. I think that's a trait that influenced me to be outspoken—to be careful and think that I can make a difference in the world... to believe that what I say and what I do is very important.

PBC: You were being groomed to be very thoughtful and mindful in your choices...very deliberate!

Charlie: I think that was instilled into all of us siblings, perhaps very fiercely 'cause my mother was orphaned.

PBC: Oh?

Charlie: Her mother died in childbirth with twins when my mother was two years old. So she was passed around from family to family. She was raised in what we would call now foster care, even though it was with other relations. But she was in some very abusive situations. At one point, when she was about four, my mother remembered being with a grandfather, a blind grandfather that she was the caretaker for. He was the one who made her feel special and took care of her. But then he died when she was 13. She went into an almost catatonic depression at that point, and the relative that she was living with wanted to hospitalize her because they thought she was crazy. But a doctor examined her and said, no, she wasn't crazy, she was just neglected, so they tried to find another place for her to be. But, the family she was with, when she told the doctor she wanted to go live someplace else, she was beaten for that. Eventually she did find another place, but then the aunt that she went to live with became pregnant and disabled in childbirth. She became the caretaker for that aunt and newborn nephew at the age of 14. My mother became very fearful that she might be put back with that other abusive family. Her aunt promised her that she would never do that. But after that birth of this baby her aunt became disabled and my mother became her caretaker and the caregiver of the infant nephew.

PBC: So at a young age, your mom had to grow up and be kind of the caregiver.

Charlie: She had to grow up beginning at about the age of three. I think, at that time, that sort of thing was normal. But I think all of those aspects made her be extremely possessive of us as children.

PBC: She didn't want the same kind of fracture to occur for you.

Charlie: Right, and I think that she wanted a family that was her family. She wanted to know this was her family and she could do what she wanted with us. She didn't have to please somebody else or be following somebody else's roles and I think that made us all develop very strong personalities. You might think that being among a 10-sibling group that we would be somewhat the same, but we're all very different from each other. But her strength transmitted to all of us. We always refer to her, even now, as a force of nature. As children, we certainly saw her as such. I think all those values developed those traits in me.

PBC: And where do you feel you've made a departure from her? She was a strong person who made a strong impact. You're a strong person and make a strong impact. Where do you feel a distinction?

Charlie: I guess for me, out of the home. She was very strong within the home and within the church. It wasn't until her death that I realized how many people she influenced. She passed away when I was 27. We perceived her as being the housemother. She stayed in the home and presented a very strong presence around her children but not in the community. At her funeral we realized her strength in the community. There were over 300 people at her funeral, and they all said the same thing over and over again. We heard from all these people, "Your mother was so important to me. I could always call your mother when I needed something. She would always know and send a note…or she would just show up at the door with dinner." We didn't all know that she was taking care of all these other people—relatives and friends. She was taking care of over 300 people for their whole lives. A lot of my cousins and aunts went into deep grief when she passed away. We didn't realize she was such a caregiver of others until after she died. My father's mother had also died when they had just gotten married, so my mother helped raise his younger siblings. He was from a large sibling group of 12. My mother raised the four youngest siblings after that loss—so they all looked to her as a mother. Of course, my mother identified with that, because she had been displaced with relatives when her mother had died. So she became the caretaker of my father's younger siblings early on in their marriage. My siblings and I were not born yet so my mother took care of my father's younger brothers and sisters when their mother, my father's mother died.

PBC: So your mother was sort of ongoing caretaker essentially her whole life?

Charlie: She was, caretaking at a very large scale that we didn't know 'till she passed away.

So I think the difference between us is that I did that on a wider level, I took those same traits but put it out more to the world.

PBC: You broadened it.

Charlie: I only had two children but I did broaden it. I was working more out in the political and the social arena. I started doing that consciously I think, when I started separating mentally and emotionally from the Catholic Church around age 16, which would have been about 1966—the era of the Vietnam War. The conscription, the draft was mandatory. While I was still in high school I started identifying with this unjust war and the fact that the males, my brothers, and the young men I knew in high school weren't going to have a choice. They were going to get drafted into this war and be forced to kill people. So I started becoming politically active in high school. Even though I was in Catholic school, I started separating from the Catholic Church.

PBC: I was going to ask about that, if that was a difference between you and your mother.

Charlie: Yeah that was a huge difference. When you ask what did we argue about, that was something we started arguing about when I was around 16. I was becoming aware that I didn't like the idea of this judgmental, unforgiving angry God looking over us. Living in Southern California where the environment is very gentle and forgiving compared to, let's say, New Mexico, which has an unforgiving desert environment—that unforgiving God didn't fit for me. I did resonate with the idea that God is within us, which the Catholic church teaches, that we carry Jesus within us, that Jesus said we're all sons or children of God. It occurred to me, Well if we're all that, why can't we just pray wherever we are? So I began to object to the idea of having to go to a church and listen.

PBC: The church felt limiting?

Charlie: Yes, it felt very limited. It felt claustrophobic. Actually even from the age of two and three I was very claustrophobic at church—I always felt I couldn't quite catch my breath. I remember an early childhood memory of being so bored in church I would gnaw on the wooden pew in front of me. And then I remember one time the priest reprimanding the parents and telling them, "Don't let your children gnaw on the pews! The pews are starting to get all chewed up!" And then—whack! The back of my head got slapped and I thought, "Oh great—now what am I supposed to do?"

PBC: Gnawing gave you some momentary relief.

Charlie: Yes—I was so frustrated.

PBC: But you've also mentioned that early on the Catholic environment with the saints was nurturing to you as a spiritual being.

Charlie: Right, it was both things. It was a dichotomy—like many things, you know...I think if I hadn't had that rich, metaphysical Mexican-Catholic or Spanish-Catholic spirituality, I don't know how I would have become. The adults around me were talking about angels and saints, and you could pray to a saint, and they would help you find things that were lost, or if you were in a scary situation, you could pray to a guardian angel and they would come help you. So that's how I learned the reality that a spirit had influence on my life. But alongside that goodness, there was this restriction within the realm of the physical Catholic Church. Being in mass on Sunday, I felt very claustrophobic. That was an ordeal for me.

PBC: When you started to differentiate at that period of time in high school where you started rebelling and becoming socially active and frowning upon the Catholic Church and it's 'judgmental-ness,' were you able to hold the blessings of it? The goodness that you had gotten early on? Or was it confusing to you?

Charlie: No, no. I was never confused. I separated it easily.

PBC: You distinguished one from the other.

Charlie: Because I think my dream realm was very rich. So I knew that that realm beyond was real. I think I started to differentiate from the dogma because I thought, "This is so real and so rich, I don't need to have this priest man telling me what to do in my daily life."

PBC: The patriarchy?

Charlie: Right, because within the Catholic school, we had to kneel down and kiss the bishop's ring when they came to visit the priest. We had to defer to them. We couldn't talk in front of them. We had to stand up whenever they came into a room…we had to kiss people's hands and like that, and I found all that really oppressive. I didn't like that.

PBC: But you were able even at that high school age to distinguish between the two. "I don't like this…and I do value this."

Charlie: I was distinguishing, I think, by the time I was nine. Because we were in Catholic schools, we would go to mass every day before we went to school. My father would drop us off at the church. We'd go to mass, then we'd walk over to school. Then, as an older kid, you know, 5th grade and beyond, I'd be responsible for taking the younger kids to mass and then take them across the street to the school. That was something I did all through my elementary and junior high school time, but not so much by high school. We did have a mandatory mass all through elementary school every day before school. I wanted to be an 'altar boy' in third grade…I wanted to be up there on the altar. I wanted to be able to ring the bells…to do all that magic stuff that was going on.

PBC: To be a leader.

Charlie: Yeah, I wanted to be seen. The altar boys got to touch the stuff and they got to move around! When we were sitting in the pews, we couldn't move. We had to sit still. We had to kneel for extended periods of time.

PBC: And you couldn't chew on the pews!

Charlie: No, no chewing. And you couldn't chew gum, you know? But, as all children do, we would have gum, and we would chew it real secret! That was a big thing from about 5th grade, trying to chew gum secretly. But we'd get in all kinds of trouble if we were caught chewing. So we'd have to be real discretionary chewers. But the altar boys got to carry all the little doilies, they got to pour the wine in the little tiny cups… I remember really wanting to touch the chalice. When I was in seventh and eighth grade I was actually going on Saturdays to help set up the mass. There was altar auxiliary were that would come and help clean the church. That's as close as I could get…I was so frustrated. I started feeling frustrated I would say about fifth grade.

PBC: And would you say there was a gender frustration? Was it becoming apparent to you that boys got more privileges than girls?

Charlie: Oh yeah, I knew at home and school my brothers were free to go outside and ride bikes or skateboards out on their own, while me and my sisters had to go in twos and threes—we weren't allowed out in the big world alone.

PBC: And what was your mom's position on that? Did you talk to her about it?

Charlie: No, we didn't talk about it. I was in a sibling group of five boys and five girls. I was in the older sibling group of the girl—I was the second daughter. So as such, I had a lot of care-taking responsibility for the younger siblings. Our roles were very defined, and there wasn't a thought to cross it.

PBC: There wasn't any place for you to say to Mom, "I wish I could be one of them."

Charlie: No, no, it was just a given. We would sort of complain, "Well, how come Chuck and Bob can go out, and not us?" And we would get slapped. It was real fast.

PBC: So you were trained to just ignore those wants, those discrepancies.

Charlie: Yes, just 'stay in your line.' We girls were confined to the house and to doing housework. Like Saturday mornings, my brothers would be outside and they would be able to mow the grass and rake leaves, which they didn't want to do either, but then after they were done with their yard work chores which took about an hour, they were free to run off to the store and go skateboarding and run around the neighborhood a bit, but we, the girls, we had to stay inside. Our chores went on much longer and then we were not free to be outside. I was never outside in the front yard without permission or alone until I moved away from my parents house.

PBC: Wow, that sounds frustrating.

Charlie: It started being frustrating around my junior, senior year. I think before that I just accepted how it was. There were a lot of dangers for girls in urban settings. As school kids, walking home from Catholic school with my younger siblings, I felt the need to protect them because the public school kids would taunt us. And I would feel the need for us to be together in a group. Our school uniforms branded us—we girls wore little bobby socks and jumpers. We had to walk home a mile. So I felt the need to be in a larger group. Initially I was the one being protected by my older sister and brother. Then as I got older, by about 5th grade, they were able to freely walk home on their own and I was put in charge of walking with my younger siblings until I got older. By eighth grade I could walk home by myself. But, except for that walking home from school, I didn't ever go out of the house. I was never alone.

PBC: And you accepted it until high school.

Charlie: Right. I did accept that. I think that we're talking about values here, and that's where I started departing from my earlier values a bit. My mother was raising us very, very strictly to be homemakers. That is what we were being trained to be. There was always a lot of pride. My mother was the only person that she knew in New Mexico that graduated from high school, and for a girl to graduate from high school in her time, which would have been about 1930, that was a huge accomplishment. So she was proud that we were doing well in high school. But in high school when I started thinking about going to college….talking about going to college…it was made clear that wasn't an option.

PBC: The only education option was high school.

Charlie: The message was: Find a good Catholic man and get married.

PBC: So it was in high school that your values started to depart from how you were raised.

Charlie: It was around 16 during my freshmen and sophomore year. I was at a mixed gender high school, which was the exception rather than the rule as far as Catholic high schools of that time frame. We had Sisters of St. Joseph, which are like the Jesuits of the priesthood, who tended towards being of a questioning nature. They thought that you should come to your faith by intellect, rather than simply by blind faith. I was at the higher level of that intellectual group, so the teachers in high school were challenging us to read Sartre… Camus, and J.D. Salinger, and then to discuss the meaning of what we were reading. I believe the intent was to come to our faith in an intellectual way. But what happened when I was exposed to the existentialism of these authors is that it took me into existentialism, rather than strengthening my Catholic faith, to my mother's chagrin. A lot of my friends whom I'd been elementary school and high school with—their faith was just strengthened by this exposure. They thought all that existentialism was weird, and they just believed in God more. Whereas, me, I just started to question everything. When I was reading those philosophers, I began to question which path I was on.

PBC: The education backfired with you.

Charlie: Right. Well, it backfired on my mother and her values.

PBC: The 'by the book' mentality didn't take with you. In other words, she was compliant, the pleaser—you were not.

Charlie: That's when I started to argue with her, and found I could out-think her.

PBC: So let's look at the arguments that you and your mom had repeatedly. Was it at that point that they began?

Charlie: Right, it was around 16 or 17 in high school. It started to heat up between us, but then I would go mostly silent, because if I ever spoke back to my mother, even at that adolescent age, I would be slapped or pushed over.

PBC: Even in high school?

Charlie: Yeah, in high school. We were still being slapped around. That was the norm in then in our community. It wasn't that unusual. It didn't seem like my parents were unusually cruel.

PBC: So you didn't talk back or argue overtly so much—just in your head.

Charlie: Yes, mostly just in my head.

PBC: And was your behavior starting to be rebellious?

Charlie: Right, my behavior, my body stances. What I did, because I couldn't argue back, is stop talking to my mother.

PBC: You withdrew?

Charlie: Right, that's how I argued, in my own way.

PBC: Passively.

Charlie: She would tell me what to do, and I would just do it, but silently. I stopped talking to her. Then she would say, "Why don't you talk to me?" But I wouldn't respond to that.

And sometimes she'd slap me and say, "You need to talk to me." And I wouldn't talk. I couldn't talk without being slapped. So I would communicate only what was essential or necessary. Otherwise, I wasn't communicative.

PBC: So there weren't actual arguments.

Charlie: Right.

PBC: You were privately differentiating, separating from your mother's mentality, and doing it as peacefully as you could.

Charlie: Right…my senior year in high school, I was still required to go to mass, but because I could drive, I was asked to drive my younger siblings to church. And what I would do is drop them off in church and then go off to the ocean myself.

PBC: And did they tell on you?

Charlie: No, no they didn't. But then something happened—they changed. I used to make them get out of the car. Then one Sunday, I stopped at church, and they said they weren't getting out of the car…they insisted I take them with me, and if I didn't, they were gonna tell on me! "We are coming with you."

PBC: In other words, "We don't wanna go in there either!"

Charlie: Right. So I threatened them, "You guys get out of the car!" You see, I raised my younger siblings the way I was raised… it was normal for us to slap each other around or wrestle, so I threatened to hit them. But they were threatening to tell on me, which I knew they would because they had all obviously talked about this. They were all in agreement. I had five younger siblings sitting there with set looks on their faces.

PBC: But you became a heavy and made them go?

Charlie: No, no.

PBC: No?

Charlie: I gave in. Because I knew that they were in agreement, that collectively they had discussed it for a period of time, and that they were gonna tell on me.

PBC: I see.

Charlie: And I had to think about…Well was I willing to be told on? Was I gonna stop going? Was I gonna start going to church and not go to the beach? And I wasn't. There was a regular bulletin that came from the mass. I said to one of the siblings, "Go get a bulletin and see who the priest is." (There were several priests that rotated at the services.) One of my siblings ran and brought that back—this was our 'proof' to convince my mom that we had gone to mass—and then we took off to the beach and had a great old time!

PBC: And you got away with it?

Charlie: We got away with it for a few months. And then, as things like that go, somebody from the church told my mother.

PBC: Oh, that you guys were all missing?

Charlie: Yeah. Well, that we were coming up to the church and somebody was getting a bulletin and then we were taking off. So we weren't caught by sand in our Sunday clothes or anything like that. And we weren't swimming in the water when we went to the beach. We would just go to the ocean and we'd walk along the beach and make sure not to have any sand in our clothes or shoes.

PBC: And how did mom respond when she got the news?

Charlie: She said, "What are you doing? I heard from so-and-so that you're going to church and just picking up the bulletin." Because she had been fooled up until then by asking "Where's the bulletin, who was the priest?" And we would always know. I challenged her, attempting to play dumb, "Well, why would they say that?" [laughs] And she persisted, "Is that what you're doing?" I said, "I don't know what you're talking about." But later, I spoke up and said, "I don't wanna take them to church anymore." Because I started to think, "Okay, what if all this God stuff is real, and I'm committing a mortal sin!" I didn't care about endangering my own soul, but I didn't want to be responsible for endangering the souls of my five younger siblings.

PBC: So you were in a bind.

Charlie: I told my mother I wasn't going to take them to church anymore.

PBC: And how'd she respond to that?

Charlie: Well, she couldn't make me, you know?

PBC: No? She couldn't hit you?

Charlie: Well, that didn't matter. I was already barely talking to her so I just said, "I don't wanna do this anymore…some other sibling that can drive should do that." This was close to the end of my senior year after which I turned 18 and about six months prior to my move away from the house. Our conflicts were becoming too evident. I just moved out quietly. Looking back I see how the withdrawing made a greater impression than arguing. I was emotionally and verbally withdrawing during that phase followed by physically withdrawing. That's when I went on to live this 'wanton life' that my mother was just horrified about. We did attempt eventually to reconcile and have a healthy adult relationship.

PBC: I'm interested in hearing you expound upon what sounds like a paradigm shift in your own personal life—this big shift as you graduated and left home. Was that a pivotal moment?

Charlie: I think so—I feel like these 'arguments' in high school shaped me to a point. But I think the movement in consciousness, the late '60s and beyond, I was advocating for young men not to sign up for the draft to go into the Vietnam War. I was doing that in school, and my mother was not aware of it. I wasn't discussing this at home with anybody. But what I was doing was going to a peace group at the high school. There were 18 year-old peers that were joining peace groups, and the guys were refusing to sign up for the draft. I encouraged them. So, when I moved away, I was hanging out with a lot of random men as friends...I became a draft counselor, and I was actively promoting refusal to sign up for the draft and abdication from the Vietnam War. It was referred to as 'passive resistance,' but it was it was **very** disobedient...to God as my mother and the church saw it...it was disobedient to the laws of the land, and people were arrested and jailed as a result of those actions or choices. So that was very 'wanton' in my mother's value system—I was disobeying laws. I was engaging with the police as part of my lifestyle. I was seen around the drug experimentation scene. Marijuana was illegal. And I started living with a boyfriend who I wasn't married to in 1969. In 1970, that was still radical in my world. At that time, we couldn't even rent a room or anything. I remember we tried to rent an apartment, and people were spitting at us. We realized, "We're not gonna be able to rent an apartment." So I just got a wedding ring, we just started saying we were married. Just my boyfriend and me went out and rented an apartment. Then our other friends moved in with us. So I was living in a house with 4 other men, which was like my family, because I was very close to my brothers. I was more energetically attuned to my brothers. Because I haven't mentioned that I have a twin brother. And my youngest brother is merely 15 months younger than us. Those were my two closest playmates growing up.

PBC: So it was natural for you to align with a clan of men when you left home.

Charlie: Right—to be linked with my boyfriend and then a lot of his friends who were also draft resisters or wanna-be draft resisters. At that time we were experimenting with LSD and marijuana and we were living together in an unmarried state.

PBC: Did mom find out about this?

Charlie: Yeah everybody heard about it. Even though my friends were the same age and we had all graduated from high school, my friends' parents forbade them to see me. It was a bigger town than some small villages. I wouldn't tell my parents where I was living.

PBC: You kept your distance.

Charlie: When I first moved out, they knew where I lived. They used to show up at the house often, unexpectedly, and try to drag me home. So then I just moved from that house into a house where they didn't know where it was. But they would take my twin brother and drive him around and say, "You have to tell us where she lives. You take us there right now!" So my siblings were under a lot of pressure to tell on me, which they didn't do. They didn't cave even though they were being pressured and threatened. They didn't ever tell. I was perceived as being very wild. Even though I wasn't promiscuous, I wasn't selling drugs and stuff like that...I was experimenting with them. I guess, actually, some of my roommates in college were selling drugs. So that was that 'wanton life.' [laughs].

PBC: It's a pretty big departure, a big rebellion from the 'by the book tow the line' values you were taught and subscribed to earlier in your childhood.

Charlie: Yes—"Be a homemaker, marry a Catholic boy, and start having babies." Yeah, they thought I was breaking laws and that I was away at college. I didn't move away to go to college even though I had a full scholarship and I was accepted into University because I decided not to work as hard as I had worked in high school. I wanted to have some carefree time, so I went to the local community college. Those classes were very easy for me. So I was working and putting myself through college, supporting myself. When I moved out I always supported myself. I didn't get married. They knew I had a boyfriend, they knew I was living with him. I would come and visit Sunday afternoons, and have dinner with the family. So, if they asked me about what I was doing I just never answered that type of question—I just talked about my studies or my job.

PBC: So they came to accept you, sort of resigned that you were living this 'wanton life?' They didn't want to lose touch with you and disown you, or anything like that.

Charlie: Right, they didn't disown me. My father was never judgmental like that. He was much more unconditionally loving. If he ever took a critical position, it was to please my mother. It wasn't 'cause he didn't believe in what I was doing. He just saw me as becoming myself. That's how he would see it. I was just becoming an adult and I was gonna be different than them. He was able to accept that. It was my mother who couldn't accept it. But then, what happened, at one point is I—deliberately and with force—moved away from the area. I kind of made a bolder shift, rather than fight with my mother. She would try to argue with me, but I wouldn't argue with her. I would freeze and just wouldn't talk about it. She would say, "I hear you're doing this and this," or "You know So-and-So told me blah blah blah...."—nothing. So she learned not to talk about it.

PBC: You just wouldn't go there.

Charlie: I would just let her say that stuff, and I then would just leave. I wouldn't say anything, I wouldn't respond. Which I think actually served me in life. I think in a lot of the political situations that I've been involved with silence is a good response to certain things.

PBC: Disengaging from a conflict.

Charlie: Right—no answer. There was a fundamental difference between my mother and me as to how to approach society. I used to tell my mother, "You know we're different from each other." I started developing the stubborn silent streak around 11 or 12—it was then that she would say that I was the devil!

PBC: And how did that feel to you?

Charlie: I just thought "Ha ha!" [laughs] I think I knew that I wasn't the devil. I felt like she was grasping at something trying to influence me but it didn't affect me. I started to realize at 16 that the bad girls were having more fun! I kind of figured if bad people went to hell, they were having more fun in hell!

PBC: What allowed you, Charlie, to know that you weren't the devil—that her perception of you wasn't real?

Charlie: This is gonna sound funny. I've never thought of that question till this moment. But I think I knew evil. And I knew that I was not that.

PBC: And do you think it was that spiritual part of you that you came in with that was what you were referring to?

Charlie: Right. I knew that I was on the side of goodness and light, and I was starting to question, actually, if the Catholic Church was 'the devil' because it felt so oppressive. I literally couldn't breathe when I was in the church. It became more and more difficult. Around age 16 or 17, the new head priest of the church that our family went to who was affiliated with all my education was very 'fire and brimstone,' and I just couldn't get there, so I had withdrawn. An example of the negativity of the church—even though I was living on my own…occurred when my mother claimed to need me to help her paint the bathroom. My dad was busy. I came and painted the bathroom. While I was doing that, there was a phone call. It was for me and I thought, "Hmmm—who would be calling me here?" It was the parish priest and he wanted me to come in to see him. I was 18 and I was living on my own. My mother pretended she didn't know what he wanted, asking, "What did he say?" And I said, "He wanted me to come down there to see him. And I said, 'I don't wanna come and see you.'" I explained that he said, "I'd like you come and talk to me. Your mother's been telling me about things. We just need to have a talk." And I replied, "Well, I don't think we do." And he said, "You just come down here at 1:00." And I said, "I'm helping her paint the bathroom." He said, "Well, you're done now, aren't you?" I said, "Well, yes, I am done."

"Well, just clean up and come down here."

I thought, "Hmmm" and considered taking him up on it. My mother asked me, "Are you gonna go there?" And I said, "I'm thinking about it." But then I did. I did go to see him.

PBC: Really! How did it go?

Charlie: I've talked with a lot of people who were raised Catholic about this, who affirmed my belief—in hindsight—that I think it was for me a very healthy response, because I was able to face what I perceived as 'the Devil'—this very oppressive, patriarchal person that I did not like. I always felt him to be oppressive. I didn't like the way he looked at me or talked to me, I never had. So now as an adult—I perceived myself as an adult even though I was maybe 18 and a half—I saw myself going into an adult dialogue with another adult. He still perceived me as a wayward child. So he came in and greeted me, "How are you?" I was in the little cloistered room with my parish priest, who kind of bears the image of the esteemed patriarch of the religion, and I had been reared to view him as having the power to send me to hell. But I just sat down, and he repeated, "How are you doing?"

"Fine."

"Well," he challenged, "you're not fine! What do you believe? Why did you stop coming to church?"

So I had an opportunity to explain to this person, this representative of the church, why I was not going to church anymore.

PBC: You were able to articulate it smoothly?

Charlie: Oh yeah, I did. I told him, "God is within us, and I feel like I can pray...I'm very close to God, I'm very close to Jesus. I believe...I carry that within me. So wherever I am, if I'm in a prayerful way, I can be with God. So I don't have to come into this church and this building. I actually find it very oppressive to come here." Then he stood up and started screaming at me that I was the devil, and I was talking to the devil, and I was on drugs. But at that time, I was not using drugs. The people around me were. I hadn't been doing what he was accusing me of. I quietly challenged, "No, actually, I'm not." He started yelling at me, and I just let him yell. He got really red in the face.

PBC: Like you had learned with your mother to keep quiet and not argue.

Charlie: Right, yes...he yelled for about 10 minutes. Then I asked, "Are you done?" [laughs] and he just looked at me baffled. His face was red, he was sweaty, and his eyes were bugging out. He was screaming at me. He wasn't cussing because he was a priest, but he was yelling very loud, and telling me I was damned and going to hell, and I was a very selfish, selfish child. I just let him say everything until he stopped…he caught his breath, and I said again, "Are you done? You don't have room for me in your world. There's no room for me here. That's why I'm leaving. I have room for you in my life and I have room for you in my heart. I can accept what you believe, and I understand it's very different than what I believe. So that's why I need to leave this place. There's no room for me here."

PBC: Wow.

Charlie: Then I turned around and walked out, and he was just stunned. He was still standing there silent. And I just left.

PBC: You left him speechless.

Charlie: Right. Since my father was working for the Catholic elementary school at that time, after I had talked with the priest, I went over to see my dad who was painting the closet at the school. I wasn't in paint clothes—I was dressed up. But I started helping him paint. We started talking, and he said, "What are you doing here?" I said, "Oh Mother kinda tricked me into come down here and talk to Father Murray." He asked, "Well how did that go?"

"Well, you know how he is."

He started laughing and said, "Yeah."

"He's kind of a stubborn bigoted man, isn't he?" My dad said. I told him I never knew. "But I know he doesn't like me."

My dad laughed and we started laughing and we were talking and painting. Then Father Murray came walking over there. He was coming to report to my father what a lawless, sinful child I was, and there I was, talking and laughing with my father, helping him paint the Catholic elementary school.

PBC: [laughs] That's quite a story—sounds like you left Father Murray flat footed and jaw dropped more than once!

So moving on, what other influences might there have been besides your mother, perhaps mentors along the way who might have seen you real or taken you under wing?

Charlie: I had a third grade teacher who was an Irish nun who integrated meditation into our daily school life. She reinforced the world of angels and saints. A part of our daily activities was meditating and praying in class. If anything sad or scary happened, we would just close our eyes, and call on our angels. She was the one who got very metaphysical...like when we went to church and when we were going to go to communion, she would have us close our eyes and imagine a little room within our hearts that we were preparing for Jesus. Then we'd go to communion, take Jesus into our hearts and notice how the room would change once he came in. That was my introduction to bring in golden light. We perceived Jesus as the golden light, and from that I learned how to bring golden light into my heart. I think she was pretty informative, because that is something I have come to practice avidly, all through my life. I never stopped doing that.

Actually, as a young adult when my kids were born—they were born at home—we lived in a country style barn house...one night I came in and I was thinking, "Why does this seem so familiar?" I realized I was in the little room I used to have in my Catholic school visions. It was exactly the little room with the wing-back chair and a small couch with doilies on the arms...it was a real cozy, soft, little place. I'd never wondered before why I put doilies on the chair arms, and then I had the epiphany: "This is my little childhood realm that I was able to create!" It was in the country-side, so I could see the sunrise from the bedroom. That's what woke us up in the morning. And from the kitchen window we could see the sunset.

PBC: Oh that's sweet.

Charlie: And that's where both my kids grew up in their early years.

PBC: So it was like the manifestation of your inner sanctuary?

Charlie: Yeah...but the unconscious manifestation. 'Cause it wasn't until I had lived there for two or three years that I made that connection. It was where the kids spent their early childhood, and that particular place has imprinted all of the children including the many, many children who used to come there to play.

PBC: So you had not only an influential third grade teacher, but also an influential space that was both inside your heart and in your actual environment that you had envisioned while you were in that teacher's care.

Charlie: Right. I feel that ability to manifest dreams into reality continued to ripple out, because several of the kids that used to come to play there have created places like that as adults. I've followed many of them and they've created their own barn houses and made sure that there was a sunrise and a sunset view in a loft room upstairs.

PBC: So they actually took that image to heart—they were children when they came there, but they replicated the image into their adult life. It was a 'dream' that has impacted at least a couple of generations.

Charlie: I've just realized from a lot of thirty-something's who have now grown into adulthood with my daughters that they always still talk about the barn, they always remember it. And three of them have now replicated that space to their own living spaces as adults.

So that's pretty strong imagery and manifesting from my third grade teacher.

I had another nun who took me aside my freshman year and said I was smart enough to go to college and asked if I had plans. I said no, I wasn't geared for that at home where there was the expectation that we merely get a high school diploma and good grades. But this nun put me specifically on a college track and made sure I was taking all the SAT tests and applying for scholarship programs and colleges. As a result, I qualified for and received full college scholarships because of the mentoring she provided through the four years in high school. But she had called me aside and encouraged me.

PBC: Isn't that great. She saw your potential, believed in you and guided you.

Charlie: She did that for a number of us—all of us college material, as she saw us; I think she mentored my whole peer group.

PBC: But it made a difference for you.

Charlie: She probably mentored countless students—I think it made a difference for all of us. But it made a difference for me because I wasn't thinking of college on my own…I wouldn't have done all of the SAT tests and all that it took to get in. So I think she was another influential mentor.

Then, all of the sisters, my high school teachers, they were real intellectuals. They strived to help us learn to be critical thinkers. We had to do speech classes; we had to read; we had to analyze; we had to be able to give presentations throughout my high school career. I received intense mentoring from them. All of them were very respectful to us as human beings and worked to bring us to our fullest potential. They made sure that we could read comprehensively, that we could understand, that we could debate, that we could present. Then even while we were presenting, we were trained to stand up to critical arguments that we had to defend.

PBC: That was a good solid education that you got.

Charlie: Right—this carried me through life 'cause in college I decided not to go into that real competitive university life…I went to the community college, in the end, and that for me was much less intense compared to the high school. It was fun and I'm glad I did it, but I just had a more light-hearted college experience. My childhood was so laden with responsibilities—I needed that break. But

I've come to realize in the work I'm doing now where we're mentoring people and trying to get them focused and set goals—working with at-risk teenagers and young people—I'm drawing upon the inspiration and confidence that those nuns instilled in me. I also think I was inspired by my aunts and uncles. I had a very large family, as I mentioned—my father was 1 of 12. My mother had a large extended family, so I had some 24 aunts and uncles [laughs].

In the last 10 years in my current life as an advocate for Native Americans, I've struggled alongside a group of fellow advocates with the challenge of how to get Native American kids who are at high risk in dangerous situations to focus on the future. I realize that in my background, my uncles especially would always—when they would see us for family gatherings, from my very young childhood on—ask the question, "What are you gonna be when you grow up?" And I never realized until recently that having adults who are regularly asking you to envision yourself becoming something from a young age creates a kind of futuristic thinking. If nobody asks you that, you don't start to formulate the picture. If you begin to formulate that when you're 16 or 20—if it's ingrained repeatedly in a kind of celebratory way, it just becomes of part of your natural thinking: "What am I gonna be when I grow up?" As youngsters, they would be grabbing us and throwing us in the air and swinging us around in the midst of these questions, so it was very fun-associated. They would remember what I'd said the previous year. They would do that with my whole sibling group. So I think that was very influential.

Then a Native American woman, Norma Knight, became my surrogate mother. I met her about two years after my mother died, she mentored me by preparing me to live in a dangerous world and taking on dangerous tasks. As advocates for and members of the Native American community trying to overcome oppression, we had to become aggressive with political and legal forces out to suppress the historical accuracies of the genocides that occurred during colonialization of the United States and face harassment. [laughs] And how to deal with that and protect ourselves…from my background I've been able to use ceremony and prayer to extend that protection into the work that we do, metaphysically, spiritually. We need a lot of protection because in the Indian world there's a lot of people like me…spirit walkers…medicine people…and in the Caucasian world, is what's called 'bad medicine' which involves very aggressive spiritual attacks from people who are seeking to harm you. So whether we find it in the FBI and the local police or just Caucasian neighbors who are anti-Indian, the challenge is how to deal with those kinds of overt, covert, spiritual prejudices and harassment.

PBC: You've also had to deal with intergenerational prejudice, haven't you?

Charlie: I think that my Native American mentors Norma and another man I haven't mentioned, Jim Big Bear, helped me. But it still goes back again to that childhood notion that there is good and evil. From a very young age, realizing you have to pray and protect yourself from these things that might harm you…having the background of angelic intervention, never doubting that we couldn't, in fact, protect ourselves. I was fortunate to get that from the nuns at a young age, and then it was reinforced with these adult mentors.

Another woman, Marilyn Fowler, CEO of Women's Intercultural Network (WIN), opened the doors to the international community and became a mentor in that way, extending what I was doing metaphysically into the physical world, and then being able to extend and reach out through the United Nations and the U.S. State Department to do citizen diplomacy…to go into dangerous war zones like Uganda…Afghanistan helping people there, women mostly, to have hope… to think creatively in very, very adverse situations. By working on a global scale, I think that shifted my focus from purely spiritual work into true action.

PBC: I wonder if you want to speak more about how your mom approached conflicts both in her primary relationship with your dad and with the family and how that either shaped or scarred you.

Charlie: My mother's dream was to be with this wild rebellious man who was her husband and my father, and also to have this big healthy, beautiful family. All her friends and family told her not to marry this extremely handsome wild card but she did! We talked about how she was the dominant person, you know. We didn't see my parents together very often, because my father let my mother be the dominant one. He came home, brought home the paycheck. She would sometimes yell at him but I don't remember him yelling back at her. When I was in the latter stages of adolescence and pretty openly rebellious, they would sometimes be fighting about me, or they would both yell at me together, but I think in their relationship that she was the dominant one.

PBC: It sounds like your dad was more forgiving and accepting of you as you went through your changes and rebellion?

Charlie: Well he was a rebel. He broke way out of what he was expected to be in an incredible way. So, I think he had a huge influence. We always felt that he accepted us. He always said, "I just want you to be happy." And then as I became an adult, he always was nonjudgmental and unconditional. What we got from him was real unconditional love. But we also saw him give that to my mother. We felt that my mother and father had a very deep love for each other and we felt held in that love. They would express affection, they held hands, they would kiss, they would say nice things to each other. They would flirt. They went out on dates, even with ten children—every Friday, even if it was just a walk to the store.

PBC: That's amazing.

Charlie: They would go out, just the two of them, and leave us at home. And they would take these wild trips even when we were small. They would leave us with our old grandmother, aunties…and they would take off for two weeks on the spur of the moment. They would go down to Carlsbad Caverns or to Disneyland. They did that until the day that my mother died, they still had that in them. Even through her suffering and death, my father was still very affectionate and caring, as she was to him. When she died, we were told that it was the most painful kind of cancer that a person could have, but she never complained, and she was one of those people who in her dying brought incredible radiance to people…certainly to my father. She would reassure us…she would tell us she believed we'd live forever and that she was in transition. I asked her once, "Are you hurting?" and she said, "What I'm going through is between me and God and I'm not going to talk about that."

PBC: Awww...

Charlie: She would say it just like that. I think she gave us the gift of being an incredible role model of how to fight fiercely for your dream. And then when it was her day to die—even though she thought she was ready to begin enjoying grandkids—at the point when she realized her death was eminent, she accepted it.

She was very sick for about a year, and during that year she was still caregiving for those around her. When her doctor who was caring for her came to tell my father that she had died, the doctor was just weeping. Nobody had ever cared for him. The doctor told us my mother cared for him more than anybody in his whole life, and that included his own mother, we guessed later. My mother said one time she was coming from her chemotherapy and she had brought some carrot-jello salad, you know, with the little marshmallows in it—she had known it was his birthday! The nurses said, "What are you doing?" My mother explained, "It's for the doctor's birthday—what are you bringing for his party?" She told us how the nurses responded, "Well, we're not having a party." My mother was shocked. "What? You're not having a party? You don't have a party for the doctor's birthday?" She described the nurses as embarrassed and said, "Well now you can start." So every time she came for treatments, she brought him something. She brought him cookies…she brought him brownies. As she was telling me this story, and she said, "You know, the nurses who were supposed to be taking care of the doctor, they weren't even celebrating his birthday. Everybody that came there was so sick. Nobody ever thanked the doctor for the work he was doing. That's just wrong. The nurses need to be taking care of him better and helping the patients to thank him back." So she just made it a point to initiate that!

PBC: Oh that's precious.

Charlie: My mother was so generous spirited. Even when she was down, she didn't lose that.

Even when she was suffering and dying, she didn't ever lose it. I think that was her greatest gift. To anybody who knew her, she maintained an incredible amount of dignity, and she never gave into whining or complaining. None of us every heard her complain, even though she was suffering. She was involved in an experimental treatment program because she wanted to help other people. So she could not receive any pain medication.

PBC: Oh wow.

Charlie: The reason the doctors were suggesting this to her is because she was managing her disease so well. I think that just speaks to her spiritual strength. I think that was what she gave to us in many unspoken ways through her whole life.

PBC: That's intense. And how did that impact you, now as an adult? Is that something you try to emulate?

Charlie: I always try to be kind, focus on the positives. I feel I know what shaped her—what got her through her extremely difficult childhood—was this belief that God was a force greater than us that watches over us, and whatever suffering we have, that's a gift from the creator which helps us help others by generating empathy and compassion. The Catholic religion and actually the Native American religion share the same belief: when you suffer, other spirits, other people that have crossed over who can't help themselves are helped. Only the strongest are given the gift of suffering on behalf of many others.

My mother was pretty expansive compared to her peer group, my maternal aunts and great aunts and relatives on her side. Most of them never left rural New Mexico. They wouldn't get on an airplane or a bus or such. They just stayed in their little space…they didn't travel beyond three or four miles from their homes. Considering what she did, by contrast, and she did that with, at the time, eight children—how they left New Mexico and came to California—that was an immense leap from their roots.

PBC: You seem to have internalized it, yes? And taken it yet another step?

Charlie: Yes I believe I took her example of generosity and helping those in need and expanded it to global or ethnic, whole cultural expressions.

PBC: So let's talk about how she saw you before she passed, in terms of what you were becoming, as a person, as a woman, as a mother. Did she admire you in any overt ways? Was there an opportunity for you to repair the disapproval or fear that she had as you were coming into yourself as a high school student still living at home?

Charlie: What I finally did in that struggle in my early 20s was leave the country. I had flown off to Western Europe with a one-way ticket to London and was gone for 20 months. I had been traveling through Western Europe and the Middle East, and they were thinking I was going to be dead. I traveled through war zones …Israel…Yugoslavia, and some of the places that I traveled through were rough. They were just delighted I returned home. When I came back, I said to her, "I'm gonna come and stay here with you until you let go of me. I'm not willing to keep having nightmares of you chasing me," which I had. So in my 22nd year I came back to my parents' home. I said to my mother, "When you're ready to let go, you tell me, and I'm gonna go. Then I need you to stop treating me like I ran away or I'm doing something wrong." And she did do that—she came to me after a month and said, "You know, we get along better when we are not trying to live together. I realize you're an adult, and you can take care of yourself." I said, "Are you willing to let me go?"

"Yes, I am willing to let you go," and then we just stood there staring at each other. She said, "What are you gonna do now?" I said, "I am gonna leave." Mom asked, "When?" I said, "Well, probably in about 20 minutes." She just stood there. I had called a few of my friends, and one of my friends was over there in actually 15 minutes, 'cause I had my little backpack packed and ready for this moment, and I just left. That shocked her. I think from that point on, she perceived me as adult and came to accept the fact that we were very different from each other.

It was about only four years later she was dying and we cried on her deathbed. I was nearly 27 when she died. I'd had my first daughter and was pregnant with my second when my mother was dying. With the birth of my first daughter I came to believe in reincarnation because of the experiences I had with my daughter's conception and then her birth and early childhood. We reflected there on Mother's deathbed the struggles we had in my process of breaking away from her and coming into my own, and she acknowledged that I wasn't a bad person. She said, "You know, I realize when I listen to you, I'm not trying to change you…I think we believe the same thing, you just use different words."

PBC: That must've been healing for you.

Charlie: It was a relief to know that I wasn't evil in her eyes. I think it was healing for us both. Because she was the one who had been so fiercely protective of her children, especially me, since I was the one who was most rebellious. Now on her deathbed I was 'Okay.' She could just love me and not be afraid of me. A lot of my siblings have told me, to this day, that they're afraid of me. I came to realize that my mother was afraid of me. I think at that point she let go of the fear.

PBC: Do you think for any reason she was threatened by the power and effect that you were beginning to have that she couldn't?

Charlie: There are still people who become afraid of me. She was afraid that I could influence the younger siblings for the worse. I think the way my mother approached conflicts was that she would withdraw, or else she would become very dominant. I think that I actually do that also.

PBC: Interesting that you objected to it then and yet you've adopted it! Maybe it actually worked in some ways? Or you became imprinted by her style?

Charlie: I become very quiet and listen and try to go into neutral. I listen carefully, and I'm trying to listen for the truth being spoken and address that. I don't address what the words might be saying but ask internally, "What's the larger picture of what they're saying?" I'll just get very quiet and listen at a deep level, then say something rather neutral—not from a place of anger. I think that that's what my mother did. She taught me this inadvertently, because if I talked back, I'd get slapped. I learned to just be quiet and listen. And then I would address the issue from a more thoughtful place than reacting. Also that's what I've been able to do on a global level, being in foreign countries, by listening. And then to say something like, "You know, how I said earlier that…" It gets received. If you're having a press conference and all the press is there say, like in East Africa or Uganda…all the leaders are present and you say something—it has huge impact. They were asking us in Uganda at this press conference, "What do you think about Uganda?" We had to be driven around by these guys with machine guns protecting us and our drivers were bodyguards. When we were leaving, we were in danger. So being asked this question, everybody in my delegation got very quiet. What could we say?? I realized: Well, we're about to leave, we might get killed or imprisoned but I have this opportunity to say something in a very important place with all of the press listening. I spoke up after the pregnant silence and said, "Your infrastructure sucks. Your roads are terrible. The women are spending way too much time hauling water. Maybe you, here in attendance, have water in your homes, but we see on the roads a lot of women and young girls carrying water all the time. They're carrying water. You know, if you could get them water from a tap nearby where they lived, that could free up a huge amount of their time to get an education or to be doing other more creative things."

Many years later, my Ugandan friend who had been there at that press conference told me in reference to a comment I made about the potholes in the roads in Uganda, "Oh that's taken care of now." And I said, "Really? When did that get taken care of?" "Well, you know, when you said that back then with the whole press there…they felt like we were just regular people but the eyes of the United States were on them." When I had spoken up, I had just taken a deep breath and said it—taking a risk and hoping they would take me seriously.

PBC: [laughs] Wow.

Charlie: We were seen as speaking for the whole country. But apparently it helped change things.

PBC: And do you think if your mother had been alive, she would be proud of you for those things that affect change, Charlie, or do you think she would have challenged you and felt like you were speaking out of turn…seen it as rude…or something like that?

Charlie: I don't know. You know, I think my mother died because she often said that the world was changing faster than she could keep up with and she was ready to go home. I think in the spirit world she's very proud of me. I've had dreams of her coming to me saying she's very proud of me. She was afraid for the courage that allows me to speak out that I would be killed by opposition. But I had a dream of her when I started going back to my indigenous roots of her standing in front of me with her arms crossed and saying, "You can't go on this road. I'm not going to let you. There's only pain, there's only suffering on this road." My reply to her in this vision was "I don't care. You know, you saved me from this place, you kept it from me intending to protect me, but now I'm an adult and I'm going this way. This is the road I'm gonna take." And I had to overcome her fear of my persecution. I hear many native women, indigenous women from around the world, they all say when they hear this story—which I share often—they don't know if they could have said that to their spirit mother. In the dream, it's more powerful than in the waking world—to stand up to her and walk around her. But then it was a few years after that, she came to me in another dream, and she was in her traditional regalia. She was with all the ancestors surrounded by these beautiful people.

PBC: Oh. Her spirit had done its own conversion to become one of those people?

Charlie: In this vision my mother said, "It's because of the work you did. You believe in the spirit world. You can't do that alone." She was able to do it because I did it. I did the work. I made the connection.

PBC: Wow. It's like she was on your shoulder.

Charlie: That world got opened for her and she was thanking me. But I think as far as going to Africa, or Afghanistan, or Ecuador in the third dimension or human world, she would have been frightened, I don't think she would have been OK with that. I did have an uncle who called me when I sent out on my Christmas letter with a picture in Africa hugging a local woman in front of a mud hut and he said, "I'm so proud of you, I'm so proud of everything you've done." That was nice.

PBC: Oh, that's sweet.

Charlie: So I think some of the uncles and the aunts have been able to embrace that return to their roots. But I think most of my relations like the 100 first cousins I have, they mostly do not understand me. They have said to me, when I see them, which isn't so often any more, "Why are you doing that?" But I'm content that my mother accepted that I was different from her, and that I was gonna have a very different life than she had.

PBC: Ah—sounds like it was a little conflictual for her—maybe, very conflictual?

Charlie: When I look to my siblings…my older sister, older brothers, my twin brother…I can't talk with them about the work I do. They would say, "Why are you doing that?" My twin brother actually said to me at one point, years ago, before I was even doing the level of work I did more recently, "Do you sit around thinking about weird things you can do or does it just come by accident?"

PBC: Ha—he sounds a little threatened or mystified?

Charlie: I feel like my whole DNA group, the ones still among us and those in the third dimension—my siblings and extended family—that's what they all think. I've actually carried my brother's question with me a lot. At the time I responded, "No, it just happens." Later I realized that I do draw this work, these situations, to me through prayer or meditation… I'm always saying to the Creator, "What do you have for me next? Help bring me to my fullest potential. Tell me what I'm supposed to do." Just that giving over of my will to a higher power, the Creator, guides me towards action. I feel called to do what I have done and continue to do.

For example, when I was going to Afghanistan on a human rights mission, which was United States State Department, sponsored. WIN was preparing to bring over and train eight emerging leaders from Afghanistan. (They came to the U.S. in 2003. We took them all over California for a month.) It was the previous spring, 2002, that our delegation traveled to Afghanistan, including five Afghan leaders who were refugees from Fremont, Ca. These women had fled Afghanistan when Russia invaded in the 1980s. There were three of us in addition—WIN's CEO (Marilyn Fowler), myself as trouble-shooter and facilitator, and a film documenter. Our delegation was having meltdowns in the London airport from the chaos we were facing and sleep deprivation. We were in the middle of a 28-hour flight with several legs. I yelled at these Afghan women who were freaking out. (Of course, they were about to return to the homeland from which they had fled years before.) A couple of them were getting scared, sensing danger when we got to our destination. They didn't want to get on the plane that was going to take us to our next connection. I said, "We are called by God to do this and if you don't feel strong enough, you should have said something in the preparation process. Now it's too late, because the ball is already rolling. And if you pull out now, you weaken all of us, and we become vulnerable. You do not have a choice to do that." When I said that, everybody just straightened up and shut-up. We completed what became a very difficult and dangerous trip. I think what I said was true, and I was speaking from a place of complete truth. I think a lot of people don't understand it. But I think when you're being guided by the Creator and you are doing what you feel asked to do, you are protected.

PBC: I'm struck by the parallel of this scene and how your mom ran her ship. Even though she was threatened when you took those same skills out into the world, into the global community, you learned it from the best of 'em in your household! You kind of slapped them into attention, didn't you?

Charlie: Right, I did. I think for her, looking at the parallel situations from my mother's generation to mine—my mother was a very light skinned woman in an indigenous community—there was danger there. But when they moved to Southern California, the Caucasian world there was still a threat. The reason we left New Mexico—a lot of my cousins and uncles didn't survive into adulthood—was to escape the dangers. The male relatives had gotten into gangs, and they were knifed to death. But in conservative Orange County, it was also dangerous for us growing up as a minority family. As a woman in 1968-'69, going out into the world without the protection of a husband or brother or father was physically very dangerous. I knew it was, I wasn't deluding myself. So I think for my mother, she was just afraid for my survival. She had real reason to be. I was able to gather these mentors that I just listed. I needed them to face dangerous situations I encountered advocating for Native Americans working with tribes where violence and oppression were prevalent. I made the decision—I'm not sure when I made it—I think around 10 or 11...to face risk and danger head on! I realized there was this big force of tension between dark and light, positive and negative, because of my belief in reincarnation, I felt that whatever I was doing, if I lost, I'd just come back again. I was able to recover my memory of previous lifetimes early on in this lifetime. I knew I was strong enough to do it again. So I think, at a very young age, I gave up my fear of death. My mother didn't get there. I think as a mother it's very hard to give up your fear for your children. My mother's fears weren't unfounded. So I couldn't reassure her, "Oh, don't be scared, I'll be alright." I never said that to her because I didn't have the assurance to offer. I was realistic about the risks and lifestyle changes I was making that were dangerous. People were being followed and tracked by the FBI because of political activism around the Vietnam war and forced conscription in the late 60s and 70s after I left home—we knew there was a chance this wasn't going to turn out well or that it might get messy.

Another example: when I started doing home births as a midwife in early the 80s, I thought, "Oh, I'm finally getting into a legitimate world." But then no, there was still the Medical Board of Quality Controllers, midwives were being followed and our phones were being tapped when we were doing home births. It was deemed illegal—a felony offense no less!—to assist women having births at home in California in the 1970s and 80s! That's about the time when my brother asked me that question, "Do you think of this weird stuff or does it happen by accident?"

We collectively ended the Vietnam War and conscription. We also made home birth a legitimate option for women in California, made midwifery a legal skill. I feel I contributed to those efforts in my work for human rights for women and children. I think that's gonna be successful in this lifetime. Unfortunately I feel we're getting further away from the demilitarization of our economy, but I think even as we get further, we get closer. I realize that may be hard for some to grasp. My understanding of life is all things move in a circle, so as we get further away from a solution we also get closer. It's a metaphysical concept. When I was working to make Napa, CA a nuclear free zone, local people were saying about our local and at that time operational Mare Island Naval Shipyard, "This is our bread and butter!" I'd say, "No, your bread and butter's killing us." But eventually Mare Island was closed. There were issues of funding of nuclear power plants and naval stations.

I spearheaded the effort of an indigenous group to purchase land in Napa Valley. It's been a huge success. Everybody told us we wouldn't be able to do it because the people here are so hostile to Native Americans. A huge lie has been told about what happened to the indigenous population in this region, Northern California. There was a lot of concerted effort to not have the true story surface…threats of violence and, "I don't want you to do that!" have been part of this journey.

PBC: REALLY??

Charlie: Yes, really! So I think my mother was afraid for me—sensing I was headed in this direction—and I couldn't reassure her. So at least we eventually made peace with those differences.

I'm sharing more now in my life about the lessons I've learned about conflict resolution. What I carry around inside me is that once you get your vision, you do deep listening from the earth and from the stars and from the living beings around you, you tune into the essence of what you're doing, and you put it into what I call the 'arrow of truth.' It's usually a very small thing. You speak to the very essence of the matter…make a concise statement that in advertising they would call a 'jingle.' You start saying it, and then it takes on a life of its own. When you say to the press: "You know your roads are bad, un-navigable and you need to put the water pump in where it's needed to free up these woman from carrying the water" and your comment has an impact, you're glad you spoke up despite the risks! In my work as a Native American advocate, we're well aware it's been barely 100 years that this population of Industrial Age Europeans has ravaged this land. I've found that just saying something short to your opponents like: "You know, the native people are still living," can shift attitudes.

PBC: You're able to draw from that sense of being protected and stick your neck out with confidence.

Charlie: It's been a huge effort to bring that truth to the surface, but I think whatever a person is doing, if they stay focused on what it is they're supposed to be doing and not get distracted by fear or greed…I think those are the primary things that would take you off the path—fear and greed.

When we had the Afghan delegation visiting in California—at one point, we all got isolated from each other, our emails, our phone calls. There was some resistance from outside forces, I believe, to our humanitarian efforts to help the women of this region. Things became quite personally difficult for awhile. There were things I couldn't talk about with my friends or clients, but I still had to deal with them and spent a lot of time and energy dealing with them. My international associates and WIN leaders had to figure out together how to deal with these tensions!

PBC: It's in keeping with your mom's practice of not complaining, even though, there were some practical reasons not to tell your massage clients the conflicts you were having that were outside of your control. I'm struck by the similarities during this period that feel a little like the meeting that you had with the priest at 17, "I'm not bitin' the bait! Not caving to your attempt to dissuade or direct me."

Charlie: That encounter did prepare me—right. One of my friends shared a pow-erful statement: "Conflict precedes clarity." I've learned not to see conflict as a problem but to realize that intense conflict actually sharpens you. It makes you very focused. Another of my friends said, "Never give in to the negative." He was another male mentor who's my age who mentored me deeply for the last 25 years. He'd say, "Don't give the negative a name. Don't call it evil. Call it the negative." Then he said: "The bigger the project the more important the work is… the larger the negative is." He was the one mentoring me when I had faced efforts to sabotage my work…trying to discredit me through the newspapers and other places… He said, "Don't feed it. Don't give into it. It's important work you're doing or the negative wouldn't be so big."

I realized more recently, when I haven't had those big negatives, it's harder to stay focused! I guess because you get a big shot of adrenaline, you have to stay focused. Without conflict it's easy to be complacent and fall short of your goals by allowing yourself to get distracted by smaller things. So constantly being challenged actually can serve a purpose. In metaphysical terms they say, "That which is to give light, must endure burning." I had a picture with that quote on it my bathroom for a long time in my early and middle adulthood.

PBC: That burned into your psyche.

Charlie: That heat. Those issues and challenges I just described brought intense scrutiny on to me. But I have come to conclude in hindsight that those doing the resistance—they have to spend their life watching and following the behavior of others. In a sense, they don't get to have real lives. I get to be the doer. I'm the one who gets to live a real life and these other people are just shadow beings watching.

PBC: Hmmm—so they seemed kind of small in your mind?

Charlie: Yes, but there were real dangers that we had to take seriously. We did get in a couple of other situations where it got scary and we just stayed calm.

PBC: You certainly have been a brave and courageous pioneer. I'm struck by the links between your mom's bravery in her childhood…then her bravery of raising 10 kids in a situation where you were the minority and when you were in New Mexico as kind of tribe-less Indians.

Charlie: Oh absolutely. Well, unrecognized landless tribe-less Indians.

PBC: I'm seeing seeds of that bravery having been set in your childhood.

Charlie: Courageous. Yes—the fact that we survived at all is in our DNA.

PBC: And all those angels and saints that you got on your side early on!

Charlie: Right. But I think also the ancestors. Our DNA goes back to our ancestors.

PBC: Let's talk about your mothering of your own daughters, because I want to make this an inter-generational experience for readers that addresses the next generation of girls and women to carry on. What are the similarities and differences between your mother's mothering—the way you were mothered—and how you mothered your own children? Especially since they are daughters, I'm very interested in how our efforts will affect our daughters.

Charlie: I think that I mothered very similar to how I was mothered. I think the one flaw that I realized after my kids were adults is how I may have over-reacted to my mother having been so possessive and controlling. I hated that as a child and as a teenager. So I went the other direction my own children, and I can see in hindsight that was a mistake I made. It would have been better to have been more controlling. I think it would have given them a tighter container within which to shape themselves.

PBC: Are you thinking of their entire childhood? Or more their adolescent time?

Charlie: Pretty much their entire childhood I gave them freedom. When they were young children, I was with them all the time and I provided the metaphysical background. My babies were home births ...I breast fed for an extended time and we had organic gardens. They ate organic fresh vegetables and drank goat milk.

PBC: You were a hands-on at-home mom.

Charlie: I was raising chickens and goats, so they were getting food that I created. We collected fresh chicken eggs from what we call now 'range free' chickens. That was their early childhood 'till they were seven and nine years old. Then we moved to an urban setting. So it was more in their junior high and high school years that I gave them way more freedom than I had, especially my older daughter. I think it would have been better had I just fought like my mother did to try to control her [laughs]. I didn't. I said, go be yourself. And I think you know, the tightness of my mother's approach actually gives you a container to shape yourself in.

PBC: Something to push back against maybe?

Charlie: A looser container is harder to shape yourself out of and to focus your direction and goals from. My mother was fiercely loving—we never doubted that as children growing up, and I think my children never doubted that they were loved and wanted. I think those were my mothering instincts, to mother very fiercely. My mother was very hands on and, and I was the same way, and now I am around my adult children a lot and my grandchildren. But I think I parented more like my father in that I want them to be happy and allowed them to figure that out. It's hard to watch them struggle to figure it out.

PBC: So moving on to any cultural figures—female role model whom readers might recognize—is there a famous person that has been influential to you?

Charlie: I'm thinking maybe Rigoberta Menchu when she was able to get the

Nobel Peace Prize. She was an indigenous woman from Nicaragua who was able to stand up for human rights in a war zone. Also Mother Theresa. In my early adulthood, there weren't female role models, not public ones. But Mother Theresa's compassionate work with poor and down-and-out people was an inspiration. She was a nun, like how I was raised by the nuns, but she did it in such a compassionate way that it made her a world famous person and somehow just doing what God was asking her to do which was to care for the poor, she was able to virtually stop wars and question the cast systems in India. Doing those kinds of things that are high risk and can be life-threatening. I admired that she just stayed focused and lived to be an old woman. Because all my grandmothers died before we were born, looking to any woman who made it into old age as a public figure was notable.

Janice Joplin was an early adult role model because she was this wild woman, but then she died. Jackie Onassis was just a typical 'Stepford Wife' who experienced trauma, and then she became very obedient and compliant. I think a lot of the famous women in our time were more about trying to survive…they were compliant, smiling women. So as I think about it, I was looking internally.

PBC: I'm asking because I think there were few in our generation, so I'm curious as to who my 'comrades' recognize as their role models, the cultural role models.

Charlie: Hillary Clinton is my age. She came into public view and was elected when I was in my fifties. But she is still somebody I admire a lot. Same with Oprah Winfrey—although she's a peer, she's almost my age; the fact that she was an ethnic minority who struggled and overcame personal hardship to become a famous and wealthy person was admirable. I think Hillary speaks to me more because she's a public servant; she is working for the public good intentionally and now is working at a global level. So I think Hillary is probably the person whom I would say speaks to me and as far as a famous female role model.

PBC: Lastly, what message do you want to give to the next generation? What are you most proud of that you want to be your impact?

Charlie: My message: We have influence beyond the physical world and this third dimension with clear intention and open heart…I hope this next generation can begin to embrace or accept the concept of multiple periods of time—to think of time in circular patterns rather than linear and the portals to other dimensions and parts of this universe. In a way, not having role models has forced us as a generation to look inside. The glitter of celebrities could distract us rather than, "This is what I feel guided to do, however small," and do it from an internal motive. Through meditations and nature walks, learn to listen inside for direction.

PBC: Well when I get done with you I'll put your name in this book. [laughs]. You'll have left your mark!

Charlie: Maybe, [laughs] but what I would like to pass on is the awareness that we can be conscious beings—aware as a species of how we exist in multiple dimensions simultaneously. It's not just hypothetical or metaphorical—to those doubters I wanna say, "Nope this is real, kiddies!" [laughs].

PBC: This is real. You've already given me some great quotes that have been meaningful to you: "That which gives light, must endure burning"... "Deep listening"... "The arrow of truth..."

Charlie: Yeah, and that we're forever—we always have been and we always will be!

PBC: I feel the appropriate response to that is, 'Ho!'

"Loretta J."

Biography

The name I chose for my mother is Ethyl. I am 65 (1948). My mother is 96 (1917).

I chose to use a different name to soften the bright light that can shine on a life obscuring the silent and undiscovered parts. I will explain later and if you read carefully the silence might speak to you.

My chosen name is Loretta J. Loretta was my mother's first choice of a name for me. My father was born in 1920 and died in 1991 of cancer. Both of my parents grew up in farming/ranching communities in different parts of the country- Illinois and the North West. They both have primarily Scotch Irish Heritage. We were Methodists as I grew up. My parents became Mormons in 1972. They lived deeply into that experience. I have 2 brothers: Hal (1942) and Brian (1950)

I got a BA in Psychology from a Cal State university, and 2 Master Degrees (education and MFC counseling) also from a State university. I have always regretted that I lost the years of my adolescence to gain academic prowess. I know I am bright. Both of my brothers went to major Universities (Harvard and Reed) and I sometimes feel a loss of that opportunity. So it is… and I wouldn't change my journey for anything really as I gain from opportunities to reflect.

I began my career as an educator in 1973. I stayed with the same job as I advanced my education and found my way into multiple facets of my career and its extensions into a community until I retired. It's complex and diverse but is primarily early education and mental health. I have been importuned through the span of my career to spread my wings and enter into these complex and diverse experiences.

I married in 1977 at the age of 28. My husband was a graduate in architecture, a pilot, a photographer, and one of the most talented people I know. I say "was" because he is my "ex". We divorced in 1994. He still is…talented. We had no children. He participated with me in a journey of infertility and a compliant partner without passion for children, really. It was the experience of trying that helped me consider what it is that children need in their lives. I am grateful to him for what he brought to me in that quest. It helped he make a very important decision, ultimately, and learn something about what is vital in a well-lived life. You will learn how much I love and respect him.

Now my mother is 96 years old. She lives in her own home with my older brother. She has other supports (including lots of me) and has had the ravages of brittle bones and dementia that elderly women often face. Because she is so vulnerable and we are so vulnerable together I could not shine too bright of a light of disclosure on our relationship by naming our names. Telling this story makes clear to me that a narrative is a moment in time. It is a truth. Real truth must be flexible, resilient, and perched for the opportunity to live the yet unlived. My choice to be opaque was to protect our opportunities. If I told undisclosed people our story by telling our names I would open my projective phenomenon to a truth that lives too deep in the psyche to receive a light that is too bright at this moment. It would betray our intimate journey. The journey between and mother and daughter is a sacred experience. I hope this bio and encounter only helps each and every one of you to live into that and to know about that, in the way still available to you. Stay open to your mothers, don't draw conclusions too soon, and stay authentic to your journey as its able to live in your intimate relationships. If it goes underground (like compost) or is undifferentiated for a moment in time (like the chrysalis) know that it is still there.

Interview

March 2012

(This is a fictitious name as this interviewee prefers to keep her actual identity private.)

PBC: Tell me how you identify yourself as being a woman who took a leap—how you see yourself having evolved beyond your mother's life and experiences.

Loretta: I feel like I have more courage to embrace novelty, to be curious about differences and people that are different. I'm more curious, I think.

PBC: Courage and curiosity are your traits. And what do you think compelled your mom's values as to how she raised you?

Loretta: I think that in her own way she wanted to protect me and wanted me to be spared the difficulties that she faced in her life.

PBC: So protective rather than courageous. Do you think that distinguishes you from her approach?

Loretta: Yes, but she didn't ultimately protect me. I think she was trying to even though her approach wasn't effective.

PBC: She was doing the best she could to protect you. Do you think she was a product of her times in terms of her protectiveness? For example, was her approach perhaps more survival based than based on what you actually needed in order to be protected?

Loretta: Yeah—she did the best she could. She was very survival based. I feel like she was challenged by circumstances, just as I in turn was really challenged by tough circumstances in my life. I think that's part of what made me and has given me the strength of being who I am, because I also had some factors that helped me build resilience. But I feel that this was true for her and her cultural time and circumstances as well. I think my leaps are fortuitous, given the particular place and time...and maybe the unique neurobiology and destiny that I brought to it.

PBC: Do you think that there is a difference in the kinds of challenges—perhaps survival challenges—that your mom faced and the kinds of challenges that you describe as tough circumstances that may have been of a different nature in our time?

Loretta: I do think they are of a different nature.

PBC: Has there been a leap in the kinds of tough circumstances you've faced from what kinds of challenging circumstances she faced?

Loretta: Yeah, there were different kinds of circumstances. She was really impacted by poverty and the Depression. In contrast to her upbringing, we were comfortable in our home. We didn't struggle in the same way with not having food and basic things that she didn't ever have when she was growing up. I believe that really marked her and her self-esteem.

PBC: But looking at your formative years, what do you think the gifts were that she gave you?

Loretta: She gave me regulation and regularity. I brought a very flexible temperament and easy to regulate system to our relationship. I was a flexible baby and an easy to regulate and interactive baby in a lot of ways, but it was lucky for her I was born that way.

PBC: Do you have an idea of what made you that way?

Loretta: Some constitutional givens. I was an easy birth. I breast-fed easily. I was an easy-to-take-care-of baby.

PBC: You were just the perfect child! [laughs]

Loretta: [laughs] I was born on the eve of Thanksgiving. We always celebrated on that night with oyster stew, like my family ate the year I was born. With that came stories of my birth and infancy. My "easiness" was distinguished from my older brother who was born during World War II—Dad was at war, Mom in grief… difficult birth and fussy baby. But because of that easiness, there were problems that came of that. Instead of feeding me on demand, she fed me on a four-hour schedule, because she thought that was what she was supposed to do.

PBC: That was the trend in those times, wasn't it?

Loretta: So I had a little bit of "failure to thrive," even though I had these qualities that made me easy to take care of.

PBC: Maybe you were too easy for your own good, huh?

Loretta: Yeah…I didn't squawk to get more from her…she said I played alone a lot, I was self-occupied. She confessed later that she wished she would have tried to engage me more—to spend more time with me and we both would have benefited from some of the net results of that.

PBC: When did she tell you that?

Loretta: She told me that as an adult. During my career, I did some training on child development. Something that we asked of the participants in our training group was what their own birth experience was like. It always made me curious to ask my mom deeper questions, and I've learned a lot over the years doing that.

And so one of the things that I've learned as I do these trainings and talking with my mom is that she regrets she didn't spend more time, she didn't try to interact more and spend more time with me. She has said that over and over.

PBC: And that's only become clear to you in these last few years?

Loretta: No, she's always said that, but the variation and the specifics have become clearer. I didn't realize that she fed me on a schedule. I knew that I was breastfed, but I didn't realize that she started out by sticking me on a schedule—a four-hour schedule, rather than on demand. As a result of that, I imagine we got off track. I wonder if it played a part ultimately with my difficulty gaining weight. I went from breastfeeding to drinking from a cup at nine months; I never had a baby bottle. And for Mom and I, one of our points of tension throughout my whole childhood relationship was food because she wanted me to gain weight. She wanted me to be heavier and to positively reflect her mothering and her nurturing, but she thought that I was too thin.

PBC: You kept getting the message that you weren't OK?

Loretta: She would take me to the doctor to try to figure out what was wrong with me, and the doctor would say, she's thin, but she's great. She's really healthy. So we battled a lot about food. But I was healthy and it was really my body type. I did fine. I ate a broad diet. I liked food.

PBC: But as we look at her style of parenting—scheduled feedings and her anxiety about your weight and your growth—it seems like there was a disconnect there.

Loretta: Yes, we battled.

PBC: Do you think she ever thought, "Maybe I need to feed my baby more often or maybe I need to feed her more?" But perhaps the times were such that she suppressed her own instincts, or her impulses? Countering those with thoughts such as: "I'm not supposed to do that, therefore I won't, but my baby is causing me some anxiety." I'm wondering if that disconnect was a source of trouble or tension for her, as well as for you in your relationship with her.

Loretta: Yeah, I think that's what happened.

PBC: She felt she had to turn to the doctor to say, "What's the matter?" and the doctor said, "Well, she looks okay to me." But there was some disconnect there.

Loretta: Yeah—she worried about this.

PBC: I'm just looking at the bind she was in. On one hand, "I'm concerned about my baby," on the other hand, "I'm not supposed to feed her too often. I'm doing this by the book you know, by the book!"

Loretta: Yeah.

PBC: And would you say as you've worked that issue through in your own life— that you've had to reckon with your tendency to be easygoing in order to get your needs met? I'm taking my own leap here, but I'm wondering if this is something you identify with?

Loretta: I would say so. I feel like I've had to learn how to stand up for myself and how to articulate my needs in relationship to other people.

PBC: And that's something Mom hasn't been able to do really, in her own life, that she's been more about being private than sticking her neck out, would you say?

Loretta: I would say so.

PBC: But back to you…

Loretta: Yeah, I've had to learn how to do that and I feel like it's been hard to do that in my family because it was hard to have a voice. Not only was my voice not heard, but also other indications that there was problem were perceived as deviant or they reflected poorly on the family.

PBC: This was a family that was rather conflict avoidant?

Loretta: Conflict avoidant until things reached a point where the parents saw the need to spank us or issued corporal punishment.

PBC: Ooh—so it was kind of all or nothing?

Loretta: Yeah. There weren't a lot of discussions along the way where you could join, connect with each other interactively nor was there much respect for another person's experience. So, emotional regulation—a term I use frequently in relation to the families and children I work with—was difficult in the family. The stress would escalate to being out of control pretty easily.

PBC: Well, you mentioned the term regulation early on in the context of the gifts that your mom gave you. I wonder if there needs to be a distinction.

Loretta: Yeah, I realize how many dichotomies there are here. It's very, very interesting because I feel like what she gave me was regulation in terms of very regular routines, especially with sleep and meals. I woke up to a complete breakfast every morning, and I knew what would be available for me for lunch. She provided really good meals.

PBC: So it was structured?

Loretta: Yes, "Everybody for dinner!" The person who would come home first would start getting things ready. So I would do it and my dad would do it. Everybody participated in getting food on the table. Everybody meaning mostly my dad and I and my mom because I don't think the boys did.

PBC: Hmm. As the girl do you think there were certain expectations of you? You were the only girl, right?

Loretta: I was the only girl.

PBC: And so it was the girl and her parents who were preparing the meals. [laughs] So, regulation in terms of structure was one of the gifts, but in terms of communication, problem-solving, emotional regulation, not so much.

Loretta: Emotional wasn't good, yeah…Emotional problem solving wasn't good.

PBC: Interesting, isn't it?

Loretta: The other thing from my infancy is that she didn't touch us or hug us very much. I don't think that she held me very much as a baby.

PBC: And what do you think the impact of that on you has been?

Loretta: I think that it's been really hard to learn how to get positive touch from other people and to learn appropriate touch. The person who touched me was my dad. The person who comforted me and hugged me and held me and loved me physically was my dad. My mom didn't touch us. She used to hug me goodbye when I would be going away to school or something, and I would hug her and her body would be really stiff—a really stiff hug and a little peck for a kiss. It wasn't a hug where you would melt your bodies into each other. It was a stiff hug. There was an incident, maybe 10 years ago where she was sick. She got really, really sick. I helped her physically by massaging her, and when she coughed, I held her. I held her ribs…I massaged her back…I helped her so that she could cough and not hurt so much, and when that was happening she said, "I have never, never had anybody do anything like this for me. I didn't do this for you kids. I didn't touch you kids."

PBC: Ah—she confessed to what she now saw as a shortcoming?

Loretta: Our family didn't touch. Mom recently said in a discussion with me, "I didn't know that we were supposed to do this for each other."

PBC: You were mothering her in a way that she could have her own catharsis of realization. It sounds like she realized what she didn't get from her family. That's speculative, yes?

Loretta: Yeah, and who knows how that played out in her family—whether it was like that for her or all of her family. I think there was a much warmer relationship between her mom and her older sister and I don't think my mom felt really nurtured by her mom. I had a really hard time getting my grandma to like me. My cousin used to say, "What happens to Grandma when Loretta's around? Look at how Grandma treats Loretta."

PBC: There was a difference in how your grandma treated you than the others?

Loretta: Yeah there was a difference. 'Cause I just set her off somehow.

PBC: And what was different about it?

Loretta: Oh, she would just correct me a lot if there was something I did that she didn't approve of. She would visit and if there was something I knew how to do that could help her, she wouldn't let me help. She'd say, "Wait, we'll let your mom do it." It's like she didn't respect me or let me be who I was.

PBC: There was something about you that was threatening, maybe?

Loretta: I'm not sure what it was. But I know that when I was an adult and I was in college in her hometown, we got along. We did pretty well. But when I was a child, we had a hard time.

PBC: Maybe there was history with your mom and her that influenced that?

Loretta: Yeah. My mom thinks there was.

PBC: Has she shared that with you?

Loretta: Yeah. My mother says that her mother didn't really look at her for the first two weeks of her life. She had a birth spot on her ear that her mom didn't notice until she was two weeks old. One of the things she always says is that her mother wanted a boy for the second child. It was a family that valued boys. So she feels that being the second girl in a family that valued boys, it became really hard to get love from her mom, and I think she had a stronger relationship with her dad.

PBC: Do you think that passed down to your family also?

Loretta: I do.

PBC: The family valued boys—such a historically traditional value. And do you think that influenced you?

Loretta: My mom said she wanted a girl when I was born. But I think sometimes there are two different things in terms of what you think you want and then how things actually feel when you are emotionally engaged.

PBC: The intellect versus the guts…the instincts.

Loretta: Yeah.

PBC: Maybe you were her teacher.

Loretta: I certainly have been a challenge. [laughs].

PBC: Teacher/challenge! Any other comments about your primary years up to age seven as to what worked for you? It sounds like the structured mealtime was actually a time of connecting with your mom.

Loretta: Ironically, it was. When I don't have that in my life, I miss having structured meal times. It's something that I value. I think it's good for people.

PBC: Are there any other positive experiences with your mom growing up, that you can recollect?

Loretta: Yeah, I can remember her reading to us. And I can remember kind of being on her chest and hearing the sound of her voice when she read.

PBC: Oh, so there was some touching there.

Loretta: Yeah, sitting by her, and feeling her body next to me, feeling the vibrations while she read.

PBC: By contrast, what did you and she argue about repeatedly as you were growing up? Any particular themes that strike you?

Loretta: Well, one of the themes was food and me being so thin. At one point, I was probably in junior high school, and she said, "In a day and age such as this when there's plenty of food around there's no excuse to go around looking like that."

PBC: You got really got chastised for your size and your weight.

Loretta: I got really chastised, yeah. And also, I think she wanted me to be more shapely, and so she would give me a padded bra, or at one time she bought me a brace to hold my shoulders back 'cause she was critical of my posture.

PBC: Ohh!

Loretta: She worried about my looks a lot. It also relates to a story about when I was born. She wanted my hair to be different. She wanted it to be more puffed and pretty and curly. I think she wanted a more feminine daughter and I was little and feminine in my own way, but she wanted something different. I didn't mirror her to her satisfaction. Maybe that I didn't look like her was hard for her. She was a beautician and so she tried to cut my hair, and then we would fight about my haircuts. She would cut my hair and I would be miserable. I would hate my haircut. I've had to learn to talk myself through haircuts as an adult, consequently! I'll go to the guy who cuts my hair and say, "It's gonna be okay, because hair grows. I learned that with my mom."[laughs] I've come to the point now where I don't get too worried about it, because it'll grow. I learned that because Mom and I used to really, really fight about it.

PBC: You had to build resilience out of that wound. You had to comfort yourself and tell yourself, "It'll grow out. This too shall pass."

Loretta: Yes, I certainly have.

PBC: So most of the arguments were about your appearance and a sense of you not measuring up?

Loretta: Yeah, not measuring up. Then the other one was my mom wanting me to show that I was happy. Like in family pictures, if I wasn't smiling, she always wanted me to smile and look different in pictures. She just didn't think I was pretty enough or she wanted something different. When I was in junior high, I was having a very hard time. My school counselor said to her, "You know, I think there's something wrong with Loretta—she doesn't smile very much, she seems unhappy." And my mom came back to me with, "Mrs. C. said that you don't smile very much. I would like you to try to smile more."

PBC: "Paste some happiness on that face!" [laughs] And when you learned about that, how did you feel?

Loretta: I felt enraged. I felt very unhappy. I was really upset because I was already upset anyway.

PBC: And what happened to that voice in you? Were you able to challenge her? Were you able to let her know you felt enraged or insulted or did you just keep it inside?

Loretta: You know, I don't think so. Because the things that were troubling me were so deeply burrowed in secrecy that I don't think I could let her know what I was so upset about. So she was trying to figure out what was wrong with me and I had a huge problem that I couldn't share with her. I don't think she knew what to do. My teenage years were a terribly out of control experience for a while.

PBC: How so?

Loretta: Because I got increasingly inside myself. I became angry and started acting out. I started smoking. My brother reminded me the other night that I ran away from home. I don't remember that very well, but it really impacted him. I cut school. I think I was trying to get some help, but I couldn't get it.

PBC: Oh, that's sad.

Loretta: Yeah, even though I cut class, I acted out in classes, and I had a grade point average of 1.9 in my sophomore year.

PBC: Really!

Loretta: And I got suspended for smoking in the girls' bathroom! And this dean who was my mentor and my friend said, "Loretta, I'm really sorry but I'm going to have to suspend you." She called my dad and I got suspended and my name was in the bulletin. At those times, the bulletins were mimeographed copies that came out every day. So your name was read out loud. [laughs] When I got home I was in trouble.

PBC: Oh gosh. So you were publicly humiliated in the school newsletter?

Loretta: Yes, but at the same time, I was home with my mom during the time that I was suspended, I learned that my mom was gonna have to have a breast biopsy to see if a lump in her breast could be cancerous.

PBC: Oh, wow. At the same time you were already struggling!

Loretta: Yeah, that kind of all happened at the same moment.

Loretta: My dad's response to my suspension was to say, "I feel like you're punishing yourself enough, so I'm not going to punish you. I can't think of anything more because you're in enough trouble, and I can see what you're doing to yourself and I can't add on to that."

PBC: Oh, interesting. Well, that was benevolent of him. How did that feel?

Loretta: He was generous in so many ways. But I couldn't be relieved because I was so ashamed. He was right. I was really punishing myself.

Loretta: And then something happened that dramatically changed my adolescence.

PBC: Can you go into that?

Loretta: I met a girl named Kathy and—it's so funny because it's such a pattern for me. She was drawn to me—I mean just as a friend—and she would call me. I think she saw me talking to a boy that she liked. So she got curious about me. She called me and we just started calling and developed a friendship. So we had this friendship that lasted for two and a half years where we were really close friends. This was in junior high, which at that time went into the 9th grade. I was between 13 and 15. We had a delightful friendship that helped lift me out of some of the angry, acting out places that I was in. I had this friendship that helped me feel lighter and more hopeful and more grounded. It was an incredible gift.

PBC: And a turning point?

Loretta: Yes, but then an awful turning point occurred when I was 15 and a half. Kathy was leaving my house and she got killed right after she left my house in an accident. She died leaving my house, on her way home and she was even wearing my clothes!

PBC: Oh, gosh. Oh, no.

Loretta: We had traded clothes. And her mom didn't know what she had on. Her mom asked me afterwards, "What did Kathy have on?" I said, "She had on my pink blouse and my black pants." Earlier, something wonderful happened that day…I bought my first Beatles album. We had walked downtown from my place to buy it. It's about a mile or so downtown. We had another friend with us named Beth, who was in the accident with Kathy. We had bought some daffodils as well as the Beatles album. Beth survived, but had a lot of surgeries.

PBC: Beth survived?

Loretta: Yes, and she and I kept in touch for a while. And then somehow I lost touch with her. The day that Kathy died we were playing in the living room. Kathy had spent the night with me that night before. We had spent the whole day together, and then before she left that day, Kathy and I were wrestling and rolling around on the floor, and both of us would put all of our strength into each other, fighting hard—rough housing, it might be called. We used to do this a lot and found it very fun. She and I wore the same size, we had the same bone structure… we kind of mirrored each other, as I look back on our exchanging clothes. You kind of mirror somebody when you really like them.

PBC: Girls that age do.

Loretta: So we would wrestle and roll around on the floor and be really vigorous and my brother Brian and his friend Chuck were there and they were laughing and we were all playing and laughing. One of the things that my brother and I reflected on later is how safe we were with our vital energies in that moment—that we didn't have anything to be afraid of. We had safety and we had a healthy, kind of lusty playfulness among all of us where nobody was in danger.

That was really one of the sweet moments. And then I walked with Kathy and Beth out the back of my house and at that time there was a field behind my house. Walking out the back of my house, we would get to the railroad tracks that crossed diagonally through the neighborhood to get to a street which would put her walking towards her house. So I walked them down the tracks, and came back home. Later, I called Kathy's house and found out she'd been hit by the train!

PBC: Oh lord!

Loretta: I had a short conversation with a person on the phone. The adult I talked with, I found out later, was her aunt. On the phone call I said, "Is Kathy there?" Her aunt said, "Is this Loretta?" I said, "Yes, it is." She said, "Loretta, Kathy's been in an accident." And I said, "Well how is she?" And she said, "Loretta, Kathy's dead."

PBC: Ohhh!

Loretta: Then she said, "She was hit by the train." And though I was reeling and in shock, I managed to say, "Thank you for telling me. I'm so sorry." And I hung up the phone. I couldn't breathe. My mom saw something was wrong and asked, "What's the matter?" I couldn't breathe. Finally, I got it out, and at that same moment there was a knock on the door and it was my friend, Jake, who took me to the hospital.

PBC: Oh gosh.

Loretta: To help me figure out what happened to Kathy. I stayed in the car and he went in and talked to the nuns.

PBC: And what did they share?

Loretta: That she had been riding in a car and the train hit the car—she died pretty immediately.

PBC: Oh, so she wasn't walking home from your house?

Loretta: No, she was in a car. She left my house walking. I walked with her and Beth along the railroad tracks behind my house. I only went part way to the street because Beth was with her. Usually I walked her half way home. Apparently when they were walking along the street, which is a major artery, a car came along driven by two guy friends who picked up her and Beth. I didn't know the driver but I knew the other person who was hit and died, three weeks after Kathy died. So two people died, one person was severely injured and the driver wasn't hurt.

PBC: So the driver and passenger were friends of hers?

Loretta: Yes. The car was hit by the train on an obscure street.

PBC: Hmm. There were no railroad gates?

Loretta: No, in fact there wasn't even a lighted signal. There was a painted RXR sign at the crossing, but the tracks were obscured by a stationary boxcar.

PBC: So no forewarning.

Loretta: No, the family won a suit. It was really tragic.

PBC: And how would you say that this profound loss affected you going forward? How did you and your family handle it?

Loretta: Well, I slept with my mom that night and she held my hand.

PBC: Ahh. She attempted to comfort you physically.

Loretta: I remember the hand holding because it was different. And then there was the viewing and the funeral. My mom took me to the funeral home to visit her. Later my dad took me to the funeral. Then, I tried to go back to school. That re-entry day, I couldn't be there.

PBC: Too distraught?

Loretta: I remember the secretary signing me in. She said, "You know we just have got to get on with our lives when these things happen. We just have to keep going and you can't let these things get you down." In those days, there wasn't support for kids when this kind of thing happened. What you did was push it under the rug. You got on with your life and you "forgot about it," you know. So, what happened to me was, I got sick.

PBC: Ooh...

Loretta: After her service and everything, and that attempt to go back to school...I was home sick for a week. I couldn't eat and I was trying to figure out how to nourish myself. I was home alone and I would make myself eggnog but I couldn't eat. I was genuinely sick, tummy sick such that I couldn't eat. I wonder now about eating raw eggs in homemade eggnog for a week. I am allergic to eggs now. So was my dad. I wonder if I made myself sicker! It came to a head with a medical emergency. And then my mom and dad were going out for an evening. As they were going out, Mom said to me, "I'm gonna be at so-and-so's house, and the number is 215...I didn't even write it down, I remembered it in my head. And so that night, the sickness continued, and while my parents were out, my appendix ruptured. This was two weeks to the day after Kathy died.

PBC: Oh horrors!

Loretta: We had a wall phone, you know, where you have to dial standing up. I was curled over, I remembered the number and I dialed the wall phone. And then I went and changed my own clothes from my pj's 'cause I knew I was gonna need to go to the hospital. I dialed my parents and said, "You've gotta come right home. I need to go to the hospital." They came home. They got me in the car. We drove to the next town to the hospital.

PBC: Gosh—they didn't have any doubt that you were in trouble?

Loretta: No, they knew I was in trouble. I was really, really sick. There would be no doubt. Let me illustrate: We arrive...my dad takes hold of me to carry me from the car into the hospital, and my mom says, "Oh Will, put her down—she can walk."

PBC: Gosh.

Loretta: So my dad said, "I'm taking her in. She's really sick." He carried me into Emergency and they took one look at me and said, "Take her right into the back." They took me back, they examined me and said, "We don't know what's wrong with you, but we're going to operate on you. We know that it's probably either your ovaries, or your appendix, or something."

PBC: My gosh.

Loretta: They put this Betadine on me and shaved me. I said, "I don't need a shave." My sense of humor kicked in—maybe they'd given me some morphine— such that I was joking with them! I guess I'm a sturdy little thing! Anyway, I had an emergency appendectomy; my appendix had ruptured. My parents were there when I came out of surgery.

PBC: This is just two weeks after Kathy died that you had this emergency appendectomy?

Loretta: Yes—I stayed in the hospital for a week because the healing wasn't so fast, and I had an infection. I remember being hooked up to a pump which was connected to a tube in my abdomen. The plug kept falling out of the wall and the pump would stop. I remember my mother coming only one time to the hospital. She stood at the door clutching her purse.

PBC: Gosh. Kept her distance.

Loretta: So I didn't know what to expect from people.

PBC: How about Dad? Did he visit you?

Loretta: My dad visited me more frequently. He touched me and knew how to comfort me, and I remember one of the nights he came. He was on his way to the Army Reserve…he came in his uniform and he smelled like Old Spice and [laughs]…Mom couldn't take his cues and follow suit. She had to stay in the doorway or not come.

PBC: Except for one time, she wouldn't join him. What a lonely time for you.

Loretta: There was a sequel to this in my life. A lot came out of this. This is a huge junction in my life. One outcome was that I had a lot of scarring from it and I developed infertility.

PBC: Through scarring?

Loretta: Inside my peritoneal cavity from the infection where my tubes were trying to move around when I was trying to get pregnant, I had a difficult time conceiving. One of the things my mother said to me after I had one of my fertility procedures and we found out about the scarring is, "We didn't know that you were actually sick. We thought you were just grieving."

Loretta: My reaction was, "So when someone's grieving you leave them alone to grieve?" She didn't tend me sufficiently but I think she did her best.

PBC: She would have done it differently had she known you were actually sick?

Loretta: I don't know…I think she didn't know how to support or tend me.

PBC: Revealing, isn't it? She wasn't equipped. She hadn't been nurtured that way herself. We could speculate that she didn't know how to tend to a grieving daughter.

Loretta: Or a sick daughter.

PBC: She knew to hold your hand that first night. She slept with you the night Kathy died and held your hand.

Loretta: Yes—but then the message was, "Now get over it."

PBC: The whole experience found her ill equipped. Except, I'm struck by her intuition knowing to give you the phone number where she was going to be that night. It's as if something in her knew you were going to need her, and you knew that too because you remembered it.

Loretta: I heard it. I didn't even write it down. But I remembered it.

PBC: You were sick as a dog, doubled over in pain and somehow you remembered a new phone number in such a moment of agony and aloneness. I'm also struck by how ill equipped your mom was to handle the whole thing, both the loss of Kathy and the drama of your appendix…that's a lot.

Loretta: Yeah, it's a lot. It would be a lot for most people, I suspect. I hate not being able to pull forward more of what is positive about my mother from my childhood.

PBC: Well, it'll probably gonna come as we go through all this. I bet there's gonna be some things that sort of weave themselves together. But right now, we're in a pretty tough juncture of your life and how it affected you.

Loretta: I almost died with my appendix ruptured. After Kathy died, I hadn't wanted to live. Initially, I thought it should have been me who died, not her. My recovery from the appendectomy was slow. I really wanted to get better. I realized that I wanted to live. When I was struggling to accept my infertility, I was angry with God. But then I had a revelation: I realized that I almost died when Kathy died and that I had gotten the opportunity to live. I imagined that God was crying, too. I wasn't angry anymore.

PBC: Wow, Loretta. What an "aha" for you! Were there any more jewels with your mom's or your own growth that you feel has come out of that traumatic experience?

Loretta: It's been wonderful to develop a relationship more recently with my mom over time since my father's death. For example, I found out, one of the times that I was talking to her that when I was born, she didn't think I was her baby.

I didn't look like particularly like her or her family. I was not the baby that she envisioned.

PBC: So this conversation explained the distance you already felt from her, yet you consider it a gift? How did you respond?

Loretta: Well, I was interested and listened—I was curious about it. I was grateful that she could tell me. I thanked her for telling me. In reflecting on this information, it helped make sense of the fact that we did have a difficult relationship and maybe this is part of the reason why. We've had a genuinely affectionate relationship in these later years, whereas we battled a lot when I was younger.

PBC: It seems there might have been a breakthrough when you were able to tend her when she was sick and she was able to acknowledge, "I don't know how to do this." Perhaps you had to break the cycle and give her the affection you had always yearned for from her before she realized it was missing. You became able to do that despite not having been mothered that way. What equipped you for the job that she hadn't been able to offer you? This is what I'm on a quest to learn—how we as daughters became able to take these leaps when there was something missing for us or even something traumatic for us in our backgrounds.

Loretta: There's another strand of the things that we fought about that includes an aspect of jealousy about the way my dad related to me and I lit up for him in a way that I didn't light up for her. It was hard for her as far back as my infancy and my toddlerhood. She didn't know what to make of it—why I didn't relate to her like I related to my dad. So there was that jealousy going on in our relationship that had an impact over time through my childhood and into my young adulthood as well.

PBC: And how do you think it impacted you, especially in those younger years?

Loretta: In my young years, I think it was very confusing and anxiety producing… because I needed my dad and yet he caused me anxiety at the same time. He was able to appreciate my accomplishments. My mom could not praise the ways that I was like my dad. Like him, I was a college graduate and a teacher—my dad was an educator. At one point when I was teaching, driving to school, getting a master's degree, I was talking to her on the phone one night and she said, "When are you going to get serious with your life? When are you are gonna get married and have a baby?" This became constant and was essentially, "When are you gonna get serious and do what a woman is supposed to do?"

PBC: Is *supposed* to do.

Loretta: Yeah, you know, by the book, by *her* book.

PBC: She stuck by the book for the feedings, and for what you were supposed to be as a girl. And it didn't allow her to embrace you for who you fully were. It didn't often allow her to follow her intuition.

Loretta: Yeah.

PBC: The instinct to feed the child who is skinny, who is hungry…got overridden it seems constantly by "the book." Later, when you were blossoming into an intellectually smart kid who was ready to get educated, she wanted you to follow a different course that was more traditional, and "by the book" that was very restrictive for girls.

Loretta: Yeah.

PBC: This must have created quite a wedge between the two of you.

Loretta: But, there's something I've gotta add that I now remember. When I was in college, I got a handwritten check from her every month for $250. I would think of her walking home from her beauty shop with the tips jangling in her pocket and saving them to write me a check to get me through school.

PBC: Her hard earned money…that was the way she could nurture you.

Loretta: At that time, for her to have any money was a pretty big deal—not like a family that has a lot money and can just throw it around…it was hand to mouth, although we didn't suffer like she did growing up. But she paid for my education. She and Dad paid for my education and she wrote me checks. It was quite a sacrifice.

PBC: So again we see a bit of a disconnect. I'm looking at the disconnect of her on the one hand pressuring you to do what a woman is supposed to do—marry and have babies, and "get over this education thing that your father is all about,"—and on the other hand, "I'll pay for your college with my hard earned wages."

Loretta: The attitude became, "Just get through college."

PBC: And yet that disconnect from her preferred value system wasn't really addressed in any kind of emotionally or verbally overt way.

Loretta: Yeah…she expected that I would go to college, but then after college I would get married and then I would be in a family way. How it's supposed to happen.

PBC: But nevertheless, she was able to stretch and do that for you. Sending you the support was one way that she could nurture you silently, [laughs] rather than the "I love you's" or the touching or stroking your hair when you were sick like you were able to do for her later. She couldn't do it so overtly.

Loretta: Yeah.

PBC: But apparently her attitude has shifted in her lifetime. Do you want to expand on that at all? From when she was with your dad, it seems like she was very much under his influence in a traditional way and, over time, it seems like she's been able to meet you more at a feeling level and look back on her own life…her attitudinal limitations, yes?

Loretta: I realize more and more that my mom is very jealous in relationships.

She has a hard time sharing in relationships. Her whole life is about relationships. For example, a cousin will email me on behalf of my mom, and then I give my mom the message. She might respond, "Well, she hasn't contacted ME," and I'll say, "Well email's faster. She wanted me to tell you through email." And she'll say, "Well, *I* haven't heard from her." Or she'll frequently ask if I've heard from my brother. She'll say, "Did Brian call you? He called me." It felt sort of competitive.

PBC: Coming from some envy of your standing with him or a chip on her shoulder?

Loretta: She felt like he was too emotive and too physically affectionate with us. So the way she coped with that was to pull herself back because she thought there was enough affection in the household. She told me that later.

PBC: She compensated for his over-affectionateness.

Loretta: Yeah. So there were many things that we couldn't talk about and ways of sharing I was not allowed to experience.

PBC: Well, the fact that she told you that later seems so significant. That she was able to look back and sort of confess her strategy, and maybe in confessing, there was some recognition that she had hurt you.

Loretta: I think what is significant is that she recognized her actions but not the next step of realizing they were hurtful. The assumption is that insight reconciles emotional incongruities but that doesn't necessarily happen. If it does for Mom, it is only very brief and then she emotionally recants.

PBC: But it seems significant that she's come to that understanding while she's still here and she can process it with you.

Loretta: It's really significant, all since my dad died. My father died over 20 years ago. It has been since his death that she is more open to reflecting on the past. Since my dad died, she is much more outgoing and initiating, not just with me, but with everybody. She's more relational than she used to be, even publicly with people that she doesn't know. It's really amazing to watch her—it's very different. Her newfound understanding about family dynamics makes me realize how defended her psyche has been as I see how layered her realizations are. She'll get an "aha" about something and remember and reveal something. But she may not realize the next layer, which is the emotional piece. That will come later. The emotional pieces have been really hard because of the way of emotion in our family. Her first responses are to go to the extreme with it. Like, "This is so awful and I feel so terrible." She will batter herself and think what a horrible person she is, and then she'll want to close it over.

PBC: You can see why she's so defended because it really devastates her when she realizes she's at fault.

Loretta: Yes. It really hurts her, and then she will close it off. And then it will pop up again, and with each revisiting of the theme, she gets a little more resilient and abundant and flexible with her ability to kinda hold this and keep some perspective with the way of our relationships.

PBC: She's pretty hard on herself.

Loretta: Yes, blaming herself for what happened, for not being able to show affection and unable to touch very much. I've shown her some of those things.

PBC: You intimated earlier that your struggle with infertility was a bit agonizing…you had Mom pressuring you to do what women are supposed to do and needed support once again for your vulnerability which she didn't know how to offer. Do you want to talk about how you dealt with this with her?

Loretta: Yes, my mom kept pressuring and pressuring and pressuring me and I couldn't do it. It was so disrespectful of what my experience was. This was really painful for me. "Mom, I wanna have a baby. It's not working! You gotta let up!"

I found out in later years that she had trouble having a baby and that she had to get help to become pregnant with me. My younger brother was a "surprise"— after that she wasn't able to have more. That devastated her. To her, having a baby was one of the most important things. So consequently, she regretted that she couldn't have one more child after the three of us were here.

PBC: So was it recently that she revealed that she had trouble having a baby and got help or during your bout with infertility and miscarriages?

Loretta: She talked about it briefly over time, but lately she's given me more details about it, like who the doctor was, that she's been thinking about him, and she's told me where his office was. I didn't realize that they had such a struggle with infertility. I had the impression that it was more like wanting to have another baby and not being able to. I hadn't realized that they sought out medical help for infertility.

PBC: I find it interesting that she went for infertility care herself but never revealed this when you were going through your tough time.

Loretta: She revealed it more recently, long after Dad's death, using humor, like, "Your dad and I had a little 'pwobwem.'"

PBC: You can see a pivotal time in your mom's life that was so private she could hardly reveal it because it was so important for her to have children. She had trouble having them and yet, she had three.

Loretta: Yeah, she wished for a fourth, and she wished it be a girl. So it was like a phantom fourth child but she never got her.

PBC: So even with the struggle in her own history, she couldn't take in your reality.

Loretta: She was very, very giving in a lot of ways to others…in the community or the church.

PBC: But my impression is that you're an intensively empathetic person by contrast. So, how do you think you became so empathetic from a mom who was so lacking in empathy? She was protective in her own way but the ability to enter someone else's emotional reality wasn't there for her. Has that let up and have there been bridges built in these last few years as she ages?

Loretta: I think so. And I think that she's learned to listen to me when I say, "This doesn't work…this is what I need."

PBC: Do you think she had to become somewhat vulnerable or needy herself in order to listen more closely?

Loretta: Yes, I think that's probably true. She needs me, and she really appreciates me.

PBC: You've done a lot of work to make sense of this, Loretta!

Loretta: I have worked very hard to make sense of my life. I have worked in therapies for over 20 years. I have a second master's degree in degree in counseling. My life is rich with grounded female friends who are constant in the way of relationship.

PBC: Are there any other influences besides your mom who were mentors along the way or who might have taken you under wing?

Loretta: Something that I always did through my school career was find a significant female to connect to. So in school I would often stay later and talk to my teachers.

PBC: Do any particular teachers stand out?

Loretta: There are from my teenage years. I used to go and talk to teachers and deans. When I was first in junior high school, I would go back to my 6th grade teacher at my elementary school. Then we built another house and I changed schools. I found and befriended the dean of girls at my new school...I really liked her. We chatted a lot in her office or out on campus. I sought her out. Even though I was acting out as I mentioned earlier, she listened and accepted me. (She's the one who suspended me when I got caught smoking, but she did it so benevolently and with empathy!)

PBC: And this was in your junior high years? That sounds pivotal, that this woman, the dean, reached out to you and was kind.

Loretta: Yeah, she was always kind, and we stayed friends. We talked, and she was always very supportive of me.

PBC: Sweet—a little bit of unconditional love. That sounds much needed. You had a lot on your shoulders and were in a world of hurt.

Loretta: Then another person in high school was a teacher who taught a clothing class. I did a lot of sewing. She taught me detailed sewing, and I used to stay and talk to her. She was another one of those people that was an extra support person.

PBC: You shared personal stories with her and she supported you?

Loretta: Yeah, she supported me. I didn't get too personal about some of the things that were really deeply bothering me. I probably toyed with it, but I never did. By the time I was in high school, some of the conflicts and issues with my parents that had been so problematic had ceased. So, I wasn't carrying that on my shoulders in the same way. But I had a boyfriend, Rob, who I started going out with after Kathy died, just before my 16th birthday. I stayed with him for six years. This teacher used to kind of mentor me about having a boyfriend and being in a relationship. It was nice to have that support, 'cause we were obviously a couple in school—we were together all the time. He was my best friend really, in high school. My teacher was a really good support for me.

Then another support was a woman who was the dean of girls at the community college. She had been a family friend, so I gravitated to her automatically. She also went to our church. I went to the local community college for one semester before I went off to college. So I did the same thing with her as the others—I found her and had grand talks with her. We had really wonderful talks about loss. I'd had a lot of loss and she was really a good support. That was really before I had any counseling or anything so it was just someone to lean on.

PBC: You gravitated towards women that you could lean on.

Loretta: I thought at times about how some people have families or alternative family members to turn to. I didn't. I had family, but I didn't use them for support. In my mom's family they were judgmental like she was and I wasn't held well by them. Not that they weren't well intended—I think they were—but there was something that went wrong for me there. I have a couple of letters that I got from people, like when Kathy died. I remember one from my cousins that was just brief.

PBC: A brief acknowledgement? But at that time, there wasn't much family that saw you for who you were.

Loretta: Yeah, it was pretty sparse.

PBC: Is there anything else in your mom's history beyond what we've covered that stands out that you feel shaped her worldview?

Loretta: She did come from a farming family in the Depression. They traveled to California from Illinois when she was 17. She had to drop out of high school. She, as well as her whole family, worked here in California when they first arrived. They were the people that worked picking olives and picking fruit. They cut and canned fruit and plucked chickens. She did all kinds of farm labor.

PBC: Agricultural people.

Loretta: Until she got the opportunity to go back to high school. She finished high school later. But she was still young. Then, she got a scholarship to go to beauty school.

PBC: Oh, she returned to high school because the family allowed her to?

Loretta: I think everybody in the family went back to high school. It was a family value. So I think that once they got their feet on the ground, there was support for all the kids to go back to high school and then go on with their lives to figure out how to work and further themselves as best they could. It really is a very highly moral family in so many ways. Their values were good, in terms of not drinking and not smoking, eating good food and going to church. It was really wholesome.

PBC: Wholesome values…are those the values around agriculture and education that nurtured you?

Loretta: Yes, very, very much. I still am nurtured by those values and still carry them forth. I've carried them through my whole life. I've always been into gardening and I continue making food from scratch. I remember watching my grandma [laughs] making her own noodles. When I went to visit my great aunt who grew up in the house that my grandma grew up in she made homemade noodles for me. And [laughs] when I used to make my own noodles, I would grind the flour from scratch!

PBC: Impressive!

Loretta: I would roll them out and then cut 'em with a knife the way my mother did. So, I have a lot of nice memories of food. I really love making food from scratch.

PBC: The garden and kitchen were some of the most nourishing parts of your childhood.

Loretta: Yeah.

PBC: There's some of that positive influence you wanted to insert earlier!

How would you say your mom approached conflict versus how you approach conflict? I'm interested in how her response to conflict scarred or shaped you.

Loretta: She had a hard time taking in the perspective of other people's subjective experience. Now, it's not so hard for her to do that. In the past, when something was troubling her, it was kind of about her and she would go on and on about it and sort of put her angst on the entire household. So when it actually came to a face-to-face confrontation about it, her manner was to project, blame or come crashing down on herself. There's not really a middle ground where we can explore this together. She's very, very critical…does a lot of self or other blaming. She's that way not just with conflict, but also with tragedy. If something troubles a person in their life, she'll cast blame to it—as in, find a problem with how that person might have caused it rather than seeing that it's just the way of the world and the pattern of the universe. She's not really willing or able to figure it out with them and hold it in an understanding way. I think it's part of her survival. But I think it's a part of a cultural survival rooted in the notion that you survive when you do right. So a part of my journey was that obstacle with her…I had to learn to hold that existentially. Those things that I suffered most from really helped me grow as a person, because I learned—eventually—that the bad things that happened to me weren't my fault. I needed to learn about my participation so that I could be more careful, and try to live a better life, but not to blame myself because it's too painful a way to live.

PBC: Having both endured and witnessed her repeatedly blaming herself or being so blaming of others perhaps has allowed you to become compassionate…forgiving…empathetic by contrast to how you were met emotionally by your mother?

Loretta: The blaming was my groundwater—that was the water I swam in. So I learned not to do it and then learned later, reflecting as an adult, that's also what she does. I would now say I learned from my mother to blame myself. I've absorbed that—it's been the only way I've known for many years, but I came to realize it's not good for me. I need to make different choices. It's still a constant edge for me when I'm in an emotional state to recognize I can choose to do it a different way. It's harder to remember when the emotions are charged to do it. I think it requires that we run interference with the patterns established by our neurobiology. I think I've developed my frontal cortex enough to be able to utilize all the multitudes of other relationships as they have imprinted me in a different way to shift. I've drawn many other mentors into my tapestry over the years. One of my reactions with being 'in trouble' in relationships is to immediately get defensive…then I've developed a compensatory response of…escaping mentally to another place [laughs] that is more affirming…gentle…allows more benefit of the doubt. It's not always immediately different than my mom's response, but it's more measured. I will look at the situation: "What part did I play in this?" And I will reveal my part in it so that it becomes a part of the conversation with my mom. It usually creates a generous space for working things through. So really it's the use of that reflective function in that has made the difference from the way my mom handles conflict. I do best with other people who can do the same thing—reflect on their part in it, because if someone else can't do the same thing, it makes it pretty tough.

PBC: What we might call evolution from your mom's way—being able to respond to a situation more kindly and gently, and more reflectively, than she has been able to. Is that what you referring to in terms of teaching her something or does she still bump up against you and try to make you wrong?

Loretta: Yeah, I think taking time and pausing has really helped our relationship a lot. I still have to be careful when I'm in an emotional place because she can get to me. But I tend to have a more benevolent reaction inside that I can now hold inside myself. A way of steering clear of both of us popping off is to just take a minute.

PBC: To deal with heightened emotions?

Loretta: Yeah. Then I'll find a way of just offering some perspective. "So it's this way for you, and it's this way for me." Often my brother Hal is in the room and chimes in that it's this way for him. I just try to slow it down and take in the different perspectives so that each person in the room can have their response. One of the things that I've learned to use with her that really helps us all is my sense of humor. We have this crazy rabbit character in my family! If I can manage to mellow out my emotions first, I'll bring the rabbit into the room.

PBC: That's cute.

Loretta: It goes like this: "The wabbit! The wabbit! Oh my gosh, the wabbit! The wabbit's back!" and then she'll get into the rabbit and we'll laugh and start talking with different inflections and use W's for R's. It's a very fun way. I think humor is congruent for her family. They used humor, but they used it in a way that made another person a target. It's like a fictitious creature [laughs] kind of confuses things and gets everything mixed up. And the 'wabbit' takes the heat and breaks up the tension. And so my brother Brian and I've talked about that, and we realize that in the constellation of our family that we both use humor to try to survive the family dynamic.

PBC: Did your family tease like this in your childhood?

Loretta: No, it's been in our adulthood.

PBC: So, it wasn't part of your family as a child?

Loretta: It's been later—in Mom's aging that I've done the 'wabbit' thing.

PBC: Sweet. Is there anything you wanna say about how the approach to conflict that you were taught and that you've learned subsequently affected your former marriage, if you don't mind my asking that?

Loretta: One of the things that I've learned since my marriage is that I was married to a man who was very forthright with his candor. It's something I really liked about him. I really liked his candor and his immediacy. It was refreshing to me and it felt good to me. But it became a double-edged sword [laughs], his candor was also his criticism, and I would get sliced. I would just get defensive and I would attack. I probably needed a 'wabbit' to lighten up! My 'wabbit' wasn't here yet. It wasn't a part of my family yet. [laughs] Now I'm out!

PBC: [laughs] Lessons learned! [laughs] I'll have to bring that in to my couples counseling!

Loretta: Something that my then husband and I did together later that was pretty awesome was that we were able, over time, to develop that function of reflection and understanding at a time when we were in a regulated place. If we're both self-regulated, we can really talk in quite depth about what happened between us and about our way of being together. But when we were in it, we didn't have the perspective or objectivity.

PBC: That only came after you separated.

Loretta: We learned to do it together before we divorced. After we separated …he would come over and sit down and we'd just chat. We did very well during that period with some distance and space. It was perhaps a time of integration.

PBC: Separation allowed you to regulate better without getting in each other's faces, yes?

Loretta: We had a period of time where our capacity for that was really good and I think we both learned a lot from each other. I think he's benefited from it. He says he has, and I have too. [laughs]

PBC: Divorce had a happy ending. [laughs]

Loretta: Yeah, really.

PBC: Sweet.

Loretta: So that's another story. It feels terrible to say, but being married was something I don't know if really, deep in my own soul I wanted. At the time I was seeing my then future husband, my mother was really pestering me to get married.

PBC: So you might have married to please your mother? And you've been a little tormented as to whether your mother pressured you or if it was in your own heart?

Loretta: Yeah, but it feels terrible to say…

PBC: But so common! People state they married for the "wrong reasons" as family pressures or other pressures…financial pressures, pregnancy pressures and so on—I find it's pretty common, especially for young love. We are the generation born from mothers who were in survival mode for the most part…as were their mothers and their mothers before them.

Loretta: Yeah. That is no disparagement of my former husband—truly not, because he's a noble and wonderful man, capable of good relationships.

PBC: If most of us in midlife look back on what influenced our choices to marry or to take jobs or whatever that were significant decisions that had consequences, I find that we weren't necessarily in touch with ourselves. Externals often influenced our choices, especially if we weren't raised to trust our instincts or to drop down and listen to our feelings. That's kind of what I'm writing about here—how we've made a shift now so that many of us have become pioneers who then pave the way for a more authentic approach. We've become better able to listen to our intuition and our feeling state and follow that as a directive rather than doubting ourselves and following the "shoulds" of the past.

To that point, Loretta, I wonder if you have dreams for this next generation of young women that might differ from what you think your mother's dreams were for you?

Loretta: For the children of our world today—including, of course, my godchildren—my wish is that they have an authentic voice that comes from and is connected to a deep source of value—God or however you name it and however you conceive it. It's beautiful if it connects to their authentic voice…their experience in relationship to value.

PBC: Spirit…Authentic voice…Value.

Loretta: To choose to have in their lives the guiding feelings and values that are authentically theirs—not shaped by nosy people who are wondering, "Well do you have a boyfriend? Are you thinking about getting married? Are you thinking about having children?" Instead, that they choose the role in life that is really right for them…the relationships that are right. My wish is that they get to choose for themselves what they want.

PBC: From within themselves, yes?

Loretta: Also, that they be free to make meaningful and intimate connections in community that shares those deep, rich values. I wish for them a broader, wider community within which they can hold those values and live fully with vitality and spirit. And I wish for them that they have support when they get into trouble—that they have somebody to go to that can help them through tough times.

PBC: Beautiful. It's inspiring to hear how despite the lack of support and the burden that your family was carrying, that you were able to find your way to your own support network of people throughout your childhood, especially women.

PBC: Are there any female role models beyond your mother who are noted figures in the culture that other people might recognize who have been influential and impactful on you? Inspiring figures? Famous woman celebrities or authors as you were coming of age?

Loretta: No, not really. My inspirations have been more local support. A local Jungian spiritual sanctuary was really influential to me. That was very, very pivotal in shifting my existential perspective. It allowed me to be able to name things and interact with things that are deep influences because I was raised Protestant with a God image that's a masculine godhead. I came to realize that I didn't subscribe to that anymore and was able to cast it out. But then it was a challenge to try to find and name my own religious or spiritual sources…a way of conceptualizing God. It was really hard when I was suffering because I needed it, but the religious framework in which I was raised wasn't working—didn't offer me comfort or guidance. I needed to be able to develop my own existential perspective and play with it—not have it be hammered into me by anybody, but just to play with it and look at how I was influenced and what different cultures do. This sanctuary, especially the women teachers, exposed me to how it's done in different parts of the world. I was able to grasp how Christianity evolved within a historical context and what might have happened. I was able to approach it with wonder and to reformulate some things for myself. So, that was poignant in its timing, as all of my miscarriages and infertility stuff had been happening and I was in great despair. I was in my mid to late thirties. Because of the vulnerability that these miscarriages stirred in me…the women there played a key role and were healing and inspiring.

Otherwise, I cannot think of female a media figure that was influential!

I watched fantasy things…Disney movies, [laughs] I do like the works of Carl Jung and reading his reflections, but that isn't a female.

PBC: I'm looking for what we might call our 'bigger mothers' beyond our families—inspirational women that we wanted to model after or found influential. It sounds like you found that in your immediate community at critical times in your life.

Loretta: I think my female inspirations have been on the "ground" in my circle of support and with some pretty incredible mentors. I did some advance training at one point and had wonderful mentors: JP who taught me that "presence" was enough and brilliance is simply stated; AL who taught me not to do it alone—to ask for help, not as a weakness but as a strength; and JJ who, in response to my questions about working with parents when I wasn't a parent myself, offered for me to consider that having the same experience does not help as much as being curious about another's experience and helping them reflect in a way that is meaningful to them. I have been trying to learn about the nature of "curiosity" that is helpful in this way ever since.

Another important female in my life was my high school boyfriend Rob's mother. She was a presence through the milestones of high school and college. When Rob and I broke up she completely surprised me. She was on board for every significant event until she died in the late 80s. She came to the hospital when I was sick. She celebrated my marriage. She always let me know if something was happening with Rob that might catch me off guard. She knew how much I had loved him and that I needed care to cope with my life as he moved on. When he married, she let me know what I needed to know so that when things came out in the newspaper, I wouldn't be surprised. She always remembered my birthday. She beckoned me as a friend and advisor as she aged, becoming a dear friend. She surprised me with the persistence of unconditional love.

PBC: Wow—that's touching! You've already answered the question about how you want to see the next generation of girls carry the torch of womanhood. In terms of you being a role model to many young women—the goddaughters and no doubt many others—what are you most proud of in terms of your own impact on this next generation of girls and young women?

Loretta: I think my courage to live a life that's different than the traditional is important, and that I hold my dignity and self-respect and viability.

PBC: What do you mean by 'viability?'

Loretta: Constancy...survival...think of a viable pregnancy. I didn't die when Kathy died. It is more than survival. In my professional world and in the world of my peers, I'm still regarded well and still valued and I'm still asked to come forth to contribute. I feel I carry the best of what came forth from my family—those deep values related to agriculture and farming. I've expanded to a different version of gardening vs. agriculture—the relationship to getting food on our planet in a more sustainable way. It is my privilege in the world we live in now to do that, and that I have this deep connection to mother earth where I really value understanding how nutrients work in the soil and how they relate to our bodies. I'm really interested in nutrition and, however I can, finding ways to help support people to be healthy. It's a very important topic for me. I talk about it all the time. [laughs]

PBC: Any message to other women in conclusion?

Loretta: Live an authentic life. Speak with an authentic voice. Be connected in whatever way you can, be conscious. Take time to invest, to be engaged, to be connected. When the emotions are really high, find another source to work things out. Sometimes you can't regulate again until you can just get it out, but it's better to get it out with a neutral party...it might be in a journal, it might be with a friend, or it might be with a therapist. It could be all three. Don't be afraid of your depths, but find a source to connect to when you take a plunge. Connect to nature and metaphors of nature. For me the chrysalis and compost inspire me.

PBC: To regulate and then look back to the source of the conflict. That's been a tough lesson for so many of us to learn the hard way. [laughs] Connect—inside and out! And play with your 'wabbit.' Love that!

Pam Burns-Clair

Biography

Birthdate: 12/29/52

Mother: Harriet (Tapp) Burns, 8/20/28, died 7/08

I was raised in North Hollywood, CA where my parents migrated from their home state of Texas after my dad returned from the Korean War when I was a toddler. They moved to LA for my dad to pursue a career in stage or screen, which didn't come to pass, and while he was trying to get "a bite," my mom had to go to work to help support the family. Long story short, she got hired by Walt Disney Studios and became a pioneer as the first female Imagineer, whose story is shared here as well in our tribute book about her.

I grew up in North Hollywood at the time that the freeways were just being built and the TV and movie studios were expanding and competing to meet the demand of more and more families owning and watching TV as a family pastime, first black and white and then color TV's. My mom, being connected with Disney, allowed us perks like going to see previews of movies at the Disney Studios, like "The Parent Trap," "The Absent Minded Professor," "101 Dalmations" and "Mary Poppins"—which my mom created the robin for on Mary's (Julie Andrews') finger! We took relatives who would visit to Disneyland every summer, and my mom showed us the attractions she had been involved with.

After getting a taste of Texas each summer with my grandma, I went to my first year of college there, but found it wasn't a fit, even though I enjoyed being so close to my grandmother "Memie" in Dallas. (I have since reconnected with Texas through family that we discovered when I was a young mom and became close with.) I wandered a bit and landed in Sonoma, CA where I got my BA in psychology at Sonoma State University ('74) at a time when psychology was very humanistic and gestalt and encounter groups were the rage. I was always drawn to working with children, and pursued a Masters Degree in school psychology at first, but then realized I wanted to work in a clinical capacity with children and their families, so I switched majors to clinical psychology and graduated from San Francisco State University ('78).

I set up my private practice in Napa and got my Marriage, Family Child Therapy license. ('79) where my emphasis was children's play therapy and women—originally to work with the children's mothers, but then I became interested in working with women of all ages and stages, which has remained an emphasis throughout my practice. I married Robert ("Bob") Clair in '81, both of us therapists. He had a son already, just a few years younger than me, which was intimidating at first, but I couldn't have scored a nicer, smarter or more talented stepson. Bob was eager to become a dad again, fortunately, since my dream was always to become a mom. We had our daughter Chelsea ('85), and even though Bob was an older dad, he was willing to go for a 2nd child—Haley arrived just in time ('90) before Bob would have concluded he was too old to keep having kids! We educated them deliberately in Waldorf schools in their elementary and Chelsea's middle school years, and I wished that I had received such a creative and respectful education when I was a child.

Our family moved to Sonoma ('98) to be closer to where the kids were carpooling to school, and I have been happy to have my therapy practice separate from my family life. Haley benefited from that locale in being close to the children's theater and dance classes in the area, later her voice teachers, and now I am fortunate that Chelsea is back in Sonoma—having gotten her college degree in design in Southern California—with her husband about to raise her family locally. She is self-employed as a successful multi-faceted designer already. Haley is in New York, having recently graduated in musical theater in Boston, pursuing her career there with the same dedication and tenacity she always brought to her performing arts activities as a child.

My dad died from a sudden heart attack when I was a new mom, ('86) shortly after my mom's retirement from Disney, and my mom's unexpected death has been quite a journey of discovery, learning more about her career, her personality, and her impact on others than I had perceived.

I have always been a writer in various forms, and my dad was a talented writer who never published. I also have been a jogger through my adult life, the jazz dance classes of my 20s have given way to yoga now, thanks to my husband—who has gotten the nickname "yogeezer"—and we love hiking and outdoor activities.

Pam's mom with baby Pam

Pam as a little girl

Pam at about age 20

Pam with her mom in 2001

Pam today

Pam's Story — My Personal Leap

The first leap began for me in my late teens/early 20s when I realized I was not willing to go the conventional art major route in my mother's footsteps, which had been my leaning throughout high school. I had won a national design contest with Seventeen Magazine through my local Broadway department store in L.A. where I worked and was sent on a five-day excursion the summer after graduation to New York, where I toured the fashion and design industry icons and landmarks. The ground was laid for my entry into that world as perhaps a textile or fashion designer already, but in my freshman year in college at my parents' alma mater—Southern Methodist University in Dallas, I found it increasingly offensive to have my artwork "graded" and judged. So I ventured away from the school and the major I had chosen. The following two years of college became a quest up and down the West Coast—and even a summer backpacking in Europe—for "Who am I REALLY and what do I want to do?" I became a psychology major and graduated from Sonoma State University, (California) as it was called back then, and went on to do graduate work in clinical psychology at San Francisco State University. I believe I was drawn to psychology and to study children and women in particular as a quest to understand my own roots and my family.

I didn't fully realize what a pioneer for women breaking through the "glass ceiling" my own mother was until after she passed in 2008 and, with help from my co-author Don Peri and my daughter Chelsea Clair Livingston, compiled a tribute book about her: *Walt Disney's First Lady of Imagineering, Harriet Burns*. My mom was among very few women of the 50s to assume a full time creative or professional career (as opposed to secretarial, teaching or nursing which were more typical of the times) as the first woman in the model shop of Disney Studios. She later became the first female Imagineer during the groundbreaking years of the development of "audio-animatronics" and their use in Disneyland and subsequently in the other Disney theme parks. She remained, despite having broken the glass ceiling in her field, allegiant to the identity of women being deferential to men in the sense of being accommodating, demure, gracious and accepting. She raised me to be similarly constricted by those values, "proper" in appearance and social manners, and as a teenager, discouraged my questioning established authority or the values of the times. She did not see how she had, in a sense, "unleashed a monster" in the ways she had modeled breaking out of convention—not only was she a successful career woman who took great pride and satisfaction in her work, but at home there was also quite a role reversal in that my dad did most of the cooking, and they remodeled the house together in a joint endeavor!

During this period of questioning and soul searching as a teen and young adult, my parents were rather mortified when I started questioning authority and became drawn towards peers who were questioning the values of the times in the late 60s/early 70s. When I veered from the art and design world that I had been leaning towards and instead went "counter culture" in my choice of colleges and majors, I'm sure I contributed to a lot of worry and sleepless nights for my mother.

My personality is much more assertive and, well…bold—than my mother's. But following her passing I also got a fuller sense of her many sides that she didn't expose me to. She kept her work life and the wide circle of colorful work friends whom she kept up with beyond her retirement in '86—fellow Imagineers and creative minds at Disney—quite separate from me, throughout her life. I knew their names and vaguely knew her relationship with them, with the exception of a dear colleague during my childhood in our neighborhood in North Hollywood that we socialized with as a family, and a couple of dear colleagues who lived close to her in retirement in Santa Barbara after my dad died and with whom she developed a special relationship. But in her passing and in the process of putting the tribute book together with stories and encounters with her former colleagues, it became clear that she deliberately sheltered me and my family from them, likely because she had a 'bawdy' and in some ways "off color" relationship with so many men (given the man's world that surrounded her at work) that didn't fit the image she wanted me and my family to have of her! Marty Sklar, her esteemed colleague throughout her career of 31 years, sized it up in his eulogy—(included in our tribute book, *Walt Disney's First Lady of Imagineering, Harriet Burns*, p. 19-21)—this way:

> *But the true heartbeat of the Imagineering Model Shop was a little corner where the Queen Bee held court…where you could find the big boys—even Walt—buzzing around Harriet.*

So there was a mystery and rather a split in my mom's persona, which I got only glimpses of as a child, but this was the backdrop of my home life.

By young adulthood, I had deliberately and, to my mother's horror, rather painfully claimed my voice and transcended the limitations from the mold that she attempted to fit me in. I was expected to please and prioritize others, and by the time I had my own daughters in my 30s, I was on my own creative path as a woman and mother, determined to raise my two girls to know themselves and to be free to express themselves in ways I was not allowed to.

My mother modeled—without realizing it—innovation and "out of the box" values at home as well as in her career...for example, the way she approached decorating and remodeling our home as I was growing up. I helped her at about age 10 make fancy bold and unusual doorknobs for her bedroom wall-to-wall closets from a mold out of a mysterious substance that had to set up...she and my dad created a dining room ceiling out of thin sheets of gold leaf mounted on panes of glass. She always brought home interesting and unusual materials from work that I was allowed to use for my junior high and high school art projects and also to decorate my room with (like a bolt of yellow felt), or spare rubber hands cast for the Carousel of Progress exhibit as props for my witch costume for Halloween. What helped to distinguish my entries in the national fashion design contest I won in my teens, I believe, is that I went 3-D with a "Disneyesque theme" for each—using materials Mom provided from surplus scraps of special paper from work. So in the context of design and Disney's cutting edge approach to the art of entertainment—she had modeled "anything goes"... "the sky's the limit." However, when I took that a step further and LEAPED BEYOND design, taking another path altogether... she became highly uncomfortable, agitated and...either afraid, embarrassed or mortified!

I believe my early years with my mom, in contrast to my later development, were smoother. She very much delighted in motherhood and, as I've seen her with other young children over the years as well as my own, I believe I brought out her own childlike playfulness and vast imagination. She thought I was precocious developmentally, so much so that it took her aback when I walked at nine months of age while my dad was away in the military. He got home from Korea as I turned one year, and she tried to push me down and discourage me from walking so he would be there to see it! But I was not deterred...potty training was also apparently early and self-imposed (in the sense that I was intolerant of wet diapers and responsive to the potty!). So she was proud of my developmental precociousness. I learned later that they put me in private school for my first three years of elementary school because the window for first grade was later; I had a December birthday and was ready to read. My dad was experimenting with entrepreneurial creative ambitions in theater and the screen in up-and-coming Hollywood (to which they had moved from Texas in my infancy) as well as in the stock market, so he was my before and after school parent as my mom was already working full time by the time I was two. I have only fond memories of my early formative years, for the most part. Although I wanted a sibling, I accepted that my mom was a career mom and that she had a difficult childbirth with me, so I was to be the only child. This allowed me a lot of time to be my own playmate, to dream, pretend and imagine, which I believe has served me well—in keeping with the Disney lyrics—"When You Wish Upon a Star":

> *When you wish upon a star*
> *Makes no difference who you are*
> *Anything your heart desires*
> *Will come to you*
> *If your heart is in your dream*
> *No request is too extreme…*

I believe I took these to heart.

My mom and I shared a love for the holidays, especially Christmas, which was four days before my birthday. Here is what I wrote in her eulogy in '08 (included in our book, *Walt Disney's First Lady of Imagineering, Harriet Burns*, p. 17):

> *No one did Christmas like my mom. The outdoor lights were subtle—blue and green, in contrast to the rest of the neighborhood—but indoors it was Santa's village! Everyone got gifts—even the mailman and milkman and piano teacher—and I'm sure many of you who worked with her watched her bring in a sleigh-full of goodies—the gift wrapping was an assembly line at our house. I helped her create magical bows with accessories tucked in. Packages were mailed to relatives…Christmas cards (including a variety of religious, non-religious or Chanukah cards suitable to the recipient!) were signed with personalized notes into the wee hours. The tree had unique ornaments, like discarded rock candy from the candy mountain model at WED Enterprises that preceded the Matterhorn, and matching beautiful glass ornaments like department stores had. Sometimes we would shop at J. Magnin's, not so much for the contents but for their magical gift boxes! Mom always hit the day-after-Christmas sale for next year's Christmas cards, etc. in her effort to be ever prepared.*

I remember the excitement and anticipation in my early years of long road trips to Texas from LA for the Christmas holidays—despite sometimes blizzardous conditions and once in Texas, my grandma would make ice cream with a crank wooden ice cream maker that I got to help crank…and I thought the ice cream was made of snow which had fallen.

My birthday is just a few days after Christmas, and my mom went out of her way to make it special even though it was so crunched with that holiday. There were always surprises, and I remember almost passing out one year when I got my first two-wheel bicycle that I had dreamed of!

Our arguments began when my assertiveness started rearing its head in junior high—she insisted I must wear corrective oxfords exclusively to school for what was deemed my "knock knees and flat feet." I became clever so as to appease them as I left for school, but then changed into my gym sneakers that I kept in my school locker. Eventually I got busted, but I wasn't going "back in the box" for long. I was required to practice piano for half-hour every day from my lesson, including the dreaded scales and metronome, but I struck a compromise with my mom by spending my own money on Beatles and popular music (not unlike my mom's preference for playing popular show tunes from her own era versus classical) and developing quite a repertoire after my half-hour duty was fulfilled.

High school is when relations became more strained with my parents when I started dating. Being an only child, my mom's fears seemed to rear up out of nowhere, and I was put on a pretty tight leash. This led to power struggles and I kept dating a boyfriend whom they didn't approve of for mysterious reasons—for longer than I might have due to my parents' resistance. As I look back, he had a mind of his own and was a critical thinker, which I craved and needed encouragement to become. (We are still friends, and my parents were foolish to judge him—he became a very successful businessman and loyal family man in his adult years.) As I reflect on those arguments, I would summarize them this way: The cat was outa the bag…there was no turning back…I was—and in many ways am— the product of the unconscious seeds that were planted in my foundation years.

I need to mention the strong influence my Texas grandma "Memie" (Leone Burns) was in my upbringing. She was my dad's mom, and I was her only grandchild for my entire childhood. I was sent each summer to spend about two months with her in Dallas. She became a widow when I was four and remained single, so it was just me and her, and she was essentially my doting fairy godmother! Where I was raised in the City of Angels, removed from the natural world of my dad's roots in Texas, and my mom was sophisticated, educated, and concerned that I would become 'spoiled' as an only child, she sent me off to the ultimate 'spoiler' each summer. I only later realized I was sent for so long out of necessity for childcare, although I loved every minute with my indulgent earthy grandma. Memie cooked up "a mess o' fixins" in her matchbox size kitchen…there were electric fans in each room…she sang off key in church and fed Sunday supper to a few stray 'brothers and sisters' and relations at a bulging matchbox-size dining room table! Memie's southern homemade biscuits and cornbread were unsurpassed (no doubt due to the "shortening"). She baked pies, shucked peas and we cracked pecans that grew all over the neighborhood, sitting out on the porch swing in the evenings and visiting with the neighbors. At age 10 or 11 she taught me to sew on her treadle sewing machine, and part of the ritual was going to the fabric store first thing during my visit and buying "material" for my school clothes that we sewed in the weeks to come. I became quite an accomplished seamstress before I ever entered junior high and took the required "home-ec" sewing class. Whereas it might have gotten lonely with just Memie for such an extended time, she was everyone else's favorite "grandma" also and accepted longterm overnight babysitting jobs over the summer for families who left their kids in her care, some of whom became my regular playmates over the years. The young ones became my charges as I became old enough to help, and I learned valuable babysitting skills.

In short, Memie was my source of unconditional love and counterbalanced my parent's "strictness" and rigidity. While I was held to a certain standard and level of achievement at home that was in many ways rigorous and disciplined, I could do no wrong in my grandma's eyes and lapped up her unconditional love. I believe this was extremely therapeutic and a healthy counterbalance. I never felt that my mother quite understood my grandmother and was judgmental of her simple earthy ways, but Memie contributed a solid foundation and sense of wellbeing and contentment in me that I would have hungered for otherwise. Sad as I was to lose her as a young mother myself, she is in my bones and my heart forever. I have been a much more 'hands-on' and earthy mother myself as a result of Memie's influence.

Another pivotal moment in my journey was my father's sudden death at age 58 from a heart attack. I was 33 and we had just celebrated my first daughter's 1st birthday three weeks prior to his passing. My husband, my mom to some degree and I had all been concerned about his health in the face of mounting stressors: their recent major move from LA to Santa Barbara in '86 shortly after my mom retired from her 31 year career at Disney…my dad continuing to commute to LA while establishing his own private consulting company…his health history that added up to Type A high risk for heart attack. And boom! It happened, and he was gone. Life wasn't the same after that.

Being tossed into grief grows us or breaks us. As boggling and upsetting and shattering as this was, now with 26 years to reflect back on its impact, I can see that one of the lessons was: don't let life yank YOU around…YOU choose life! It's precious…it's a privilege. My dad was overextended and bullheaded. I became determined to challenge my own bullheadedness and smell the roses more. I had a young baby I had waited and yearned for. "Don't blow this," I told myself. "Don't let his demise become your own undoing."

Then there was my anxiety about what impact his death would have on my mom, who was in so many ways his sidekick. They had become so intertwined, and she was dependent in particular ways on my dad. She was pretty helpless regarding managing finances and legal matters—those had been his department, yet she was stubbornly independent so didn't want my/our help or our concern. For an agonizing couple of years, we watched her get taken advantage of by an accountant and lawyer. I had to sit myself down at one point and recognize that if I kept pestering her about my concern and insisting she listen to my perspective about her affairs, I would lose her emotionally. She proved herself amazingly resilient and tough at the same time as I began surrendering my sense of protectiveness towards her. It wasn't easy…there was the constant battle over her vision, which was failing little by little. In retirement she became quite involved in her local community, and wasn't about to give up her car keys, at least locally.

Raised in the depression, she was "programmed" to save and re-use scrounged materials. "Raised" by Disney, Imagineers had to be inventive and create with scrounged materials. I too have tendencies to collect "stuff" with the notion that someday these things will be put to use.

She and my dad prided themselves on being fiercely independent. I had lost him to his own denial resulting in lousy self-care. I was so afraid of losing her to her own poor judgment. For example, she told me after the fact that she'd had a breast lumpectomy—as if she had had a tooth filled! Another time she told me after the fact by a couple of weeks that she had taken quite a spill at the farmers market while carrying a bouquet of flowers (obstructing her vision, no doubt)—this was after she had been dealing with both glaucoma and macular degeneration for years. She passed out, paramedics had been called, she had a black eye and swollen toe and gash above her eyebrow…and the way she brought this up was asking me what shoes she might wear to a party with her foot so swollen.

Given my parents' predictable work hours and our location to the neighboring freeway underpass, our house was robbed repeatedly during my childhood. We installed burglar alarms and the burglars uninstalled them and robbed the house. We installed rod iron bars on the side windows and they removed the bars. I have developed abhorrence for secrecy and as a kid, wondered why they didn't just leave the house unlocked? It would have been less hassle! My mother had a very private side that I was constantly trying to draw out from under the covers, whatever forms this took during our journey together.

These were some of my mother's shortcomings that made me crazy periodically. I had to keep coming back to how much I valued the relationship over and beyond power struggles. It was not easy. We got into plenty of power struggles, and I knew I saw a side of her that her many friends and fans did not see! And her pride and stubbornness was not completely foreign to me. It's humbling to see your own weaknesses in your loved one—whether parent, child or spouse, and to apply the lessons of humility by surrendering that darned ego! In many ways, this has been my life's work. This is what has kept me married for over 30 years and has allowed me to weather the storms of parenting teens and young adults. This lesson is what

I attempt to teach my clients as a psychotherapist, but it is a constant challenge to walk the walk.

The other thing I learned and absorbed from my mom—humility of a different sort—is to LAUGH at ourselves…not take our human dramas and ourselves so seriously. She had a lot of fun with her colleagues and told uproariously entertaining stories about these "kooky artists" she worked with (with funny names like T. Hee and X. Atencio and Rolly Crump) who were a barrel of fun and practical jokes. Likewise, she could make fun of herself and aspects of our household that were kinda wacky! That was her nature from childhood. She was nicknamed "Tippy Tapp" because she was tiny, her maiden name was Tapp and she taught herself to tap dance watching Shirley Temple movies. She named her childhood goldfish "Tackaonsitgo Popeye-Gotsinyammar Cockapinany-Kasuzyanna-Karcachi Dinanashey-Brianashey Jickalicky-Jackaboney Christianna-More", as my daughter Chelsea begins her tribute in our Harriet book recounting. This is the wacky mom who raised me, and you just can't take yourself too seriously around that kind of whimsy! I would say humor and our ability to laugh at ourselves has been the strongest enduring glue of my marriage and sailed us through the most challenging years of parenting our daughters.

In identifying other women who have shaped and inspired me along my way, several were important influences in my 20s and 30s: Anais Nin (*The Diary of Anaïs Nin*) introduced me to journaling, which has become a lifelong therapy for me as a writer and a therapist. I resonated with what seemed a juicy life that she led, and her belief and conviction "that self-knowledge through journaling was the source of personal liberation." I was mesmerized by the songs of Judy Collins and Joni Mitchell and played the albums as well as the sheet music on the piano of "Both Sides Now," "Court and Spark," "Blue," and "Big Yellow Taxi." In my 30s Sarah Ban Breathnach taught me about making a practice of gratitude and embracing simplicity, and I taught women's workshops based on this work. I found Dr. Christiane Northrup's *Women's Bodies, Women's Wisdom* as a feminist OBGYN riveting in my personal journey as a woman and in my work. I have found her approach to women's health and wellness refreshing and empowering as she teaches women how to thrive at every stage of life, and recently gave her book to my pregnant daughter to continue the cycle. But perhaps the most influential of my female role models from my 20s on has been Jane Goodall, British primatologist, ethnologist, anthropologist, and UN Messenger of Peace whom I've heard speak a number of times. She is still my role model for someone who, with grace, warmth, and humor, has been able to weave together activism and spirituality and make such a difference! When she talks about her observation of the chimp in the wild of Gambe, Africa, (whom she named David Greybeard) using a tool to catch fish, it's thrilling, and it changed the world of anthropology.

Louis Leakey responded to her reporting of this discovery to him this way: "Now we must redefine tool, redefine Man, or accept chimpanzees as humans." Jane was a groundbreaker because of her willingness to be a pioneer and follow her passion and conviction. Jane credits her mother as a crucial part of her foundation and vision and for supporting the early venture to study chimpanzees in Africa, which led her into her life's work. Nearly 80 now, Jane is still traveling and speaking about 360 days a year all around the world with standing ovation audiences wherever she goes. She is truly a steward of the planet and such an endearing activist! So of all the female role models, she is my greatest hero.

Another major influence on my evolution of consciousness and our journey as women has been facilitating women's therapy support groups over many years in my psychotherapy practice. For several years I led as many as four weekly ongoing evening groups for six to eight women. Periodically I have run workshops or taught classes on women's issues. What a privilege it's been to witness and encourage women to see themselves as journeying together as we learn to claim the voices our mothers often didn't have…set boundaries on our personal space and time and tasks that may be expected of us…choose where and how we invest our energy and express ourselves rather than have these choices handed to us or dictated for us. We can feel so alone, take things too personally and feel guilty for making these shifts individually, but in concert with each other, we can borrow each other's courage, strength and perspective as we forge our way into unknown territory. This opportunity to bear witness and observe patterns among many women over the last 20 years has been a key factor in my own personal journey as a woman as well as prompting me to write about the "paradigm shift" in female consciousness that is occurring in my generation of mid-life women.

What I wish for the next generation of women is:

Gather your tribe—we can't and shouldn't go it alone. We need trusted girlfriends and role models…"sisters" and people we can journey with. Seize by the tail the work that has been done by our generation and continue! The world needs your feminine presence and influence…give it all you got!

The Tapestry of Women Who Took a Leap

Clients and friends who fall into the category of "mid-lifers" often feel like their experience is deviant and alone. They don't realize that we're all going through a cultural paradigm shift together. Previous generations of women—as we can see in the mothers in these stories—were confined by roles and traditions rooted in survival. As most of us in modern times expect to be able to buy milk and eggs as opposed to milking an animal or raising chickens to feed our families...as we either rely on cars or public transportation to get through our day rather than our feet...few of us are bearing as many as 10 children now in modern times...this allows us and affords us some different values than our mothers and grandmothers were trained to live by, and that they trained us to live by.

As I weave together these stories, what comes to mind is quotes like "What doesn't kill you makes you stronger"... "Every cloud has a silver lining"... "It turned out to be a gift in disguise." How did these women transcend, survive and even thrive in the face of such adversity? Whether we hear the stories of the mothers—Myrna's mother enduring her baby dying for mysterious reasons while her husband was away in the military or saying goodbye to her roots and familiar culture in China to immigrate to a foreign land with no money, determined to pursue a college education for her girls...or Anne's mother's heart being broken as she was beckoned back from Japan by her family, forcing her to leave her true love behind to take care of her siblings at home in Hawaii...or the challenges the daughters faced, such as Loretta enduring the back-to-back losses of her best friend's sudden death followed by appendicitis without support, only later to find yet another related loss of her fertility in the chain of events...Charlie growing up in a culture that didn't acknowledge or respect her people whether in New Mexico or Southern California, always having to watch her back...Hope being raised in the throws of a mother with mental illness...Anita's alcoholic and domineering father who was both a respected professional in public but at times violent at home who intimidated her mother into submission—we see remarkable strength, resilience, hope, and courage in these women.

Cyndi's mother—though working long hours as a single mom—managed to convey her love, devotion and be a fierce role model for her daughter's work ethic but also inspire her to become a respected pillar in her family at a young age. Despite her mom never marrying, Cyndi has had a very enduring successful marriage and realized her dream of the "traditional" two-parent family.

Just as I recognize, in hindsight, my mother—subconsciously and by being a pioneer herself—handed me the torch for breaking loose and becoming a woman empowered with options, Hope was able ultimately to take the unchanneled restless and adventurous spirit of her mother and make a life's work out of it, both in her early travels and as an educator.

Loretta, having been misread and criticized by her mother throughout her childhood, managed to seek out other mother figures and healers as resources, making peace ultimately with her losses by generating compassion both for herself and for young children and families in her work. Not only has she allowed her mother to be her catalyst for inner exploration and discovery, she has been able to gently teach her mother to be more accepting and receive nurturing that she was never able to give as a young mother herself or perhaps ever receive in another relationship.

Anita's persistent vision that she was more than her family credited her for and her passion for the underdog led her to her life's work of healing and activism, now expanding from working with individuals to focusing on communities of people around the globe. Where her background and the oppression she and her mother experienced should, by all accounts, have broken her spirit, her spirit could be described as tenacious and effervescent!

Charlie's mother of 10 was a force to be reckoned with in the home, and Charlie took that modeling the next step—she has become a force to be reckoned within the politics of human rights and as a leader in restoring culture and dignity among indigenous people. She has been able to carry forward her mother's torch of being so generous to those in her community to Charlie carrying that spirit of generosity both locally—in her non-profit which is realizing its dream after years of patience and persistence under Charlie's direction—as well as making a difference internationally as an advocate and representative for women's human rights.

Myrna has picked up the ingredients of quality mothering from her mother coming out of a very prescribed culture and modernized it, making the conscious choice to be a full-time mother and creating a balanced home over a career while her daughters are still school age, but making sure her daughters have unbridled options. Just as her mother did for her and her sisters, Myrna is encouraging and nurturing their educational opportunities. In Myrna's case—she being the youngest of this sampling of interviewees—her mother took a giant leap out of her own background, ahead of her time, and Myrna is carrying it proudly a step further.

Anne, also coming out of a family of immigrants (like Myrna and Charlie) with very restrictive expectations of women, has managed not only to speak up and express herself, but also to become a healer and professional helper of others. But why stop there? She fits the description of a lifelong learner—taking one "aha" moment after another and transforming her lens into something even more expansive and life affirming.

The dichotomy that I experienced with my mother—on one hand, finding her expectations and standards impossible to meet, and on the other hand, she was delightfully creative and imaginative and had an endearing sense of humor— became my threads to weave into something more integrated. She had a wide circle of friends but kept her categories and pockets of friends and family separated from one another, yet she was loyal and special to each of them. I am a networker, by contrast, but also have the loyalty "gene." I am grateful to have generated a wide circle of enduring friends (I cherish several junior high and high school girlfriends still whom I keep up with) despite having been raised as an only child. It has been and continues to be an honor and a pleasure to share in the journeys of my clients, so many of us on a quest to bridge the gap between our "programming" from our mothers and backgrounds and claiming/discovering our authenticity and our voices…our natural expression. We need each other's stories for perspective.

In these stories it's notable how several of the mothers of these women came alive and tapped into undiscovered or unexpressed aspects of themselves AFTER they were widowed: Anita's, Anne's, Loretta's, Hope's stories all share this theme. Myrna's mom also found her stride and embraced her family anew after the loss of her beloved husband. Something in their spirits got freed up in their loss.

Is this the generation of mid-lifers who manage at last to claim our personal power and truth separate from how our forbearers and we have been defined in our roles as wives, partners or mothers? Can we borrow from the leaps and accomplishments of other trailblazers and "sisters" on the quest for self-discovery…recovery…self empowerment and leave a rich tapestry of stories, of little and big victories to the next generation? Are we ready to cultivate the kernels and seeds we were handed, to gather the tools needed to forge into the unknown, to make a giant leap and departure from what constrained past generations of women? My hope and vision is that collectively we can lend courage and vision to those still confined or crawling out of the straightjackets and ditches that entrapped their mothers and weave a future rich with possibilities. Our journey is just beginning.

Acknowledgments

Such DEEP GRATITUDE and appreciation for these women who said yes to being interviewed for this purpose, completely voluntarily and with courage and curiosity about my project:

Hope Boylston, Cyndi Willams Carter, Anita Casalina, "Loretta J.," Charlie Toledo, Anne Uemura, and "Myrna Yi."

This has no doubt been more involved and intense than they expected, in that it requires the subject to reflect and drop down into themselves, and since the editing process occurred over more than a year, it offered up yet another look back…and another and another. Some of the material is tender, charged, and painful, and they had to deal with exposing their rawness and history to the wide unknown public. I am so impressed and moved by their stories, and can only hope I've done justice in sharing them here. I hope each of these women—even though two have chosen to protect their identities—holds their head high and trusts that their sharing goes forward in ways that we can only imagine will empower and en-courage others.

I am incredibly grateful for my daughter Chelsea—the designer—venturing through this with me, though her wedding and now pregnancy have certainly at times delayed and distracted this project from being my top priority! This is the second book that she's helped design and been my assistant for. But more than being my design and tech partner, I am so proud of her as a young woman, as I am my younger daughter Haley, for who they are becoming. My girls have already leaped light years ahead of me from where I was at their age in their sense of self, their confidence, strength and vision. They both have delightful sense-of-humors, are incredibly talented artists, and loving friends and partners. What I cherish most is that we have a great mother-daughter relationship. They share their stories with me, and I am so honored to be their mom!

Then there's my husband, Bob Clair, who was really nervous when I shared that I had another book in me. He's known my aspirations for years to write about the path that women are embarking on in a meaningful way. But I gotta say, he not only accepted that the time had come, he's tolerated my buzz and fervor, my many plates spinning at once with patience, friendliness, humor and love. He's not always available to hear my little victories—for example, "Wanna see my new website that Chelsea helped me put together?" "No, not right now. I'm sure I'll see it!" But he's been there to handle all the household "to-do's" that I haven't been able to manage as this project heated up. Most of all, I'm amazed and grateful he's stuck by me through all this journeying over 30 plus years…he also loved my mom and they jested plenty over the years, and he's helped me honor her legacy since she passed in ways neither of us ever imagined.

Next there's my two "right hand gals" who were willing to look at my pieces with their professional editor's eye—Mary Jo Gibson and Lori Howard. They were invaluable at sharpening, clarifying, and tightening—they thought amazingly alike (there are many fewer exclamation points as a result!), and they were already my longtime cherished friends.

And finally, there's my team: publicist and marketing specialist Denise Cassino who was willing to take the project on when it was merely an idea but who lit a fire under me in the final month to complete it on schedule, and my newest members of the team: publishing expert Chris O'Byrne and his crew at JETLAUNCH (www.jetlaunch.net).

Here's to all of us taking this leap of faith together!

About the Author

Pam Burns-Clair, MFT, is a licensed psychotherapist in private practice in Napa, California, specializing in women's issues and child/parenting issues. She is the daughter of the late Disney Legend, Harriet Burns, who was in many ways a pioneer for women entering the professional world in the '50s. Together with co-author Don Peri, Pam authored a tribute book about her mom, *Walt Disney's First Lady of Imagineering, Harriet Burns*, in '09. Pam has facilitated women's support groups in her practice for 30 years, authored several articles, taught classes and workshops in her field, and lives in Sonoma, California, with her husband. She has two daughters, both artists. Chelsea Clair Livingston has collaborated on cover and book design for both books, and is starting her own family with her husband in Sonoma, CA. Haley Clair is making her way into the world of musical theater in New York.

www.ingramcontent.com/pod-product-compliance
Lightning Source LLC
Chambersburg PA
CBHW071527040426
42452CB00008B/912